NEW CUTTING EDGE

PRE-INTERMEDIATE

photocopiable resources by Chris Redston

TEACHER'S RESOURCE BOOK

helen barker

with sarah cunningham peter moor

Contents

Introduction

New Cutting Edge Pre-Intermediate is aimed at young adults studying general English at a pre-intermediate level and provides material for approximately 120 hours of teaching. It is suitable for students studying in either a monolingual or multilingual classroom situation.

<table>
<tr>
<td>STUDENTS' BOOK

CLASS CDS/CASSETTES</td>
<td>The New Cutting Edge Pre-Intermediate Students' Book is divided into fifteen modules, each consisting of approximately eight hours of classroom material. Each module contains some or all of the following:
• reading and/or listening and/or vocabulary – an introduction to the topic of the module, and incorporates speaking
• grammar – input/revision in two Language focus sections with practice activities and integrated pronunciation work
• vocabulary – includes a Wordspot section which focuses on common words (have, get, take, etc.)
• task preparation – a stimulus or model for the task (often listening or reading) and Useful language for the task
• task – extended speaking, often with an optional writing component
• Real life section – language needed in more complex real-life situations, usually including listening and speaking
• writing skills
• a Study ... Practise ... Remember! section – to develop study skills, with practice activities and a self-assessment section for students to monitor their progress.

At the back of the Students' Book you will find:
• a Mini-dictionary which contains definitions, pronunciations and examples of key words and phrases from the Students' Book
• a detailed Language summary covering the grammar in each module
• Tapescripts for material on the Class CDs/Cassettes.</td>
</tr>
<tr>
<td>WORKBOOK

STUDENTS' CD/CASSETTE</td>
<td>The New Cutting Edge Pre-Intermediate Workbook is divided into fifteen modules, which consist of:
• grammar – consolidation of the main language points covered in the Students' Book
• vocabulary – additional practice and input
• skills work – Improve your writing and Listen and read sections
• pronunciation – focus on problem sounds and word stress.

The optional Students' CD/Cassette features exercises on grammar and pronunciation. There are two versions of the Workbook, one with and the other without an Answer key.</td>
</tr>
<tr>
<td>TEACHER'S RESOURCE BOOK</td>
<td>The New Cutting Edge Pre-Intermediate Teacher's Resource Book consists of three sections:
• an Introduction and some Teacher's tips on:
  – helping students with pronunciation
  – working with lexical phrases
  – making the most of the mini-dictionary
  – making tasks work
  – responding to learners' individual language needs
  – using the Study ... Practise ... Remember! and Mini-check sections
• Step-by-step teacher's notes for each module, including alternative suggestions for different teaching situations (particularly for tasks), detailed language notes and integrated answer keys
• a photocopiable Resource bank, including learner-training worksheets, communicative grammar practice activities and vocabulary extension activities.

The teacher's notes section is cross-referenced to the Resource bank and the Workbook.</td>
</tr>
</table>

The thinking behind *New Cutting Edge Pre-Intermediate*

Overview

New Cutting Edge Pre-Intermediate has a multilayered, topic-based syllabus which includes thorough and comprehensive work on grammar, vocabulary, pronunciation and the skills of listening, reading, speaking and writing. Structured speaking tasks form a central part of each module. The course gives special emphasis to:

- communication
- the use of phrases and collocation
- active learning and study skills
- revision and recycling.

Topics and content

We aim to motivate learners by basing modules around up-to-date topics of international interest. Students are encouraged to learn more about the world and other cultures through the medium of English, and personalisation is strongly emphasised. The differing needs of monocultural and multicultural classes have been kept in mind throughout.

Approach to grammar

Learners are encouraged to take an active, systematic approach to developing their knowledge of grammar, and the opportunity to use new language is provided in a natural, communicative way. There are two *Language focus* sections in each module, in which grammar is presented using reading or listening texts. Each *Language focus* has a *Grammar* box focusing on the main language points, in which learners are encouraged to work out rules for themselves. This is followed up thoroughly through:

- a wide range of communicative and written practice exercises in the *Students' Book*
- the opportunity to use new grammar naturally in the speaking tasks (see below)
- the *Study ... Practise ... Remember!* and *Mini-check* sections, in which learners are encouraged to assess their progress and work on any remaining problems
- a *Language summary* section at the back of the *Students' Book*
- further practice in the *Workbook*.

(See *Teacher's tips: using the* Study ... Practise ... Remember! *and* Mini-check *sections* on pages 13–14.)

Approach to vocabulary

A wide vocabulary is vital to communicative success, so new lexis is introduced and practised at every stage in the course. Particular attention has been paid to the selection of high-frequency, internationally useful words and phrases, drawing on information from the British National Corpus.

Vocabulary input is closely related to the topics and tasks in the modules, allowing for plenty of natural recycling. Further practice is provided in the *Study ... Practise ... Remember!* section at the end of each module and in the *Workbook*.

In order to communicate, fluent speakers make extensive use of 'prefabricated chunks' of language. For this reason, *New Cutting Edge Pre-Intermediate* gives particular emphasis to collocations and fixed phrases. These are integrated through:

- *Wordspot* sections, which focus on high-frequency words such as *get*, *have* and *think*
- the *Useful language* boxes in the speaking tasks
- *Real life* sections, which focus on phrases used in common everyday situations such as telephoning or making arrangements
- topic-based vocabulary lessons.

(See *Teacher's tips: working with lexical phrases* on pages 8–9.) In addition, more straightforward single-item vocabulary is also extended through the *Vocabulary booster* sections of the *Workbook*.

'Useful' vocabulary is partly individual to the learner. With this in mind, the speaking tasks in *New Cutting Edge Pre-Intermediate* provide the opportunity for students to ask the teacher for the words and phrases they need. (See *Teacher's tips: responding to learners' individual language needs* on pages 12–13.)

To encourage learner independence, *New Cutting Edge Pre-Intermediate* has a *mini-dictionary* which includes entries for words and phrases appropriate to the level of the learners. Learners are encouraged to refer to the *mini-dictionary* throughout the course, and there are study tips to help them to do this more effectively. (See *Teacher's tips: making the most of the* mini-dictionary on pages 9–10.)

The speaking tasks

New Cutting Edge Pre-Intermediate aims to integrate elements of a task-based approach into its overall methodology. There are structured speaking tasks in each module which include interviews, mini-talks, problem-solving and storytelling. Here the primary focus is on achieving a particular outcome or product, rather than on practising specific language. Learners are encouraged to find the language they need in order to express their own ideas.

The frequent performance of such tasks is regarded in this course as a central element in learners' progress. The tasks provide the opportunity for realistic and extended communication, and because learners are striving to express what they want to say, they are more likely to absorb the language that they are learning. Much of the grammar and vocabulary input in each module is therefore integrated around these tasks, which in turn provide a valuable opportunity for the teacher to revisit and recycle what has been studied.

In order to make the tasks work effectively in the classroom:

- they are graded carefully in terms of difficulty
- a model/stimulus is provided for what the student is expected to do
- useful language is provided to help students to express themselves
- thinking and planning time is included.

(See *Teacher's tips: making tasks work* on pages 10–11 and *Responding to learners' individual language needs* on pages 12–13.)

In addition to the tasks, *New Cutting Edge Pre-*

Intermediate offers many other opportunities for speaking. For example, through the discussion of texts, communicative practice exercises and the wide range of games and activities in the photocopiable *Resource bank* in the *Teacher's Resource Book*.

Other important elements in *New Cutting Edge Pre-Intermediate*

Listening

New Cutting Edge Pre-Intermediate places strong emphasis on listening. Listening material consists of:

- short extracts and mini-dialogues to introduce and practise new language
- words and sentences for close listening and to model pronunciation
- longer texts (interviews, songs, stories and conversations), some of which are authentic, often in the *Preparation* section as a model or stimulus for the task
- regular *Listen and read* sections in the *Workbook* to further develop students' confidence in this area.

Speaking

There is also a strong emphasis on speaking, as follows.

- The tasks provide a regular opportunity for extended and prepared speaking based around realistic topics and situations (see page 4).
- Much of the practice of grammar and lexis is through oral exercises and activities.
- The topics and reading texts in each module provide opportunities for follow-up discussion.
- There is regular integrated work on pronunciation.
- Most of the photocopiable activities in the *Resource bank* are oral.

Reading

There is a wide range of reading material in the *Students' Book*, including factual/scientific texts, stories, quizzes, forms, notes and e-mails. These texts are integrated in a number of different ways:

- extended texts specifically to develop reading skills
- texts which lead into grammar work and language analysis
- texts which provide a model or stimulus for tasks and a model for writing activities.

Note: for classes who do not have a lot of time to do reading in class, there are suggestions in the teacher's notes section on how to avoid this where appropriate.

Writing

Systematic work on writing skills is developed in *New Cutting Edge Pre-Intermediate* through:

- regular writing sections in the *Students' Book*, which focus on writing e-mails and letters, composing narratives and reviews, drafting and redrafting, using linkers, etc.
- *Improve your writing* sections in the *Workbook*, which expand on the areas covered in the *Students' Book*
- written follow-up sections to many of the speaking tasks.

Pronunciation

Pronunciation work in *New Cutting Edge Pre-Intermediate* is integrated with grammar and lexis, and in the *Real life* sections in special *Pronunciation* boxes. The focus in the *Students' Book* is mainly on stress, weak forms and intonation, while the *Workbook* focuses on problem sounds and word stress. A range of activity types are used in the *Students' Book*, including discrimination exercises and dictation, and an equal emphasis is placed on understanding and reproducing. In addition, there are *Pronunciation spots* in the *Study ... Practise ... Remember!* sections, which focus on problem sounds. These activities are intended as quick warmers and fillers, and can be omitted if not required.

Learning skills

New Cutting Edge Pre-Intermediate develops learning skills in a number of ways as follows.

- The discovery approach to grammar encourages learners to experiment with language and to work out rules for themselves.
- The task-based approach encourages learners to take a proactive role in their learning.
- Looking up words and phrases in the *mini-dictionary* gives students constant practice of a range of dictionary skills.
- The *Study* ... section of *Study ... Practise ... Remember!* focuses on useful learning strategies, such as keeping notes and revision techniques. Learners are encouraged to share ideas about the most effective ways to learn.
- The *Resource bank* includes eleven learner-training worksheets aimed at developing students' awareness of the importance of taking an active role in the learning process.

Revision and recycling

Recycling is a key feature of *New Cutting Edge Pre-Intermediate*. New language is explicitly recycled through:

- extra practice exercises in the *Study ... Practise ... Remember!* sections. These are designed to cover all the main grammar and vocabulary areas in the module. After trying the exercises, learners are encouraged to return to any parts of the module that they still feel unsure about to assess what they have (and have not) remembered from the module. (See *Teacher's tips: using the* Study ... Practise ... Remember! *and* Mini-check *sections* on pages 13–14.)
- *Consolidation* spreads after Modules 5, 10 and 15. These combine grammar and vocabulary exercises with listening and speaking activities, recycling material from the previous five modules.
- three photocopiable tests in the *Resource bank* for use after Modules 5, 10 and 15.

In addition, the speaking tasks offer constant opportunities for learners to use what they have studied in a natural way, and for teachers to assess their progress and remind them of important points.

Teacher's tips

Helping students with pronunciation

When people say that you speak good English, very often they are reacting to your pronunciation – this is very important in creating a confident first impression as a speaker of a foreign language. Although most students today are learning English for communication in an international context (so the perfect reproduction of British vowels, for example, is not essential), a high frequency of pronunciation errors can make students hard to understand, and listeners, whether native speakers or not, may just switch off. Setting high standards for pronunciation, even if you are not aiming for native-speaker-like production, will help to achieve the right kind of comprehensibility.

1 *Give priority to pronunciation ... but be realistic*

Don't wait for a *Pronunciation* box to come along in the *Students' Book*. Integrate pronunciation work whenever students have a problem. 'Little and often' is a particularly good principle with pronunciation.

On the other hand, think about what you want to achieve: clarity and confidence are what most students need, rather than perfection in every detail. Individuals vary widely in what they can achieve, so don't push too much when a particular student is getting frustrated or embarrassed. Leave it and come back to it again another day. A humorous, light-hearted approach also helps to alleviate stress!

2 *Drill ...*

Choral and/or individual repetition is the simplest pronunciation activity to set up and possibly the most effective. It can help to build confidence, and is often popular with low-level students as long as you don't overdo it (see above). There are models on the CDs/cassettes that students can copy for most key language in *New Cutting Edge Pre-Intermediate*.

3 *... but make sure students can hear the correct pronunciation*

Even if students cannot yet produce the target pronunciation, it will improve their listening skills if they can at least hear it; and it goes without saying that you cannot reproduce something that you haven't heard clearly!

There are various ways of doing this. At low levels, it is often helpful to repeat the word or phrase two or three times yourself, before you ask students to say it. Sometimes you need to isolate and repeat individual syllables or sounds, and exaggeration of features like stress and intonation can be helpful. Or you can contrast the correct pronunciation with what the students are producing, either with the way that that word or syllable is pronounced in their own language, or with a similar sound in English.

4 *Pay particular attention to words with irregular spelling*

One of the biggest problems for learners of English is the relationship between sounds and spelling. Highlight and drill problem words on a consistent basis. Think about teaching students the phonemic alphabet – this gives them a valuable tool for dealing with problematic pronunciation by themselves, and for recording it. You can use the list of sounds on the inside front cover of the *mini-dictionary* to teach it – but only teach a few symbols at a time, and make constant use of them, otherwise students will soon forget them again.

5 *Focus on the sounds that most affect students' comprehensibility*

Consonants (particularly at the beginning and end of words) are probably more important than vowels here. Use any tips you know for helping students to reproduce them. You might focus them on a similar sound in their own language and then help them to adapt it, or use a trick like starting with /uː/ to get students to produce the /w/ sound. Anything that works is valid here! Sometimes it is useful to contrast the problem sound with the one that students are mistakenly producing, via a 'minimal pair' such as *tree* and *three*. Say the pair of words several times, then ask students to say which they can hear, before asking them to produce the words themselves.

6 *Pay attention to schwa /ə/*

This is one vowel sound that you shouldn't ignore. It is by far the most common vowel sound in English, occurring in a very high percentage of multi-syllable words. Using it correctly will help students to sound more fluent, and increase their comprehensibility. At the beginning of the course, make sure that students can produce this sound, and focus on it whenever it occurs in new words. Be careful not to stress it accidentally though – syllables with schwa in them are not normally stressed. To avoid this, drill new words starting with the stressed syllable, then add the schwa sounds either before or afterwards, for example:

/ə/ /ə/
ten ... atten ... attention

Consistently marking schwa sounds when you write words on the board will also help:

/ə/ /ə/
attention

7 *Focus consistently on word stress ...*

This is an easy area in which to correct students effectively. Get into the habit of focusing on word stress whenever you teach a new word with potential problems. If students have problems, try one of the following ideas when you drill.

- Exaggerate the stress.
- Clap, click your fingers, etc. on the stressed syllable.
- Mumble the stress pattern, before saying the word: *mm-MM-mm attention*.
- Isolate the stressed syllable first, then add the other syllables.

Don't forget to mark stressed syllables when you write new words on the board, by underlining or writing a blob over them, and encourage students to do the same when they write in their notebooks. Make sure that students know how word stress is marked in the *mini-dictionary*.

8 *... and sentence stress*

Sentence stress is one of the most important elements in helping students to be easy to understand when they speak, just as punctuation makes their written work more comprehensible. Try to focus on it little and often, for example, when you teach a new structure or phrase. You can use the same methods as for word stress to help students to hear and reproduce the sentence stress.

9 *Make students aware of weak forms and word linking*

As students become more advanced, these features will also contribute to comprehensibility and fluency, and at any level they are important for the purposes of listening. As you teach new phrases and structures, draw students' attention to weak forms and word linking as appropriate, and give students the opportunity to practise them. You can use the same method as for schwa sounds if they have problems. However, do not worry too much if students do not produce the weak forms and word linking spontaneously – this is more likely to come naturally when students are more fluent. All you can do at this stage is to sow the seeds for the future.

10 *Make students aware of intonation*

Intonation is a source of worry to many teachers and, consequently, students. Teachers worry that their students (or they themselves) cannot hear it, and that whatever they do their students don't seem to 'learn' it. In reality, there are few situations in which wrong intonation leads to serious misunderstanding. Where problems do occasionally occur is in the area of politeness, and sounding sufficiently enthusiastic (although, even here, in real life many other factors – such as facial expression – can counteract 'wrong' intonation!).

In *New Cutting Edge Pre-Intermediate*, we focus on these limited areas for intonation work. Again the key idea is 'awareness': you probably won't 'teach' students the right intonation overnight, but by focusing on this problem you can help them to see the importance of it. They are more likely to improve their overall intonation via plenty of exposure to natural-sounding English, and this is something that will take time. If students have problems hearing and reproducing the intonation patterns that you choose to focus on, try some of the following ideas.

- Exaggerate the intonation pattern, before returning to a more normal model.
- Hum the intonation pattern before repeating the words (incidentally, this is very useful for hearing intonation patterns yourself, if you have difficulty).
- Use gestures to show the intonation pattern (rather like a conductor).
- Mark the intonation on the board using arrows.

Remember, though, that if students are getting frustrated, or cannot 'get' the correct intonation, it is probably best to leave it and come back to it another time!

Working with lexical phrases

❶ *Become more aware of phrases and collocations yourself*

Until recently, relatively little attention was given to the thousands of phrases and collocations that make up the lexis in English, along with the traditional one-word items. If necessary, look at the list of phrase types, and start noticing how common these 'prefabricated chunks' are in all types of English. They go far beyond areas traditionally dealt with in English-language courses – phrasal verbs, functional exponents and the occasional idiom, although of course they incorporate all of these.

a **collocations** (common word combinations), including:
- verbs + nouns (*leave school*, *have a drink*)
- adjectives + nouns (*best friend*, *bad news*)
- verbs + adverbs (*work hard*)
- verbs + prepositions/particles, including phrasal verbs (*listen to*, *wait for*)
- adjectives + prepositions (*interested in*)

b **fixed phrases**, such as: *Excuse me. / Here you are.*

c **whole sentences which act as phrases**, such as: *I don't know. / I agree with you.*

Such phrases blur the boundaries between 'vocabulary' and 'grammar' – in teaching these phrases, you will find that you are helping students with many problematic areas that are traditionally considered to be grammar, such as articles and prepositions. Many common examples of these structures are in fact fixed or semi-fixed phrases. We are not suggesting that work on chunks should entirely replace the traditional grammatical approach to such verb forms, but rather that it is a useful supplement.

❷ *Make your students aware of phrases and collocations*

Students should also know about the importance of such phrases. *Learner-training worksheet C* on page 123 of the *Resource bank* aims to develop students' awareness of such collocations.

❸ *Feed in phrases on a 'little but often' basis*

To avoid overloading students and ensure that your lexical input is useful, teach a few phrases relating to particular activities as you go along. For example, in a grammar practice activity, instead of simple answers such as *Yes, I do* or *No, I haven't*, feed in phrases like *It depends* or *I don't really care*. The same is true of discussions about reading/listening texts and writing activities.

❹ *Introduce phrases in context, but drill them as short chunks*

Phrases can be difficult to understand and be specific to certain situations, so it is important that they are introduced in context. However, students may retain them better if you drill just the phrase (for example, *have lunch*, *go for a walk*) rather than a full sentence with problems which might distract from the phrase itself. The drilling of such phrases can be a valuable opportunity to focus on pronunciation features such as weak forms and word linking.

❺ *Point out patterns in phrases*

Pointing out patterns will help students to remember phrases. Many do not fit into patterns, but you can often show similar phrases with the same construction, like this:

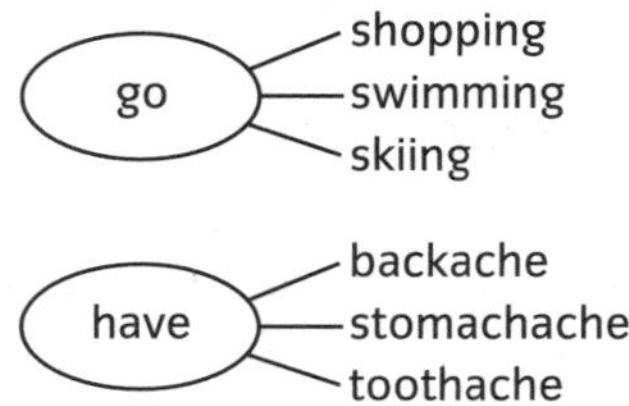

❻ *Keep written records of phrases as phrases*

One simple way to make your students more aware of collocation is to get into the habit of writing word combinations on the board wherever appropriate, rather than just individual words. The more students see these words together, the more likely they are to remember them as a unit. Rather than just writing up *housework* or *piano*, write up *do the housework* or *play the piano*. In sentences, collocations can be highlighted in colour or underlined – this is particularly important when the associated words are not actually next to each other in the sentence. Remind students to write down the collocations too, even if they 'know' the constituent words.

❼ *Reinforce and recycle phrases as much as you can*

This is particularly important with phrases which, for the reasons given above, can be hard to remember. Most revision games and activities that teachers do with single items of vocabulary can be adapted and used with phrases. You may find the following useful in addition.

- **Making wall posters**: help students remember collocations by making a wall poster with a spidergram like those in the *Wordspot* sections of the *Students' Book*. Seeing the phrases on the wall like this every lesson can provide valuable reinforcement. There are many other areas for which wall posters would be effective, for example, common offers with *I'll* or common passive phrases. Always write the full phrase on the poster (*get married* not just *married*) and remove the old posters regularly, as they will lose impact if there are too many.

- **Making a phrase bank:** copy the new words and phrases from the lesson onto slips of card or paper (large enough for students to read if you hold them up at the front of the room) and keep them in a box or bag. This is a good record for you as well as the students of the phrases that you have studied – you can get them out whenever there are a few spare moments at the beginning or end of a lesson for some quick revision. Hold them up and, as appropriate, get students to give you:
  - an explanation of the phrase
  - a translation of the phrase
  - synonyms
  - opposites
  - the pronunciation
  - situations where they might say this
  - a sentence including the phrase
  - the missing word that you are holding your hand over (for example, *to* in the phrase *listen to the radio*)
  - the phrase itself, based on a definition or translation that you have given them.

Making the most of the *mini-dictionary*

The *New Cutting Edge Pre-Intermediate mini-dictionary* has been especially designed to be useful to, and usable by, pre-intermediate students. It contains examples of most words, which are as self-explanatory as possible. We realise how difficult it may be for students at this level to understand definitions in English, although we have made a big effort to make these as simple as possible. We hope that students will develop the habit of using a monolingual dictionary, even if they cannot understand everything in it straight away. Obviously, however, students will still need support from the teacher to use the *mini-dictionary* effectively.

1 *Show students the* mini-dictionary *at the beginning of the course*

Explain what the *mini-dictionary* is, and reassure students that they don't need to understand all the definitions to use it. Obviously, students will not understand all the definitions immediately. Show them all the other information they can still find, such as opposites or word stress. Point out, too, that it is often easier to work out the meaning of a word from an example, rather than from a definition.

2 *Use the* mini-dictionary *together as a class, or in pairwork*

This will help to build up confidence in using a monolingual dictionary, as students work out together what they understand. Especially in the initial stages, it will help to make dictionary work less arduous and more sociable!

3 *Use it where appropriate in grammar lessons*

Whenever you teach a grammatical area that is covered in the *mini-dictionary*, for example, the Past simple or the comparative and superlative of adjectives, show students how the *mini-dictionary* can help to answer their questions, even when you are not available to do so!

4 *Draw students' attention to information about collocation*

The *mini-dictionary* provides a lot of basic information about collocation, which will help students to use what they know effectively. Pre-intermediate students might not always be aware that collocations in English are often different from those in their first language, so whenever you look up a word together which has a problematic collocation, show how the *mini-dictionary* examples can help with this.

5 *Vary your approach*

If you always use the *mini-dictionary* in the same way, students may get tired of it before long. Try using the *mini-dictionary* in the following ways instead for a change.

a **Matching words to definitions on a handout:** make a worksheet with the new words in column A and their definitions from the *mini-dictionary* mixed up in column B. Students match the words with the definitions.

b **Matching words to definitions on cards:** the same idea can be used by giving each group of students two small sets of cards with definitions and words to match.

c ***I know it / I can guess it / I need to check it:*** write the list of new words on the board, and tell students to copy it down marking the words ✔✔ if they already know it, ✔ if they can guess what it means (either from the context or because it is similar in their own language) and ✘ if they need to look it up. Students then compare answers in pairs to see if they can help each other, before looking up any words that neither of them know.

d **Looking up the five words you most need to know:** instead of pre-teaching the vocabulary in a reading text, set the first (gist-type) comprehension activity straight away, instructing students not to refer to the *mini-dictionary* at this point. Check answers or establish that students cannot answer without some work on vocabulary. Tell them that they are only allowed to look up five words from the text – they have to choose the five that are most important to understanding the text. Demonstrate the difference between a 'key' unknown word in the text and one that can easily be ignored. Put students into pairs to select their five words, emphasising that they must not start using the *mini-dictionary* until they have completed their list of five. After they have finished, compare the lists of words that different pairs chose and discuss how important they are to the text, before continuing with more detailed comprehension work.

e ***True/False*** **statements based on information in the *mini-dictionary*:** write a list of statements about the target words on the board, then ask students to look them up to see if they are true or false, for example:
The phrase ... is very informal – true or false?
The phrase means ... – true or false?

Making tasks work

Treat tasks primarily as an opportunity for communication. Remember the main objective is for students to use the language that they know in order to achieve a particular communicative goal. Although it is virtually impossible to perform many of the tasks without using the language introduced earlier in the module, in others students may choose to use this language only once or twice, or not at all. Do not try to 'force-feed' it. Of course, if learners are seeking this language but have forgotten it, this is the ideal moment to remind them!

❶ *Make the task suit your class*

Students using this course will vary in age, background, interests and ability. All these students need to find the tasks motivating and 'doable', yet challenging at the same time. Do not be afraid to adapt the tasks to suit your class if this helps. The teacher's notes contain suggestions on how to adapt certain tasks for monolingual and multilingual groups, students of different ages and interests, large classes and weaker or stronger groups. We hope these suggestions will give you other ideas of your own on how to adapt the tasks.

❷ *Personalise it!*

Most tasks in *New Cutting Edge Pre-Intermediate* have a model to introduce them. Sometimes these are recordings of people talking about something personal, for example, describing their family or finding something in common with other people. However, finding out about you, their teacher, may be more motivating, so you could try providing a personalised model instead. If you do this, remember to:

- plan what you are going to say, but do not write it out word for word, as this may sound unnatural
- bring in any photos or illustrations you can to help to bring your talk alive
- either pre-teach or explain as you go along any problematic vocabulary
- give students something to do as they are listening (the teacher's notes give suggestions on this where appropriate).

This approach may take a little courage at first, but students are likely to appreciate the variety it provides.

❸ *Set the final objective clearly before students start preparing*

Do not assume that students will work out where their preparations are leading if you do not tell them! Knowing that they will have to tell their story to the class, for example, may make a big difference to how carefully they prepare it.

4 Pay attention to seating arrangements

Whether you have fixed desks or more portable furniture, when working in groups or pairs always make sure that students are sitting so that they can hear and speak to each other comfortably. Groups should be in a small circle or square rather than a line, for example. Empty desks between students may mean that they have to raise their voices to a level at which they feel self-conscious when speaking English – this can have an adverse effect on any pairwork or groupwork activity.

5 Give students time to think and plan

Planning time is very important if low-level students are to produce the best language that they are capable of. It is particularly useful for building up the confidence of students who are normally reluctant to speak in class. The amount of time needed will vary from task to task, but normally about five minutes will suffice.

This planning time will sometimes mean a period of silence in class, something that teachers used to noisy, communicative classrooms can find unnerving. Remember that just because you cannot hear anything, this does not mean that nothing is happening! With storytelling and other activities, it may be useful to get students to go over what they are going to say, silently in their heads.

It may help to relieve any feelings of tension at this stage by playing some background music or, if practical in your school, by suggesting that students go somewhere else to prepare – another classroom if one is available.

Students may well find the idea of 'time to plan' strange at first, but, as with many other teaching and learning techniques, it is very much a question of training.

6 *Make the most of the* Useful language *boxes*

The *Useful language* boxes are intended to help students with language they need to perform the tasks. It is important to get students to do something with the phrases in order to help students pronounce them and begin to learn them. Here are some suggestions.

- You can write the useful language on an overhead transparency. Give a definition/explanation to elicit each phrase, and then uncover it.
- Give some group and individual repetition if necessary, first with students looking at the phrase and then covering it up to encourage them to remember it.
- When you have looked at all the phrases, give students a minute to try and memorise them. Then remove the prompts, and students in pairs can try to say them to each other, or to write them down.
- If the *Useful language* box has a lot of questions, you could write the answers on the board and see if students can provide the questions. Don't write the questions. Give group and individual repetition practice of each question as needed, continually going back to earlier questions to see if students can remember them. At the end, students can look at the questions in the book.
- Elicit each phrase, as above, and write them up on the board until you have all the useful language up. Then ask students in pairs to read the phrases aloud to each other, and when they finish they should start again. Meanwhile you can start rubbing off individual words from the phrases and replace them with a dash. Start with smaller words, so that you leave the main information words. Keep rubbing off more and more words until only dashes are left! See how much students can remember of this missing language.
- Write the phrases on cards and cut the phrases into two, for example, *I was ten / at the time*, so that students in groups can try to match the two halves. They can then check the *Useful language* box, and you can give group and individual practice.

7 Insist that students do the task in English!

It may not be realistic to prevent students from using their own language completely, but they should understand that during the performance of the task (if not at the planning stage, when they may need their mother tongue to ask for new language) they must use English. At the beginning of the course, it may be useful to discuss the importance of this, and the best ways of implementing it. Students will be more tempted to use their own language if they find the task daunting, so do not be afraid to shorten or simplify tasks if necessary. However, planning and rehearsal time will make students less inclined to use their first language.

8 Let the students do the talking

If students are hesitant, it is easy (with the best of intentions!) to intervene and speak for them. Some students will be only too happy to let you do this, and before long they won't even attempt to formulate full sentences, knowing that you will usually do it for them. Don't worry if they have to think for a little while before they can string their words together – they will get better at this eventually, but only if they have the opportunity to practise!

9 Give your feedback at the end ... and make it positive!

Students at this level are bound to make a lot of errors in any kind of extended communication, and you may feel that you need to deal with these. It is usually best not to interrupt however, but to make a note of any important points to deal with at the end. Keep these brief though, and remember that at low levels any kind of extended speaking is a considerable challenge. Keep the emphasis on praise and positive feedback, and hopefully your students will be eager to do this kind of speaking task again!

10 Use written follow-up as consolidation

Learners have more time to focus on correct language when writing, so encourage them to make use of any suggestions and corrections you made during the oral phase of the task. You could get them to read through and correct each other's written work if you have time.

Responding to learners' individual language needs

At appropriate points throughout the *Students' Book*, during the tasks and speaking activities, students are instructed to ask their teacher about any words or phrases they need. The ability to respond to students' individual language needs is central to a task-based approach, and you may find yourself doing this during pair/group/individual work and during preparation stages. The following suggestions are designed to help teachers who may feel daunted by the idea of unplanned, unpredictable input.

❶ *Encourage students to ask about language*

Students who take an active approach to their own learning are far more likely to succeed than those who sit back and expect the teacher to do it all for them. It is important to make students aware of this, and to convey to them your willingness to deal with their queries. Circulate during pair/group/individual work, making it clear that you are available to answer questions. Even if you cannot answer a query on the spot, let students know that you are happy to deal with it.

❷ *Be responsive, but do not get sidetracked*

One danger of this approach is that a teacher may get sidetracked by dominant students who want all their attention, leading to frustration and irritation among others. If you feel that this is happening, tell these students that you will answer their questions later, and move quickly on. Make sure that you keep moving round during pair/group/individual work. Keep a 'bird's-eye' view of the class, moving in to help students if they need it rather than spending too much time with one pair/group/individual.

❸ *Encourage students to use what they already know*

There is also a danger that students will become overdependent on you, perhaps asking you to translate large chunks for them, which they are very unlikely to retain. Always encourage students to use what they know first, only asking you if they really have no idea.

❹ *Have strategies for dealing with questions you cannot answer*

Have at least one bilingual dictionary in the classroom (especially for specialised/technical vocabulary) for students to refer to, although you may still need to check that they have found the right translation. If students ask for idioms and expressions, make sure you keep it simple – in most cases you will be able to come up with an adequate phrase, even if it is not precisely the phrase the student wanted. Finally, if all else fails, promise to find out for the next lesson!

❺ *Note down important language points to be dealt with later*

Note down any important language points that come up during tasks and discussions, and build in time slots to go over these later on. Write the errors on the board, and invite students to correct them, think of a better word, etc. Remember that it is also motivating (and can be just as instructive) to include examples of good language use as well as errors. Feedback slots can either be at the end of the lesson or, if time is a problem, at the beginning of the next.

❻ *Select language points for correction slots carefully*

Students are more likely to retain a few well-chosen points in these correction slots than a long list of miscellaneous language points. The following are helpful things to bear in mind.

- **Usefulness:** many items may only be of interest to individual students – only bring up general language with the whole class.
- **Quantity/Variety:** try to combine one or two more general points with a number of more specific/minor ones, including a mixture of grammar, vocabulary and pronunciation as far as possible.
- **Level:** be careful not to present students with points above their level or which are too complex to deal with in a few minutes.
- **Problems induced by students' mother tongue:** correction slots are an excellent opportunity to deal with L1-specific errors ('false friends', pronunciation, etc.) not usually mentioned in general English courses.
- **Revision:** the correction slots are a very good opportunity to increase students' knowledge of complex language covered previously, as well as to remind them of smaller language points.

❼ *Don't worry if you cannot think of 'creative' practice on the spot*

If students encounter a genuine need for the language as they try to achieve a particular goal, it is more likely to be remembered than if it is introduced 'cold' by the teacher. In many cases, elaborate practice may be unnecessary – what is important is that you are dealing with the language at the moment it is most likely to be retained by the student. With lexis and small points of pronunciation, it may be enough to get students to repeat the word a few times and for you to write an example on the board, highlighting problems.

❽ *Try some simple 'on the spot' practice activities*

If you feel more work is needed, the following box includes some well-known activities which are relatively easy to adapt 'on the spot' (you can always provide a more substantial exercise later). A few examples should be enough for students to see how the structure is formed, and to increase awareness of it. These activities are also useful for practising phrases in the *Useful language* boxes in the tasks.

a **Choral and individual drilling**

b **Questions and answers:** ask questions prompting students to use the language item in the answer. For example, to practise the phrase *famous for*, ask questions such as:

What's Monte Carlo famous for?	*It's famous for its casinos.*
What's Loch Ness famous for?	*It's famous for the Loch Ness Monster.*

Alternatively, give an example, then prompt students to ask each other questions, like this:

Monica, ask Henri about Venice.	*What's Venice famous for, Henri?*

c **Forming sentences/phrases from prompts:** for example, to practise the construction *is worth* + verb *-ing*, provide the example *The National Gallery is worth visiting*, then give prompts like this:

ROYAL PALACE / SEE	*The Royal Palace is worth seeing.*
THIS DICTIONARY / BUY	*This dictionary is worth buying.*

d **Substitutions:** give an example phrase/sentence, then provide prompts which can easily be substituted into the original. For example, to practise the non-use of the article, start with *I hate cats*, then prompt as follows:

LOVE	*I love cats.*
BABIES	*I love babies.*
DON'T LIKE	*I don't like babies.*

e **Transformations:** these are useful if there is another construction with almost the same meaning. Give one construction and ask students to say the same thing using another. For example, to practise *although*:

He's rich, but he's very mean.	*Although he's rich, he's very mean.*
She's over eighty, but she's very active.	*Although she's over eighty, she's very active.*

f **Combining shorter sentences/phrases:** give two short sentences and ask students to combine them with a more complex construction. For example, to practise *too … to*:

She's very young. She can't do this job.	*She's too young to do this job.*
He's too old. He can't drive.	*He's too old to drive.*

g **Dictating sentences for students to complete:** dictate a few incomplete sentences including the phrase/structure, which students complete themselves, then compare with other students. For example, to practise *It takes … to*, dictate:

It takes about three hours to get to …,	*It only takes a few minutes to …,*
It took me ages to …	

Using the *Study … Practise … Remember!* and *Mini-check* sections

These sections are a fresh component in *New Cutting Edge Pre-Intermediate*, replacing and extending the old *Do you remember?* sections. They occur at the end of each module except Modules 5, 10 and 15, where there is a more extensive *Consolidation* section.

The *Study … Practise … Remember!* and *Mini-check* sections have the following main aims:

- to ensure systematic consolidation of new language before learners move on to the next module
- to encourage learners to take responsibility for and assess their own progress
- to cover problem sounds which are not covered elsewhere.

1 *Use the different activities as warmers and fillers*

The activities in the *Study … Practise … Remember!* sections are not intended to be used all together. They can be broken down into 'bite-sized' chunks and used as warmers or fillers when you have ten or fifteen minutes to spare. For example, you could do the *Study …* section at the end of one lesson, use the *Pronunciation spot* as a warmer in another lesson and set the exercises in the *Practise …* section (either together or separately) as warmers or fillers in other lessons. The *Mini-check* could be done as a short slot in the final lesson before you move on to the next module.

2 *Set homework based on these sections*

If you are short of time in class, the *Practise …* section could easily be set as homework. If you do this, draw learners' attention to the *Need to check?* rubric at the end of each exercise. It might be useful to explain in class where students should look (for example, in the *Language summary*) if they need to do further revision.

3 *Set aside time to answer students' questions*

If you set the *Practise …* section for homework, in the next lesson set aside some time for students to ask any questions they have, and to complete the *Remember!* self-assessment section, before getting students to do the *Mini-check*.

4 *Encourage students to take responsibility for their own progress*

The approach throughout the *Study … Practise … Remember!* section is intended to encourage learner independence and personal responsibility for progress, and the *Mini-check* should also be presented to students in this light. Of course, it would be possible for learners to cheat and prepare beforehand (which in itself might be perfectly valid revision!), but explain to learners that these checks are for their own benefit and that if they cheat, they are cheating themselves. Of course, it is also a good opportunity for you to check informally how well they are progressing.

5 *Select the* Pronunciation spots *that are most useful for your learners*

More than any other part of these sections, the *Pronunciation spots* are intended to stand alone. They can be used at any time as a warmer or filler. Some areas covered may not be a problem for your learners, in which case they can easily be omitted.

module 1

Leisure and lifestyle

Vocabulary and speaking

(PAGES 6–7)

Leisure activities

See *Teacher's tips: working with lexical phrases* on pages 8–9 and *Making the most of the* mini-dictionary on pages 9–10.

1 a Introduce students to the *mini-dictionary*, showing them how to find one or two of the words and phrases, and pointing out how the stress is marked in the dictionary entries. Students work individually or in pairs to match the pictures to the correct vocabulary. Check answers with the whole class.

ANSWERS
clockwise from top right: skiing, surfing the Internet, playing the guitar, clubbing, rollerblading, going for a run

Pronunciation to check: *guitar* /gɪtɑː/, *skateboarding* /skeɪtbɔːdɪŋ/, *surfing* /sɜːfɪŋ/.

b Before you start this activity, point out that the *-ing* form is used for the names of activities, but students should use the Present simple to say what activities they do and when.

2 [T1.1] Words to check: *survey*, *musical instrument*. Students listen to the whole recording once before checking answers in pairs, and listening again if necessary.

ANSWERS

playing video games	11%
going **for a run / to the gym**	28%
going to the cinema	46%
renting a video/DVD	40%
reading a **newspaper/magazine**	100%
going for a **walk**	93%
going to a **restaurant**	64%
listening to the **radio**	71%
playing a **musical instrument**	8%

3 Students discuss the questions in groups. Each group presents their ideas to the class.

ANSWERS
Most popular activities: reading a newspaper/ magazine (100%), going for a walk (93%), listening to the radio (71%), going to a restaurant (64%)
Least popular activities: playing a musical instrument (8%), playing video games (11%), going for a run / to the gym (28%), renting a video/DVD (40%), going to the cinema (46%)

4 Tell students that word locusts are useful for recording word combinations (collocations), because they can add new collocations at a later date. Check answers with the whole class.

ANSWERS
a **going to:** the gym, the cinema, a restaurant, a football match, a yoga class
b **going for a:** run, walk
c **going + -ing:** swimming, clubbing, skateboarding, snowboarding, rollerblading, skiing
d **playing:** video games, the guitar, football, a musical instrument
e **doing:** yoga
f ***other verbs***: renting a video, surfing the Internet, renting a DVD, reading a newspaper/magazine, listening to the radio

5 Regroup students to work with a new partner. Emphasise that students can use the words and phrases from exercise 4 and any other examples they know. Each pair reports back briefly to the class.

ADDITIONAL PRACTICE

RB **Resource bank:** 1A Get to know the *Students' Book*, page 112; Learner-training worksheet A (using the *mini-dictionary*: introduction), page 113

Workbook: Vocabulary booster: sports, exercise 8, page 9; Vocabulary, exercises 9–10, page 10

Language focus 1 (PAGES 8–9)

Revision of question forms

1 Check students understand the difference between *a sport* and *a game*. Put them into pairs to discuss the questions.

2 Pre-teach *a dice*, *a referee*, *a match*, *a race*. Students do the quiz in groups with a time limit of five minutes. Remind them to check any unknown vocabulary in their mini-dictionaries.
Give three points to any group which has answered all the questions after five minutes. Then give one point for each correct answer (see exercise 3).

3 [T1.2] Ask a spokesperson from each group to give the answer to each question before you play the recording. Stop the recording before the next answer and repeat the procedure.

ANSWERS
See tapescript for recording 2 on page 162 of the *Students' Book*.

Grammar

Question words

Students work individually or in pairs. As you check the answers, highlight the difference between *what* and *which*: *what* = many possible answers, *which* = only a few possible answers. Also elicit some other examples of compound question words to show students how common they are, for example, *How much* ...? *What time* ...?

ANSWERS
1 who 2 where 3 what/which 4 when
5 how long 6 what kind 7 how often 8 how

Word order in questions
- in questions where the subject is known, the verb *be* (as an ordinary or auxiliary verb) and other verbs such as *do* (as an auxiliary verb) go before the subject.
- the subject can be a phrase like *the Winter Olympics* or a pronoun like *they*.

ANSWERS
1 Is James good at sport?
2 Do your friends play football?
3 When does the match start?

Refer students to *Language summaries A* and *B* on page 148 of the *Students' Book* for more information.

PRACTICE

1 Students work in pairs on the matching activity. It could be done as a race. Check answers with the whole class.

ANSWERS
a 1 On Sunday mornings.
2 My friends from college.
3 In the local park.
4 Because it's fun and it's good exercise.
b 1 Twice a week.
2 Ninety minutes.
3 Tuesdays and Thursdays.
4 Two.
c 1 Nearly three o'clock.
2 Five forty-five.
3 Monday.
4 The sixteenth of May.

Pronunciation

See *Teacher's tips: helping students with pronunciation* on pages 6–7.

1 [T1.3] Highlight that the main stress falls on the words carrying information, for example, *long, lessons, who, play*. Play the recording. Pause after each question for students to repeat the stressed words only.

2 [T1.4] Show students how *be* as an ordinary verb and *do* as an auxiliary verb are squashed in between the (stressed) information words by drilling the information words first, then adding the relevant verbs.

How long … lessons? How long** are the **lessons?

Who … play football with? Who** do you **play football with?

Play the recording again, pausing after each question for students to repeat.

For extra practice, students choose five questions from exercise 1 to ask a partner, paying attention to their pronunciation.

2 **a** Emphasise that the words in **bold** should be used to decide which question words to use. Students work in pairs to write questions. Monitor their use of question words.

ANSWERS
1 How often do you go to the cinema?
2 How do you come to school?
3 When's your birthday?
4 What kind of music do you like?
5 What's your favourite colour?
6 How many people are there in your family?
7 How long does your journey to school take?
8 Where would you like to visit?

b Draw students' attention to the example. Get a student from each pair to ask you a question in turn. If you prefer, students can work in small groups to ask and answer questions. Encourage them to ask follow-up questions as in the example.

ADDITIONAL PRACTICE

RB **Resource bank:** 1B Me too! (Present simple and question words), page 114

Workbook: Question forms, exercises 1–3, pages 5–6

Reading (PAGES 10–11)

1 Students discuss the questions in small groups or as a whole class.

2 Students look at the photos and guess what the people in each are doing before they read. Words to check: *opponent*, *attack*, *defend*, *martial art*, *get rid of stress*, *fantasy world*. Students match the pictures to the three paragraphs of the text as quickly as possible.

ANSWERS
a Tai-Chi b gaming for fitness c korfball

3 Students read and make notes before comparing answers in pairs. Check answers with the whole class.

ANSWERS

	Where it began	When it began	Adjectives/ Phrases to describe it
Korfball	The Netherlands	About 100 years ago	Fast, exciting, terrific
Tai-Chi	China	Thousands of years ago	Very gentle
Gaming for fitness	Japan	Very recently – it's brand new	Physical

4 Demonstrate the activity using sentence a as an example. Refer students to line 3 and ask them to underline *It's*. Show them how the description relates back to the game korfball. Students then work in pairs before checking answers with the whole class.

ANSWERS
a korfball b korfball c Tai-Chi d Tai-Chi
e Tai-Chi f most gamers

5 Tell students your answers to these questions first. Then put students into pairs to discuss their answers.

Language focus 2 (PAGES 11–12)

Present simple

1 Discuss what students know about the lifestyles of the people in the pictures. Words to check: *weigh*, *earn*. Students decide which person each question relates to.

2 [T1.5] Emphasise that students don't need to understand everything they hear. Check the answers to exercise 1 with the whole class before students discuss the final question in pairs or as a class.

ANSWERS
Toshi: a, e, g, i, k
Ania: b, d, f, h
João: c, j

Grammar

Present simple

1 Check: *habit*. Students work in pairs to match the sentences. To check that students understand the meaning of the Present simple, write up some more examples on the board, for example, *has two brothers*, *enjoys her job*. Ask students which things are habits and which are always true.

ANSWERS
A habit: sentence b
Something that is always true: sentence a

2 Elicit the question and negative forms of the examples, and write them on the board. Refer students to *Language summary C* on page 148 of the *Students' Book*. Highlight:
- the *-s* or *-es* on the third person in the positive form
- the use of *do/does* in negative and question forms, with the main verb remaining in the infinitive without *to*
- the contractions *don't* and *doesn't*
- the short answer forms:
  Yes, I/you/we/they do. *No, I/you/we/they don't.*
  Yes, he/she does. *No, he/she doesn't.*

ANSWERS
Question forms
Does Ania come from Lublin in Poland?
Does he have a big lunch and then go to sleep for a few hours?
Negative forms
Ania doesn't come from Lublin in Poland.
He doesn't have a big lunch and he doesn't go to sleep for a few hours.

How often?

1 Give students a few minutes individually to match the halves before checking answers with the whole class. Emphasise the position of the time phrases.
- They cannot go between the subject and the verb, for example, ~~*We every day go swimming*~~.
- The meaning is more emphatic if they are placed at the beginning of a sentence.

ANSWERS
every month on Sundays five times a week

Elicit other time phrases using *every* ..., *on* ... and ... *a* ... Check answers with the whole class. For consolidation, refer students to *Language summary D* on page 148 of the *Students' Book*.

POSSIBLE ANSWERS
every day, week, year, morning, afternoon, evening, night
on Mondays, Tuesdays, Wednesdays, Thursdays, Fridays, Saturdays
once **a** day, month, year
twice **a** day, month, year
three times **a** day, month, year

2 Students work in pairs to order the adverbs before checking answers as a class. Write the adverbs in the correct order on the board. Ask students for some more example sentences with these adverbs. Show students that the adverbs are often used in combination with other time phrases, for example, *I **usually** go shopping **on Saturdays***. Practise the pronunciation of *usually* /juːʒuəli/ and *occasionally* /əkeɪʒənəli/ with a repetition drill.

ANSWERS
1 always 2 usually 3 often 4 sometimes
5 occasionally 6 never

PRACTICE

1 The focus here is on word order. Students work individually to make sentences using the prompts.

ANSWERS
a All of them train for many hours every day.
b Ania and Toshi don't earn much money.
c Ania usually gets up at seven.
d She never goes to bed before midnight.
e Toshi lives in a special training camp called a *Heya*.
f He often sleeps on the floor.
g He receives lots of fan letters every week.
h João doesn't play in every match.
i He owns two sports cars.
j He misses his family in Brazil.
k He phones his mother about four times a week.

To make the exercise more challenging for your students: encourage them to do it orally in pairs rather than writing out the sentences.

2 a Before you start this activity, do a couple of examples on the board, reminding students that *Do you …?* is used with a verb, and *Are you …?* is used with an adjective. Put students into Groups A and B. Then refer Group A to the text on page 12, and Group B to the text on page 140. Words to check: *get up, get ready, healthy, unfit, wake up, awake, sleepy, energetic*.

b Pair up A and B students. Ask a pair to demonstrate an example. When students have finished, ask two or three of them to tell the class how energetic or healthy their partner is.

ADDITIONAL PRACTICE

RB **Resource bank:** 1C Connected lives (Present simple questions with *How often …?* and adverbs of frequency), pages 115–116

Workbook: Present simple, exercises 4–5, pages 7–8; Frequency, exercises 6–7, page 8

Task: Compile a fact file

(PAGES 12–13)

See *Teacher's tips: making tasks work* on pages 10–11 and *Responding to learners' individual language needs* on pages 12–13.

Preparation: reading

1 Focus students' attention on the pictures. In pairs, students discuss the five things they know, or the five questions they have, about Orlando.

2 Give students two minutes to read the fact file to check. Students close their books and work in pairs to remember as much as they can about Orlando. Words to check: *fan, up-to-date*.

3 Put students into pairs to work on the questions and remind them to write them down, as they will need to refer to them later. Make a note of any questions that are causing problems. Go over these at the end.

Task: speaking

1 Make sure students understand that they are going to interview someone they don't know well in the class. Get them to decide at this point who it will be. Elicit ideas for other topics, for example, *favourite TV programme/sport/book/magazine, best friend, favourite school subject*. Allow ten minutes for students to work individually on their questions.

2 Put students into pairs to interview each other and complete the fact file. As they do this, note down examples of good language use and/or errors to focus on later. Concentrate on the use of question forms and the Present simple.

3 *Either*: put students into groups in order to tell each other about their partner. *Or*: with smaller groups, ask one student from each pair to report back to the class.

After this feedback, write on the board examples of language students used well and/or errors. Ask students in pairs to note the examples of good language use and/or to correct the errors. Go through the answers with the class.

***Task*: alternative suggestions**

a *If you want to provide more language input before* Task: speaking: do the *Real life* section before students start preparing their questions and answers.

b *If you are short of time*: ask students to read the fact file about Orlando Bloom for homework and to come to class prepared to tell a partner what they can remember about it.

c *If your students already know each other well*: ask them to try one of the following ideas.
- Students pretend to be someone else in the class and answer all the questions as if they are that person. Their partner guesses at the end who they are.
- Students interview other English-speaking members of staff in the school.
- Students interview people in another class with roughly the same level of English.

Optional writing

Students make any corrections to the fact files they completed during *Task: speaking*. The fact files can be displayed on the wall or put together in a class magazine. Alternatively, you could start a website for the class with the fact files. For more ideas, see the *Cutting Edge* website: www.longman-elt.com/cuttingedge

Real life (PAGE 14)

Questions you can't live without

1 Discuss with the class who/where the people are in the pictures. Students work in pairs to allocate questions to pictures. Emphasise that there will be more than one question for each picture, and that students should decide which they would actually hear or ask.

POSSIBLE ANSWERS

a **In the street:** What time is it? Where's the nearest (bank)? Do you speak English?
b **Filling in a form at the bank:** Where are you from? What's your date of birth? How long are you going to stay? How do you spell …?
c **In a restaurant:** Anything else? Can we have the bill, please? Where are the toilets, please?
d **In the classroom:** How do you spell …? Sorry, could you repeat that, please?
e **In a shop:** Can I help you? How much does this cost? Anything else?
f **When you start talking to someone for the first time:** Where are you from? Which part of (Poland) are you from? How long are you going to stay?

2 a [T1.6] Students listen and write the letter for the appropriate situation before checking answers in pairs and with the whole class.

ANSWERS
1 c (In a restaurant) 2 a (In the street)
3 e (In a shop)

b [T1.6] Play the recording for students to tick the questions. Replay the recording if necessary.

ANSWERS
1 Can I help you? Where are the toilets, please? Can we have the bill, please?
2 Do you speak English? Where's the nearest (underground station)? Where are you from? How long are you going to stay?
3 How much does this cost? Anything else?

Pronunciation

See *Teacher's tips: helping students with pronunciation* on pages 6–7.

1 [T1.7] Pause the recording after each question to allow students time to write their answers. Replay the recording if necessary.

2 Refer students to the tapescript to check their answers.

ANSWERS
See tapescript for recording 7 on page 162 of the *Students' Book*.

3 [T1.7] Although *wh-* questions do not always go down at the end, this is a useful general rule.
Play the first three or four examples for students to listen to. Then play the recording, pausing after each question for them to copy the intonation. If they have trouble hearing the falling intonation, get them to add a person's name to the end of the question, for example, *Where are you from, Dr Jones?* This will help them to hear the voice falling after the final stress (*from* in this case).

Study ... (PAGE 14)

Using the *mini-dictionary* (1): Checking word class

1 Ensure that students understand how to use their mini-dictionaries to check word class by asking students to look at the entry for *fit*, reproduced on page 14 of the *Students' Book*.

As a class, brainstorm one or two words to go into each category. Students work in pairs. Set either a time limit or a limit to the number of words they add.

2 **a** Students work in pairs to look up the words in **bold**.
b In pairs, students look up half the words each to check their word class. Check answers with the whole class.

ANSWERS
1 adjective 2 preposition 3 modal verb
4 verb 5 adverb 6 noun 7 adjective 8 noun
9 preposition

Practise ... (PAGE 15)

1 Question words

Students work in pairs before checking answers as a class.

ANSWERS
a When b How long c Which d Who
e How f What kind of g What h Where
i What colour j Why k How often l How many

2 Word order in questions

This activity could be done in pairs with the questions cut up on pieces of card. Students put the cards into the right order.

ANSWERS
a Will you be at the concert tomorrow night?
b Does Cristina like skateboarding?
c Can you play football tomorrow night?
d Why was the train late this morning?
e Where did you have lunch today?
f Is your brother at home today?

3 Present simple

Students do this activity orally first, in pairs. They write their answers for homework as consolidation.

ANSWERS
a 1 I don't like wet days.
2 My brother doesn't live in the town centre.
b 1 Do you know my cousin?
2 Does your friend like snowboarding?
c 1 She speaks perfect Spanish.
2 She flies home once a year.
3 She has lunch at home.
4 She catches the early train to work.

4 *How often ...?*

Students work individually before checking their answers in pairs and then with the whole class.

ANSWERS
a We go to our holiday home once a month.
b I always go for a walk before going to bed.
c I am usually tired when I get home.
d We go to the beach every day in summer.
e Juana is never late for class.
f We often go swimming before breakfast.

5 Leisure activities

First, students cover up column A and try to think of a verb to put before each of the items in column B. Then, they uncover column A and see how many they remembered.

ANSWERS
a 5 b 4 c 1 d 2 e 6 f 3

6 Questions you can't live without

Students work in pairs. Check answers with the whole class, asking students where they might use each phrase.

ANSWERS
a 4 b 2 c 8 d 3 e 5 f 6 g 1 h 7

Pronunciation spot

The sounds /w/ and /v/

See *Teacher's tips: helping students with pronunciation* on pages 6–7.

1 [T1.8] [T1.9] Play the two recordings several times. Show students how to form the sounds, highlighting the need for the top teeth to 'bite' the bottom lip for /v/, and also the fact that this sound is voiced, whereas /w/ is unvoiced, and the lips form a tight circle.

If students have problems distinguishing between the two, write the two sounds on the board, and read a list of words aloud to the class. Some of the words should begin with /w/ and some with /v/. Students listen and, after each word, they say *One* if it begins with /w/ and *Two* if it begins with /v/. This helps to build their confidence in recognition before they are required to produce the sounds for themselves.

2 Students work in pairs to complete the spellings.

3 [T1.10] Play the recording. Students check their answers. Play the recording again for students to repeat.

ANSWERS
a weekend b video games c when d visiting
e women f vegetarian g watch h words
i which j very

Remember! (PAGE 15)

Students do the *Mini-check* on page 158 of the *Students' Book*. Check answers with the whole class, and ask students to tell you their scores.

ANSWERS AND LANGUAGE NOTE
1 *How* 2 *many* 3 *Which* 4 *does* 5 *often* 6 *long*
7 *play* 8 *go* 9 *rent** 10 *go* 11 *lives* 12 *has*
13 *doesn't use* 14 *goes* 15 *catches* 16 *every day*
17 *How long* 18 *always* 19 *How long* 20 *Where*

**Watch* is also possible, but *rent* is used in Module 1.

module 2

Important firsts

Language focus 1 (PAGES 16–17)

Past simple

1 Before you start the activity, check students know the TV programme genres listed using the photos. Put students into pairs or groups to discuss the questions. After the discussion, ask one or two people to report back any interesting points.

If you have a mono-nationality class: give students names of some well-known TV programmes and ask them which genre each one belongs to.

2 [T2.1] Words to check: *appear*, *inventor*, *chef*. Draw students' attention to the information they need to find before playing the recording. Students read the text as they listen. Encourage students to check their answers in pairs before checking with the whole class.

ANSWERS
The 'father' of TV: Russian
The inventor of TV: Scottish
The first person to appear on TV: English
The first TV chef: French

Grammar

To clarify the use of the Past simple before looking at the form, use the following examples from the text: *Vladimir Zworykin … **went** to live in the United States in 1919* (= single finished action); *Not many people **watched** them* (= repeated action); *not many people **had** a TV* (= state).

If this is revision for your class, students can work on exercises 1–4 in pairs before checking answers with the whole class.

1 As you elicit the answers, focus on the spelling. Encourage students to tell you the rules and give you more examples. Refer them to the spelling rules in *Language summary A* on page 149 of the *Students' Book* if they are not sure.

ANSWERS
Past simple of regular verbs: verb + *-ed*
Examples from the text: *worked, invented, watched*

2 As you check the answers, refer students to the list of irregular verbs on page 157 of the *Students' Book*. Emphasise that the verb forms simply have to be learnt. Ask if students have ideas for how best to learn the verbs and/or suggest some ideas such as the following.

- Choose ten verbs to learn every week.
- At the end of every day, remember all the 'irregular' things you did, for example, ***went** to work*, ***bought** a book*, ***had** coffee with …*

ANSWERS
went – **go** made – **make** had – **have**
were – **be** became – **become**

3 Highlight the fact that there are two possible past forms of the verb *be*.

ANSWERS
I/he/she **was** you/we/they **were**

4 Elicit a table of the negative and question forms onto the board. Alternatively, students check by referring to the table in *Language summary A* on page 149 of the *Students' Book*. Highlight:

- the use of *did* for all persons (but not with *be*)
- the fact that the main verb remains in the infinitive without *to*
- the contraction *didn't*
- the inversion for the question form of *be*, and the formation of the negative *was/were not*.

If necessary, explain that *could* operates like *was/were* and *had to* operates like a normal verb using *did … have to*.

ANSWERS
Questions forms:
Did he go to live in the United States?
Were cookery programmes popular in the 1930s?
Negative forms:
He didn't go to live in the United States.
Cookery programmes weren't popular in the 1930s.

PRACTICE

1 [T2.2] Word to check: *advert*. Students work in pairs to complete the sentences. Encourage students to use their instinct or to make guesses about the Past simple forms. Play the recording, pausing after each sentence if necessary for students to check their answers. Remind students of the list of irregular verbs on page 157 of the *Students' Book*, or refer them to the *mini-dictionary*, to check whether verbs are irregular.

ANSWERS
a began, was b lasted, cost
c came, were, bought d made

2 Use the first two questions as examples to remind students that they should use *was/were* if the main verb is *be*, but that otherwise they should use *did*. Students work in pairs to complete the quiz. Emphasise that they do not need to try to answer the questions at this stage.

ANSWERS
1 was 2 did 3 was 4 were 5 did 6 was
7 did 8 were

Pronunciation

See *Teacher's tips: helping students with pronunciation* on pages 6–7.

1 Focus students' attention on the pairs of regular Past simple forms. Allow a few minutes for students to check the infinitives and their meaning. Either explain unfamiliar verbs yourself or ask students to look in their mini-dictionaries.

2 [T2.3] Use the recording to model the three different verb endings, or model them yourself. Point out that the *-ed* ending on regular verbs is pronounced /ɪd/ only when the infinitive ends in *-t* (*lasted*) or *-d* (*ended*). This will help students to see that verbs like *appeared* and *worked* are not pronounced /aˈpɪərɪd/ and /wɜːkɪd/.
Students often find it difficult to distinguish between /d/ and /t/ endings. Highlight that:
- /d/ follows voiced sounds
- /t/ follows unvoiced sounds.

It may be useful to show them the difference between voiced and unvoiced sounds. A finger placed gently on the throat should vibrate when a voiced sound is produced, but not with unvoiced sounds. It should be easier for students to hear /ɪd/, as this is different and adds a syllable to the base form of the verb. This is the most important of the three different endings.

3 [T2.4] Use the first two pairs of past forms as examples. Pause the recording after each pair of verbs, and allow students time to compare their ideas in pairs before repeating the recording if necessary. Check answers with the whole class.

ANSWERS
b D c S d D e S f D g D

4 Students work individually to practise pronouncing the endings. Emphasise that the /ɪd/ endings are the most important. If students find this difficult, model and drill the verbs chorally and individually before students work on their own.

Pronunciation, exercise 3: additional suggestion

Put students into groups and give each group a ball. One student says the infinitive of a verb and throws the ball to another student, who has to say the Past simple form. That student then says another infinitive form and throws the ball to someone else, and so on. After a minute or two, introduce the rule that anyone who answers wrongly (with the wrong form or the wrong pronunciation of the *-ed* ending) drops out, until there is only one student left.

3 Set this up as a competition. Students work in pairs to complete the quiz, and then check their answers on page 140 of the *Students' Book*. In class feedback, find out which pair had the highest score.

4 **a** Demonstrate the activity using the board. Write up five sentences about yourself, and invite students to guess which are true and which are false. Give students a few minutes to write notes about themselves. Circulate and help with vocabulary.

b Focus students on the example in the speech balloons. If necessary, get a student to demonstrate one of their own examples with you. Tell students to change over after each sentence. This can also be done as a mingling activity, where students move on to the next person after each correct guess.

c Have some brief class feedback to find out who was good at guessing correctly.

ADDITIONAL PRACTICE

RB **Resource bank:** Learner-training worksheet B (Using the *mini-dictionary*: irregular verbs – part 1), page 117; 2A Dead famous (Past simple yes/no questions and short answers), pages 118–119

Workbook: Vocabulary booster: TV Programmes, exercise 8, page 15; Past simple, exercises 1–4, pages 12–13

Language focus 2 (PAGE 18)

Time phrases often used in the past: *at, on, in, ago*

1 Demonstrate the activity using the first sentence as an example. Ask students if they believe that you started learning English six months ago. Students work individually to decide which sentences are true for them before comparing their answers in pairs, justifying their choices. Circulate and note down any time phrases which cause problems to focus on later.

2 Explain that the most recent time phrase has already been numbered for the students. Then, elicit and number the time phrase which is least recent. Students work individually or in pairs to number the remaining phrases. If you want to encourage some discussion, ask students to try to remember something about each time/date and to tell each other about it. Check answers with the whole class. Write the answers along a timeline on the board as you elicit them.

ANSWERS
1 f 2 g 3 h 4 c 5 b 6 a 7 j 8 e 9 d 10 i 11 k 12 l

3 Demonstrate the activity using the first sentence, rewriting it to make it true for you. Give students a few minutes to work individually before they share answers in small groups.

Grammar

1 Refer students back to the time phrases in exercise 1. Give them a few minutes individually or in pairs to complete the rules. As you elicit the answers, ask students for more examples of each rule. Alternatively, refer them to *Language summary B* on page 149 of the *Students' Book* to check their answers and to see more examples.

ANSWERS
a at b on c in d fl

2 Students work individually or in pairs to identify which phrase is wrong with *ago*.

ANSWER AND LANGUAGE NOTE
The phrase *the summer ago* is wrong.
Explain that we don't use *ago* after specific periods of time with *the*. We use *ago* for a period of time from the present to the past, in order to show how far in the past something happened.

PRACTICE

1 [T2.5] Do this as a written or oral exercise. *Either*: play the recording while students write their answers. Ask them to compare their answers in pairs, and to try to remember what each question was. *Or*: stop the recording after each question and ask students to tell each other their answers in pairs without writing.

2 Words to check: *stay up*, *lose/lost*, *journey*, *sing/sang*, *rent*. Give students a few minutes to complete the sentences individually before comparing in pairs. Encourage them to ask follow-up questions to find out more about their partner's answers. Circulate and note down good examples of language use and/or problems with time phrases or the Past simple. Have some brief class feedback on what you noted.

ADDITIONAL PRACTICE

RB **Resource bank:** 2B The millionaire's ball (Past simple and time phrases), pages 120–121

Workbook: Time phrases often used in the past, exercises 5–6, page 14

Vocabulary (PAGE 19)

Words to describe feelings

See *Teacher's tips: working with lexical phrases* on pages 8–9 and *Making the most of the* mini-dictionary on pages 9–10.

1 Students work in pairs or groups to match the words to the pictures, using their mini-dictionaries if necessary. Some of the words are similar in meaning, and the photos can be interpreted in different ways, so students may not agree on all the answers. Encourage any useful discussion.

POSSIBLE ANSWERS AND LANGUAGE NOTES
a *bored, disappointed* b *excited, surprised*
c *nervous, worried* d *angry, disappointed, impatient*
e *excited; in a good mood* f *scared*

Note the following points.

- If *nervous* is a 'false friend' for your students, check it carefully with examples. You can feel *nervous* about an exam because you are worried about it and can't relax.
- *Nervous* and *worried* are similar in meaning, but *nervous* implies an element of fear, whereas *worried* implies that you are unhappy and cannot stop thinking about the problem.
- *Angry* and *impatient* are similar in meaning, but *impatient* means being bored with a situation and wanting it to change immediately. There may be an element of anger, but this is usually only temporary. The cause is less serious than for *angry*.

2 [T2.6] This activity checks that students have understood the meaning of the words. Demonstrate the activity using the first conversation. Emphasise that students do not need to understand every word. Pause the recording after each conversation to allow students time to compare their answers in pairs. Replay the recording if necessary. Check answers with the whole class.

ANSWERS
a nervous b disappointed c surprised
d impatient e in a good mood f embarrassed
g bored h worried

3 Words to check: *purse/wallet*, *miss a train/bus*, *a spider*, *cancelled*. Emphasise that students need only write a word or phrase, not a whole sentence, as their answer. Give them a few minutes individually to answer the questions. Suggest that students take turns to ask and answer, and that they choose questions at random, to keep the pace going. Have some brief class feedback on any unusual answers.

Pronunciation

See *Teacher's tips: helping students with pronunciation* on pages 6–7.

[T2.7] Students listen and mark the stress patterns. Demonstrate the activity using the first word, and show students how to mark stress by writing a circle above the stressed syllable. Check answers with the whole class.

If you have time: ask students to group words with similar stress patterns together. Write them on the board to check.

ANSWERS
See tapescript for recording 7 on page 163 of the *Students' Book*.

Groups of words with similar stress patterns

● •	• ● •	• ●
angry	embarrassed	relaxed
nervous	excited	surprised
worried	impatient	
• • ● •	**• • ● ●**	
disappointed	in a good mood	

ADDITIONAL PRACTICE

Workbook: Vocabulary, exercise 7, page 14

Wordspot (PAGE 20)

feel

See *Teacher's tips: working with lexical phrases* on pages 8–9.

1 Explain that in each of these *Wordspot* sections, students are going to look at a word with several meanings which is used a lot in English. Do an example with the class, then give students time individually or in pairs to study the diagram. Circulate to help and assess the level of knowledge. Elicit more examples for each category in the diagram, and highlight the following points.

- *Feel* is followed by an adjective when referring to a person or thing: *He feels stupid. The room felt hot.*
- *Feel* is followed by *about* when it means 'have an opinion' or 'think'.
- *Feel like* is quite informal and is followed by a noun or an *-ing* form.

If you have a mono-nationality class: consider using translation to help students check the meaning against their own language.

2 **a** Students work individually or in pairs to match the sentences.

b [T2.8] Play the recording. Students check their answers in pairs before checking with the whole class.

ANSWERS
1 d 2 g 3 a 4 f 5 h 6 c 7 e 8 b

3 Give students a few minutes to study the conversations. Put them into pairs to practise. Demonstrate with a strong student if necessary.

Wordspot, exercises 2 and 3: alternative suggestions

- Put the lines of the conversations on separate pieces of paper (either one set per pair, or one large set stuck to the board that all students can see). Students put the lines next to each other when they are matching the lines of conversations in exercise 2. In exercise 3, turn over B's part so that students have to remember it.
- Instead of remembering B's part in exercise 3, students invent their own lines (trying to use a phrase with *feel*).

Task: Tell a first time story

(PAGES 20–21)

See *Teacher's tips: making tasks work* on pages 10–11 and *Responding to learners' individual language needs* on pages 12–13.

Preparation: listening

1 **a** Start by telling students how many of the firsts you remember. Ask them to guess which ones they are. Students then work individually for a few minutes, ticking the appropriate boxes on the list.

b Focus students' attention on the pictures. Students work individually to decide which firsts the pictures show before comparing their answers in pairs. Check answers with the whole class.

ANSWERS
a the first time you went shopping or bought something alone
b your first day at school
c the first time you met someone important in your life
d your first car

2 **a** [T2.9] Play the recording. Give students a few minutes in pairs to discuss which pictures illustrate the stories. Check answers with the whole class.

ANSWERS
b and c

b Students stay in their pairs to discuss which phrases come from each story, and what Helen and Josh say about them. They should check any of the unknown words in their mini-dictionaries. (The words in the box are key to the stories, so make sure that students understand them all.) Check answers with the whole class.

ANSWERS
b *secondary school* (Helen's first day there); *a video camera* (Helen's mum took it out and filmed her); *a big smile* (Helen had a big smile); *embarrassing* (the video)
c *crowded* (room); *a get-together* (at a ski resort)

3 [T2.9] Focus students' attention on the questions. Play the recording, giving students time to discuss their answers in pairs before checking with the whole class.

ANSWERS

	Helen	Josh
a **Where and when did it happen?**	In the road outside her house; on her first day at secondary school, in September 1990	At a get-together in a ski resort in Yugoslavia; twelve years ago
b **Who else was in the story?**	Her friend and her mother	The staff who worked at the ski resort, and the woman who became his wife
c **How did they feel?**	Helen and her friend felt very nervous. The story doesn't say how Helen's mother felt.	Josh felt shy and strange. The story doesn't say how the woman or the other staff felt.

d What happened in the end?	Her mother filmed her on a video camera. When Helen saw the film recently, she was embarrassed.	Josh smiled at the woman and she smiled back. Two years later, they got married.

***Preparation:* listening: alternative suggestions**

a *If you want to personalise this stage*: tell the story of one of your firsts. Speak from notes and, if possible, bring in maps, photos, souvenirs, etc. to illustrate your story. Students answer the same questions as for the recording (exercise 3, questions a–d).

b *If you are short of time*: play the recording of only one of the stories in exercise 3.

Task: speaking

1 Refer students back to the list of firsts that they ticked in *Preparation: listening*, exercise 1a. Explain that you want them to choose two or three to speak about. Elicit any ideas for other important firsts that were not on the list. If any of your students seem reluctant to talk about themselves, give them the option of talking about another person's first, and refer them to the pictures on page 141 of the *Students' Book*.

2 Encourage students to spend some time thinking, and to make notes to help them remember and structure what they want to say. Show students what you mean by notes with an example on the board: *first pet – 8 or 9 – mum and dad bought – puppy – fell in love – so sweet – got up at five every morning – ran home from school – played with puppy all the time*.

Circulate, feeding in language, and prompting less confident students with questions, for example, *Why was it important for you? Why did you feel worried?* Focus students on the *Useful language* box. They could spend a minute or two thinking about how to improve their story by the addition of any of the phrases.

The size of the groups will depend on the size of your class, and on how long your students can concentrate on listening to other people's stories. While you are listening to the stories, collect examples of good language use and/or errors to focus on later. When the groups have finished, ask one person from each group to report on the funniest/saddest/strangest story.

***Task: speaking*: alternative suggestions**

a *If any of your students lack the confidence or ability to speak at any length*: ask them to write their stories down to present to the other students in written form in a future lesson, or to tell just one short story.

b *If you want to record students telling their story*: ask them to follow one of the following procedures.
- Students record their stories in a language laboratory, then change places and listen to each other's stories.
- Students record their story on cassette at home, then give you the cassette for correction in the same way as for a piece of written homework. (Comments and corrections can be written on a separate piece of paper.)
- Groups work in different rooms and record their two or three stories, to listen to and comment on later. (This is obviously more suitable for smaller classes.)

Writing (PAGE 22)

Linking ideas in narrative

1 **a** Students read phrases 1–9 and in pairs discuss what first experience they describe. Words to check: *a silver ring*, *coach*, *youth hostel*. Students work individually or in pairs to complete the text before checking answers with the whole class.

ANSWERS
a 1 b 6 c 7 d 2 e 9 f 5 g 3 h 8 i 4

b *Either*: ask students to underline the linking words in their books. *Or*: write the complete text on the board or an overhead transparency, and go through the text with the class. Clarify that:
- *and* joins two clauses: *I went to London **and** stayed for six months.*
- *because* introduces a reason: *I stayed at home **because** I was ill.*
- *so* follows a reason: *I was ill **so** I stayed at home.*
- *then* shows a sequence: *I went to the supermarket, **then** to the post office.*
- *but* introduces information which is contrasting or unexpected: *The weather was terrible **but** we had a good time.*

If your students seem fairly familiar with the words, point out *First* (used at the beginning of a sequence of events) and *Unfortunately* (used to introduce something negative).

To give students some controlled practice of the linking words, put them into pairs, A and B. Student B closes their book, and Student A reads Marcos's story, saying *Beep* instead of the linking words. Student B calls out the correct word as soon as they can. Students A and B change over.

ANSWERS
2 because 3 and 4 because 5 but 6 so
7 but 8 so 9 then

2 Refer students back to the notes they made for their story in *Task: speaking*. The notes can be used to help structure their writing. Encourage students to plan their writing. *If you have time*: ask them to write a first draft in class, and then a second draft for homework. This will enable you to give them some help in the initial stages.

ADDITIONAL PRACTICE

RB **Resource bank:** 2C Invent a story (Past simple and linkers), page 122
Workbook: Improve your writing, exercise 13, page 17

Study ... (PAGE 22)

Using the *mini-dictionary* (2): Word stress

1 Students work individually or in pairs, saying the words aloud quietly to help them decide on the number of syllables. Check answers with the whole class.

ANSWERS
angry (2) colourful (3) electronic (4)
expensive (3) popular (3) inventor (3)
programme (2)

2 Students use their mini-dictionaries to check where the main stress is in each word. This could be done as a race. Encourage students to record where the stress is for each new word they learn, as pronunciation is an integral part of 'knowing' a word. You could show students different ways of marking/recording word stress, such as writing a small circle (the method typically used in this course) or square above the stressed syllable; underlining the stressed syllable; or inserting a primary stress mark (') of the kind used in the *mini-dictionary* before the stressed syllable.

ANSWERS
● ● ● ● ●
angry colourful electronic expensive popular
● ●
inventor programme

Pronunciation spot

Stress and the /ə/ sound

See *Teacher's tips: helping students with pronunciation* on pages 6–7.

1 [T2.10] Play the recording or model the words, exaggerating the stressed syllables so that the contrast is greater, for students to hear the schwa sound.

2 [T2.11] Students work individually or in pairs, saying the words aloud to help them decide where the stressed syllables are. Play the recording for them to check, or model the words yourself. Students listen again to help them decide where the schwa sounds are. If students find this difficult, tell them how many schwa sounds there are in each word. Students listen and check.

ANSWERS
● /ə/ /ə/ ● ● /ə/ ● /ə/
inventor afternoon November summer
/ə/ ● ●/ə/ ● /ə/ ●/ə/
Japanese television person colour

3 Students practise saying the words. Drill the words chorally and individually before students work in pairs.

Practise ... (PAGE 23)

1 Past simple

ANSWERS
a The programmes were extremely popular.
b Did you watch television?
c I took my exams.
d My brother stayed up late.
e I didn't get home until midnight.
f I bought presents for everyone in my family.
g We watched a video in the evening.
h Renate sang beautifully.
i The match began at 8.30.
j I felt so tired.

2 Time phrases with *at*, *on*, *in* and *fl*

ANSWERS

at	on	in	fl
eleven o'clock	June 18th Friday afternoon	2002 the 1990s the twentieth century	a minute ago last night last year

3 Words to describe feelings

ANSWERS
a nervous b scared c disappointed
d good mood e surprised f worried g bored
h excited i embarrassed

4 *feel*

ANSWERS
a about b sad c better d going e ill f fine

5 Linking words

ANSWERS
a so b then c so d but e because f and
g so h because i then

Remember! (PAGE 23)

After looking back at the areas they have practised, students do the *Mini-check* on page 158 of the *Students' Book*. Check answers with the whole class, and ask students to tell you their scores out of 20.

ANSWERS
1 cost 2 were 3 watched 4 bought
5 Did you feel 6 began 7 in 8 fl 9 at 10 in
11 on 12 fl 13 bored/excited 14 nervous/relaxed
15 fed up / in a good mood 16 going 17 better
18 disappointed 19 felt 20 worried

module 3

At rest, at work

Vocabulary (PAGE 24)

Daily routines

See *Teacher's tips: working with lexical phrases* on pages 8–9 and *Making the most of the* mini-dictionary on pages 9–10.

1 Students discuss the questions in pairs. Have some brief class feedback on students' ideas.

2 Demonstrate the exercise by eliciting the activity which usually happens first in the morning. Start drawing a diagram of the activities in order. Students work in pairs or small groups, checking any unknown words in their *mini-dictionaries*. Check answers with the whole class by completing the diagram.

Remind students of the usefulness of word locusts (see *Vocabulary and speaking*, exercise 4, on page 7 of the *Students' Book*) for collecting phrases with a common verb, for example, *have a bath/shower*, *have something to eat*.

POSSIBLE ANSWERS
your alarm goes off
you wake up
you switch off the alarm
you get out of bed
you have a bath/shower
you get dressed
you have something to eat
you go to school/work
you come home
you feel tired
you get into bed
you set your alarm
you turn off the light
you fall asleep
you dream about something

3 Use the order of activities in exercise 2 to elicit or explain the meaning of *routine*. Students work in pairs to talk about their daily routines. Choose one or two pairs to report back to the class on similarities and differences.

ADDITIONAL PRACTICE

RB **Resource bank:** Learner-training worksheet C (Noticing and recording collocations), page 123

Reading and speaking (PAGES 24–25)

1 Start the discussion by telling students about some of your sleep habits. Give students a few minutes to discuss the questions in pairs.

2 Draw students' attention to the title of the text and explain that it gives advice on falling asleep and waking up. Demonstrate the activity using the first paragraph. Give students a few minutes to read individually before checking answers in pairs and then as a whole class.

ANSWERS
(*in order of paragraphs*)
F F W W F F F F W

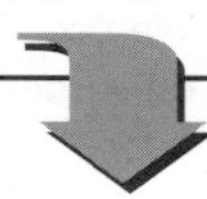

***Reading and speaking*, exercises 1 and 2: additional suggestion**

Before reading the text in exercise 2, students spend a few minutes working in small groups to think of advice they would give to people who have sleep problems such as the ones highlighted in exercise 1. Students feed back briefly, writing their ideas on the board. As students read, they check to see if their ideas are mentioned in the text as well as writing *F* (falling asleep) and *W* (waking up).

3 Demonstrate the activity using the board. Write up the first phrase from column A and the choice of three definitions from column B. Elicit the correct answer. Students work individually or in pairs to complete the matching.

ANSWERS

a	Get	1	Buy
b	light	2	small
c	fast	3	after the correct time
d	Get	4	Ask
e	they	5	people in general
f	great	6	wonderful
g	avoid	7	do not have

4 Students discuss the questions in small groups or as a class.

Language focus 1 (PAGE 26)

should, shouldn't

1 Words to check: *ashtray*, *cigarette end*. Ask students when they last had to study for an important exam, how they prefer to study and how organised they are. Give students a few minutes to search the picture for the items listed in the box. Encourage comments about how successful Bruce is in his studies!

2 Discuss the sentences briefly with the class. Emphasise that whether students agree with the sentences or not depends on their view of the right/wrong thing to do.

Grammar

1 Give students a minute or two individually or in pairs to choose the correct ending to the rule. As you check the answer, highlight the following points.

Should is less strong than *have to* (and *must*, if students ask about it). We use *should* to talk about what is a good idea or the right thing to do. This general meaning is more helpful to students than limiting it to *should* = advice.

- We use the infinitive without *to* after *should*.
- *Should* does not change in the third person.
- The letter 'l' in *should* is silent: /ʃʊd/.
- We often use *Perhaps* ... or *I think* ... in front of *should*, in order to make it less direct.

ANSWER
We use *should/shouldn't* when it is/isn't a good idea to do something.

2–3 Ask students to read the rules, then refer them to *Language summary* A on page 149 of the *Students' Book* for more information.

PRACTICE

1 a Students discuss their ideas in pairs, then make a written list. Circulate and help with vocabulary. Students compare ideas with other pairs or with the whole class. Encourage them to give reasons for their ideas.

POSSIBLE ANSWERS
He should tidy his room.
He should organise his notes and books.
He should empty the ashtray.
He shouldn't play computer games / read the newspaper when he's studying.
He should have a short break every hour / every two hours (to read the newspaper or play a computer game).
He shouldn't phone friends when he's studying.
He should put his answering machine on.
He shouldn't listen to loud music when he's studying.

b [T3.1] Students listen and write any sentences they haven't already written. Pause the recording after each sentence to allow students time to write.

Pronunciation

See *Teacher's tips: helping students with pronunciation* on pages 6–7.

1 Model the two sentences for the class, taking care to use a natural speed and rhythm.

ANSWER
The negative form *shouldn't* is stressed.

2 [T3.1] Pause the recording after each sentence to allow time for students to repeat the sentence. Alternatively, model and chorally drill the sentences.

2 Check the meaning of *be annoyed with someone*. Give students a few minutes to read about the situations and to think about what the people should/shouldn't do. Then put students into pairs to discuss their ideas.

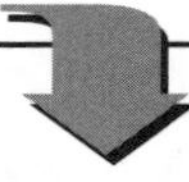

Practice, exercise 2: additional activity

Students work in pairs or small groups on one of two situations. *Either*: ask them to think of three pieces of advice for someone who wants to practise their English outside the classroom in their own country. *Or*: ask them to think of some advice for someone going to stay in the UK or another English-speaking country. (The advice can be about language learning and/or about other things, for example, money or things to take with you.)

Emphasise that students should use *should/shouldn't* in their discussions. Elicit an example before putting them into pairs or small groups to discuss their ideas. If some of your students have experience of both situations, get some pairs/groups to discuss the first situation and some the second. They can then exchange ideas.

If your students need more input: refer them to the following ideas for advice concerning each situation. They can then use these ideas to discuss what the person in each situation should/shouldn't do.

a *In the student's own country*
- Listen to radio programmes in English (for example, on the BBC World Service).
- Find books, newspapers, etc. in the library.
- Subscribe to an English magazine.
- Find a cinema which shows English films in the original language with subtitles.
- Find a speaking partner (in your class or another class) and arrange to meet for an hour or so every week to speak English.

b *In an English-speaking country*
- Make friends with students from other countries, rather than your own country, so that you have to speak English.
- Don't forget to take some warm clothes and an umbrella.
- Arrange a conversation exchange with an English-speaking person. Meet for an hour. Speak for half an hour in English, half an hour in your own language.
- Don't take too much cash. Take traveller's cheques and a credit card.

Practice, exercise 2: alternative suggestions

a *If your students enjoy roleplaying*: ask them to imagine they are a famous person with a problem situation. Give students a few minutes to decide on a problem and to prepare what they are going to say. Then put them into groups to tell each other about the problem and to give advice.

b *If you have access to an English magazine with a problem page* (those written for teenagers are best in terms of language level): collect some examples of letters and distribute them, one per student or one between two. Students read their letter, then mingle and tell each other about the problem and ask for advice.

ADDITIONAL PRACTICE

RB Resource bank: 3A The secret of successful language learning (Vocabulary extension – word building), page 124

Workbook: *should/shouldn't*, exercise 1, page 18; Vocabulary booster: studying, exercise 10, page 22

Language focus 2 (PAGE 27)

can, can't, have to, don't have to

1 [T3.2] Focus students' attention on the pictures and ask them to guess what Mayo is studying to be. As students discuss their ideas as a whole class, note their ideas on the board. Play the recording for students to check their ideas. Words to check: *circus*, *acrobat*.

ANSWER
She's doing a course in Circus Studies. She wants to be a circus entertainer / an acrobat.

2 [T3.3] Students listen again before checking their answers in pairs and as a whole class.

ANSWERS
a False b True c False d False e True f False

Grammar

1 Give students a few minutes individually or in pairs to complete the sentences before looking at the tapescript for recording 3 on page 163 of the *Students' Book*. As you check the answers, highlight:

- that *can* operates like *should* (it does not change in the third person and it is followed by an infinitive without *to*)
- that *have to* does change in the third person, for example, *he/she has to …*
- the negative forms and their contractions *can't* and *don't/doesn't have to*
- the question forms *Can I/you/he/she/we/they …? Do I/you/we/they have to …? Does he/she have to …?*

ANSWERS
a don't have to b have to c can d can't

2 Students work in pairs to complete the sentences. Go through the answers with the class, then refer students to *Language summary B* on pages 149–150 of the *Students' Book* for more information.

ANSWERS AND LANGUAGE NOTES
a *Have to* means that something is necessary.
b *Can* means that you are able to do something.
c *Don't have to* means that something is not necessary.
d *Can't* means that you are not able to do something.

Must is not treated here, to avoid confusion at this level. *Have to* can be used safely by students instead. However, if students ask about *must*, explain that:

- *must* and *have to* are very similar in meaning
- *mustn't* and *don't have to* are different in meaning (*mustn't* = it's prohibited, *don't have to* = it's not necessary, but you can if you want).

Can is also used to ask for permission, for example, *Can I leave work early today?*

PRACTICE

1 Draw students' attention to the two written examples. Students work individually to write sentences which are true for them. Circulate, noting any problem areas to focus on later.

2 Students work in pairs to compare their answers.

Pronunciation

See *Teacher's tips: helping students with pronunciation* on pages 6–7.

[T3.4] Play the recording or say the sentences yourself at natural speed. Ask students to write *can* or *can't* for each sentence. As you check the answers, highlight the following points.

- Can is unstressed. Help students to hear this by first drilling I … see much better now. Then show them how can is squashed in between I and see.
- Can't is stressed.

ANSWERS
See tapescript for recording 4 on page 164 of the *Students' Book*.

ADDITIONAL PRACTICE

RB Resource bank: 3B Parents and children (*can, can't, have to, don't have to, should, shouldn't*), page 125

Workbook: *can/can't*, exercise 2, page 18; *have to / don't have to*, exercises 3–4, pages 18–19

Vocabulary (PAGE 28)

Jobs

See *Teacher's tips: working with lexical phrases* on pages 8–9 and *Making the most of the* mini-dictionary on pages 9–10.

1 Students work individually or in pairs to complete the alphabetical list of jobs. Emphasise that they should check the meaning of any unknown words in their mini-dictionaries. Check answers with the whole class.

ANSWERS
A accountant B bus driver C chef D dentist
F firefighter J judge L librarian N nanny
P plumber S secretary T translator W waitress

2 Students work in small groups before discussing their ideas with the whole class. Point out that the answers are not fixed.

POSSIBLE ANSWERS
Can make a lot of money: accountant, architect, civil servant, dentist, doctor, journalist, judge, lawyer, psychologist, writer
Can be dangerous: bus driver, firefighter, journalist, police officer, taxi driver
Have to study a long time: accountant, architect, dentist, doctor, judge, lawyer, psychologist
Can work at home: accountant, architect, journalist, translator, writer
Can really help people: doctor, lawyer, nurse, psychologist
Have to be very patient: librarian, nanny, nurse, psychologist, secretary, shop assistant, taxi driver
Have to be good at languages: translator
Have to be very good with people: barman, nanny, nurse, police officer, psychologist, secretary, shop assistant, waitress

3 Give students a few minutes to prepare what they will say and to ask you for any vocabulary before putting them into small groups.

4 Students work individually for five minutes to categorise the jobs before discussing their ideas in small groups. Have some brief class feedback, recording the most and least popular jobs on the board.

Task: Choose the right job (PAGE 29)

See *Teacher's tips: making tasks work* on pages 10–11 and *Responding to learners' individual needs* on pages 12–13.

Preparation: listening

[T3.5] Focus students on the pictures. Make sure they understand that the first time they listen they should only try to complete the column about interests in the table. Emphasise that they should write brief notes. Play the recording, pausing after each person to allow students time to write. Students compare answers in pairs before checking with the whole class.

ANSWERS

Person	Interests
Morgan	Loves music and going to the movies; really interested in people and making friends
Luke	Money; would like to work for himself; not really into computers; likes to be independent
Carmen	Studying languages (English, French and maybe Chinese); likes reading and meeting people from all over the world
Jong	Likes hard work; wants to improve his English, get a good job and become a millionaire

Task: speaking

1 **a** Ask students to look at the jobs on page 28, and then to think of a few of their own. Set a time limit of five minutes for students to work individually. They should suggest two or three different jobs for each person, and give reasons for their suggestions, completing the table in note form.

b Draw students' attention to *Useful language a* and *b*, and point out the different ways of comparing ideas and of agreeing and disagreeing. Working in small groups, students discuss the suggestions they made in exercise 1a. Circulate and note down good examples of language use and/or problem areas to focus on later.

2 Give students a few minutes to prepare what they will say and to ask you for any vocabulary. Ask the spokesperson from each group to present their ideas to the class. Tell students to make a note of any ideas that are different to theirs. Then set up a class discussion and/or vote to decide on the best job for each person.

3 [T3.6] Play the recording, asking students to listen for each person's ideal job. Check answers with the whole class and discuss any they are surprised about.

ANSWERS
Morgan: psychologist
Luke: plumber
Carmen: translator
Jong: trader on the stock market

***Task*: alternative suggestions**

a *If you are short of time*: spread *Preparation: listening* and *Task: speaking* over two lessons. This also gives students time to think of ideas between lessons, so that they come to the second lesson with a completed table and are ready to discuss their ideas.

b *If you have a large class or your students are not confident at speaking in front of the class*: instead of having a spokesperson presenting each group's ideas to the class, regroup students (in groups of three/four) into groups with students who worked in different groups. Ask each student to present their previous group's ideas to the rest of the new group.

Real life (PAGE 30)

Making requests and asking for permission

1 **a** Ask students to look briefly at the conversations. Establish where the conversations take place and what each person wants. Ask students to guess the missing words in pairs, or as a class, but tell them not to write yet.

ANSWERS
1 A man is outside a neighbour's house, and wants his neighbour to turn her music down.
2 An employee/student is at work / in class, and wants to leave early.

3 Someone is away from home, and wants to borrow a friend's mobile phone.
4 A student is in class, and wants to change seats because of the sun.

b [T3.7] Play the recording. Pause after each conversation for students to write in the missing words. Students compare answers in pairs and/or as a class.

ANSWERS AND LANGUAGE NOTE

1 *could you; thanks*
2 *is it OK if I; go ahead; telling me*
3 *Can I borrow; here you are*
4 *Do you mind if I; What's the problem*

In 1, the speaker is making a request, asking someone else to do something: *could you turn the music down …?*

In 2, 3 and 4, the speakers are asking for permission, asking if they can do something: *is it OK if I leave …? Can I borrow …? Do you mind if I change …?*

Although, strictly speaking, the positive response to *Do you mind if I …?* is *No*, in practice English speakers are inconsistent about this. They simply make it clear through the other words they use whether the response is positive or not.

Pronunciation

See *Teacher's tips: helping students with pronunciation* on pages 6–7.

1 [T3.8] Ask students to look at the tapescript for recording 8 on page 164 of the *Students' Book*. As they read, play the recording or say the examples yourself. Students will sound more polite if they start at a high pitch. It can be useful to demonstrate this by raising your hand at the start of each sentence.

2 [T3.8] Play or say the examples again, pausing for students to repeat. If necessary, extend this controlled practice by giving students prompts to substitute in the examples. For example:

T: *say that again*	S: *Could you say that again, please?*
T: *borrow your pen*	S: *Can I borrow your pen, please?*

2 Give students five to ten minutes to choose the situations and to prepare their conversations. *If you are short of time*: ask them to prepare two conversations.

Check the use of *keep* + verb *-ing* to talk about repetitive/annoying behaviour. Circulate and help with vocabulary. Depending on time, choose two or three pairs to act out their conversations. Other students tick the situations from the list that they are acting out and/or the request/permission phrases that they use.

ADDITIONAL PRACTICE

Workbook: *have to / don't have to*, exercise 5, page 19

Study … (PAGE 31)

Class rules

1 Make sure that students understand the idea of classroom guidelines, which have been negotiated and agreed between teacher and students. Elicit one or two ideas, for example, how much the teacher should speak English or the students' language. Students work individually to choose rules they would like to have in class before discussing their choices with the whole class. If students are reticent, explain that it is useful for the teacher to know what students think: it can be beneficial for their learning, the class dynamics, etc.

2 Encourage students to collaborate in groups to write up their class rules on poster-size paper. The rules can be reviewed at a later stage in the course, to see how well everyone is keeping to the guidelines.

Pronunciation spot

Silent letters

See *Teacher's tips: helping students with pronunciation* on pages 6–7.

1 Students work in pairs, saying the words aloud to help each other hear where the missing letters are. Tell them to guess if they are not sure.

2 [T3.9] Write the words on the board. Play the recording, pausing after each word to allow students time to confer with their partner, if necessary, before checking answers with the whole class. Underline the silent letters on the board. Model any problematic words for students to repeat. Students practise in pairs.

ANSWERS
(*answers in* **bold**)
cou**l**d frien**d** ha**l**f **h**our somethin**g** li**gh**t
shou**l**d midni**gh**t ca**l**m interesting

Practise … (PAGE 31)

1 *should, shouldn't* and forms for giving advice

Students work individually before checking answers in pairs.

ANSWERS
a Why b should c Try d shouldn't e Should

2 *can, can't, have to, don't have to*

Do this exercise orally. Say the phrase in **bold** and students change the sentence using *can*, *can't*, *have to* or *don't have to*. Make sure that students use weak forms appropriately. Students write the answers for homework to consolidate the practice.

ANSWERS
a You can b You don't have to c Can my friend
d Do I have to e You can't

3 Daily routines

Put the phrases from boxes A and B onto different coloured card. Students work in pairs or small groups to match the beginnings with the endings. This could also be done as a race.

ANSWERS
fall asleep feel tired get dressed get into bed
have a shower set the alarm turn off the light
wake up

4 Jobs

Students work in pairs to match pictures and jobs. Check answers with the whole class and ask students to tell the class something about the job, for example, for a firefighter: *You have to work late at night. You should be good at driving*.

ANSWERS
a shop assistant b taxi driver c farmer
d chef e nurse f firefighter

5 Making requests and asking for permission

Set this up as a race. In small groups, students compete to be the first person to write the question out in the correct order.

ANSWERS
1 Could you open the window, please?
2 Do you mind if I smoke?
3 Can I borrow your newspaper, please?
4 Could you phone back later?

Remember! (PAGE 31)

After looking back at the areas they have practised, students do the *Mini-check* on page 158 of the *Students' Book*. Check answers with the whole class, and ask students to tell you their scores out of 20.

ANSWERS
1 shouldn't 2 can't 3 have to 4 can 5 should
6 don't have to 7 architect 8 taxi driver 9 nurse
10 shop assistant 11 journalist 12 off 13 up
14 ahead 15 off 16 to do 17 doing 18 Do
19 don't 20 does

module 4

Special occasions

Vocabulary and speaking (PAGE 32)

Dates and special occasions

See *Teacher's tips: working with lexical phrases* on pages 8–9 and *Making the most of the* mini-dictionary on pages 9–10.

1 Check that students can say the months of the year in English. Revise ordinal numbers briefly as students will need them for saying dates.

Students discuss the questions in pairs or groups. Have some brief feedback on which months are the most/least popular, and why.

2 **a** Word to check: *celebrate*. Ask students to tick the days celebrated in their country. Go through the days with the class, making sure that they understand them all. You may find it useful to refer to some of the facts listed below.

Chinese New Year: a day in the Chinese calendar when people celebrate the New Year.

St Valentine's Day: a day when people send anonymous cards to their boyfriend/girlfriend/husband/wife or somebody they like romantically. People often call it *Valentine's Day* for short.

Mother's Day: a day when children send cards and flowers to their mothers, to show how much they appreciate them. It is always on a Sunday.

Easter: a Christian festival, which people celebrate on a Sunday in March/April. It is also a holiday weekend.

May Day: a holiday on the first Monday in May, traditionally a day when all workplaces closed. In some countries, people call it *Labour Day* instead.

Father's Day: a day when children send cards and presents to their fathers, to show how much they appreciate them. It is always on a Sunday.

American Independence Day: a day when Americans celebrate independence from the British.

Halloween: a night when children in the UK/USA play games and dress up as ghosts etc. It is the evening before *All Saints' Day*, a Christian festival in which people honour the dead.

Christmas Day: a day in the Christian calendar when people celebrate the birth of Jesus Christ. Most people spend a few days with their family, and exchange cards and presents.

New Year's Eve: the last day of the year. People usually have parties in the evening, and stay awake until after midnight.

Put students into pairs or small groups to discuss the questions, and see if they know when the days are.

b [T4.1] Students listen and make notes. In pairs or groups they compare answers and discuss the differences between the UK/USA and their countries.

ANSWERS
See tapescript for recording 1 on page 164 of the *Students' Book*.

Pronunciation

See *Teacher's tips: helping students with pronunciation* on pages 6–7.

1 [T4.2] Demonstrate the activity using *January* as an example. Model the word and show the number of syllables and the stress at the same time. Play the recording, pausing after each month to give students time to mark the stress. Students check answers in pairs and then as a whole class.

ANSWERS
February April July August September
October November December

2 [T4.3] Emphasise that students can write the answers in full (for example, *August 23rd*) or in numbers (for example, *23.08*). Pause the recording after each date to give students time to write their answers.

ANSWERS
See tapescript for recording 3 on page 164 of the *Students' Book*.

3 [T4.3] Using the first date as an example, highlight how the date is said. Play the recording or say the dates yourself, and point out the difference between the voiced sound /ð/ in ***the*** and the unvoiced sound /θ/ in *ten**th*** and ***th**irtie**th***. Students listen again and repeat the dates.

3 **a** Students match the phrases in pairs, using their mini-dictionaries to look up any unknown words. Check answers with the whole class.

ANSWERS
2 dress up 3 eat out 4 exchange presents
5 have a day off work 6 invite people to your home
7 make a cake 8 send cards to people
9 stay up late 10 visit relatives 11 buy flowers

b Give students an example of something you do on one of the special occasions, for example, *I visit relatives on Christmas Day*. Then elicit one or two more examples of why people might do these things, for instance, *You visit relatives when they are in hospital. You dress up when you go to a wedding*. Give students a few minutes to think about what they do, and to give other reasons why people do these things. Students compare their ideas.

ADDITIONAL PRACTICE

Workbook: Vocabulary, exercise 6, page 26; Vocabulary booster: special occasions, exercise 9, page 27

Reading (PAGE 33)

1 a Give students a few minutes individually to think about their birthday and what they do.

b Students look at the picture and find the things, using their mini-dictionaries if necessary. Check answers with the whole class.

2 Students read the text individually before comparing their answers in pairs.

3 Students work individually before checking answers with the whole class.

ANSWERS
b particularly c brand-new d several e ceremony
f the armed forces g shape h City Hall

Language focus 1 (PAGES 34–35)

Present continuous and Present simple

1 Students look at the picture and discuss what they think it is like working for a fashion magazine. Words to check: *choose articles*, *earn money*. Do the first example with the class. Students then work in pairs to decide what the three people do in their jobs.

POSSIBLE ANSWERS
Juliet: a, c, f **Imogen:** b, e, g **Carlos:** d, h

2 Remind students about the topic of special occasions. Set the context, for example, *It is the May Day holiday*. Explain that students are going to find out about the three people from *Glitz* magazine, who have got the day off. Tell students to read the paragraph about Imogen. Establish that she is relaxing at home with her husband.

Grammar

1 Students work individually to underline the examples.

ANSWERS
is spending aren't doing they're … sitting
she's … doing She's finding

2 Give students a few minutes in pairs to complete the rules and to find examples. As you check the answers, highlight:
- the use of the Present continuous for actions happening in a present period (*this year*, *this week*) and for actions in progress at this moment
- the contracted form of *be*
- the spelling of the present participle, e.g., *making*, *running* (see *Students' Book* page 150 *Language summary A*)
- the inversion of the subject and *be* to form a question
- the short answer forms:
  Yes, I/you/we/they are. *No, I/you/we/they aren't.*
  Yes, he/she is. *No, he/she isn't.*

ANSWERS
a We use the Present simple for things that are generally or always true.
Example: *Imogen and Alex usually go away at the weekend.*
b We use the Present continuous for things happening at this moment.
Example: *Imogen is spending her day off with her husband, Alex.*
c We use the Present continuous for things happening in the present period, but not at this moment.
Example: *she's also doing a course in fashion design.*

3 Students work in pairs to decide which sentences are correct. As you feed back, contrast the examples of state verbs with sentences containing verbs expressing activity or processes, for example, *do*, *go*, *work*. Point out that state verbs are often used with feelings and the senses, for example, *love*, *hate*, *think*. Refer students to *Language summaries A* and *B* on page 150 of the *Students' Book*.

ANSWERS
a ✘ b ✔ c ✘ d ✔

PRACTICE

1 Students predict from the pictures what Carlos and Juliet are doing. Check the meaning of *wedding anniversary*. Students work in pairs before checking with the whole class.

ANSWERS
1 is spending 2 live/lives 3 doesn't see
4 are celebrating 5 spends 6 doesn't like
7 is looking 8 wants

2 Do an example with the class first, to show that there are no set answers here. Students work in pairs before checking with the whole class.

POSSIBLE ANSWERS
Juliet is spending her day off with her family / her mother and her husband.
At the weekends, she usually goes shopping / does housework.
Today, she's painting/decorating her house. (She isn't shopping / doing housework.)
Her husband is reading a newspaper / relaxing.
He doesn't help her / like decorating.
Juliet doesn't like her job/life.
One day she wants to go and live by the sea / leave her husband.

3 a Do the first sentence with the class as an example. Students need to choose the correct form of the verb.

ANSWERS
1 'm learning 2 speak 3 don't like 4 never read
5 'm reading 6 'm wearing 7 go 8 usually spend
9 'm looking 10 'm trying

b Students work individually to decide if the sentences are true for them, changing the untrue sentences with information about themselves. Students compare answers.

ADDITIONAL PRACTICE

RB **Resource bank:** 4A Party guests (Present continuous and Present simple), pages 126–127

Workbook: Present continuous, exercises 1–3, page 24

Listening (PAGE 36)

New Year in two different cultures

1 Students discuss the questions in pairs.

2 Ask if anyone knows of any customs relating to New Year in Scotland or Hong Kong. Students check unknown words in their mini-dictionaries. Put students into pairs, and give them a few minutes to predict who mentions the words in the box.

3 [T4.4] Play the recording once. Tell students that they only need to understand enough to complete the table. Play the recording again before they discuss their answers in pairs.

ANSWERS

	Karen/Scotland	Johnny/Hong Kong
When it happens	December 31st	The end of January or the beginning of February
Special food/ drink	Shortbread	Mushrooms, oysters and sweets (for luck and money)
Things people give to each other	The first foot (the first person to visit your house) brings shortbread, coal and something to drink.	Adults give children a small red envelope with money in it.
Other customs	People clean the house in the evening. They open the door at midnight to let in the New Year. The first foot brings luck for the year.	People wear new clothes.

4 [T4.4] Write prompts on the board, for example: *food*; *good luck*; *children/adults*; *clothes*; *the house*; *when are the celebrations?* Put students into pairs to think of similarities and differences. Play the recording again if necessary before checking answers with the class.

POSSIBLE ANSWERS

Similarities

In both countries, good luck is important.
In both countries, people eat special food.

Differences

Chinese New Year involves children, but New Year in Scotland is more for adults because most of the customs happen at midnight or after.
New Year in Scotland (or New Year's Eve) is on December 31st, whereas Chinese New Year is either at the end of January or the beginning of February.
Scottish people clean the house; Chinese people wear new clothes.

Language focus 2 (PAGES 36–37)

Present continuous for future arrangements

1 Word to check: *rent*. Give students time to think which verb goes in each gap before they write.

2 [T4.5] Play the recording, pausing after each person. Highlight that the verb form is the Present continuous, but that in this context it is not being used to talk about the present. Have class feedback, and discuss whose plans sound the most interesting.

ANSWERS

a are renting b are coming c am having
d is cooking e are going f are meeting

Grammar

Write on the board a couple of examples of the Present continuous from recording 5. Ask students to tick the best explanation. Highlight:

- the use of the Present continuous for future arrangements. This often means that you have arranged something with another person or told them about it.
- the fact that the future time is usually given (*This New Year*) or is understood from the context.

Refer students to *Language summary C* on page 150 of the *Students' Book* for more information.

ANSWER

The best explanation is c.
Going to is covered in Module 6.

PRACTICE

1 Check the meaning of *go abroad*. Students work in pairs to complete the questions with the most suitable verb. As you check the questions with the whole class, drill them, demonstrating appropriate intonation for questions.

ANSWERS

a going b doing c meeting d going e having
f cooking, having g taking h going

2 Give students a few minutes to think about the questions and to practise saying them. Students choose one of the two options. *If you have a large class*: you may find the second option easier to manage.

ADDITIONAL PRACTICE

RB **Resource bank:** 4B I'm having lunch with Madonna (Present continuous for future arrangements), pages 128–129

Workbook: Present continuous for future arrangements, exercises 4–5, page 25

Wordspot (PAGE 37)

day

See *Teacher's tips: working with lexical phrases* on pages 8–9.

1 Elicit suggestions for the first gap. Students work individually or in pairs to predict the others.

2 [T4.6] Play the recording. Students check answers in pairs before checking as a whole class.

ANSWERS
a the other day b a day off c one day
d every day e the day after tomorrow
f Have a good day g the day before yesterday
h all day i twice a day j six days a week
k go out for the day l bad day

3 Students work individually or in pairs before checking with the whole class. Highlight the following points.

One day can refer to the past or the future, for example, *One day he left work early and ...* and *One day I'll be rich*.

Go out for the day means to go somewhere for pleasure, like the beach or a place of interest. A related term (used in exercise 4) is *a day out*, which means a day when you go somewhere for pleasure.

ANSWERS
a **the past:** the day before yesterday, the other day, one day
b **the future:** one day, the day after tomorrow, Have a good day
c **how often / how long:** all day, every day, twice a day, six days a week
d **other:** a day off, go out for the day, bad day

4 Refer students to page 140 of the *Students' Book*, and give them five minutes to answer the questions. Put students into pairs to ask and answer the questions.

Task: Talk about a personal calendar (PAGES 38–39)

See *Teacher's tips: making tasks work* on pages 10–11 and *Responding to learners' individual language needs* on pages 12–13.

Preparation: listening

1 a [T4.7] Elicit some examples of important dates, for example, *your birthday*, *the day you start a new job*. Play the recording twice. The first time, students should write only the dates mentioned, in the *Date* column. Emphasise that they will not hear a date for every month. Play the recording through without stopping. Students then compare answers.

ANSWERS
February 14th March 23rd May 8th
June 20th July 15th September 7th
October 23rd December 25th

b [T4.7] Tell students they only need to write a few words or the name of a special occasion in the *Why it's important* column. Play the recording again. Students compare answers.

ANSWERS

Month	Date	Why it's important
January		
February	14th	Valentine's Day
March	17th	St Patrick's Day
April		
May	8th	Passed driving test
June	20th	Father's Day
July	15th	Going on holiday
August		
September	7th	Birthday
October	23rd	Wedding anniversary
November		
December	25th	Christmas Day

Task: speaking

1 Word to check: *anniversary*. Students draw a blank calendar in their notebooks. Remind them to include dates from the past and future arrangements, as well as events that happen every year.

2 Students look at *Useful language a*, and think about what they will say.

3 Put students into pairs or small groups. Ask students to look at *Useful language b*. Drill some examples of questions to help students with their intonation. Students take turns to talk about their calendars. Students listening make notes so that the group can decide afterwards which was the most interesting thing, and report back to the class.

Real life (PAGE 39)

Phrases for special occasions

1 Words to check: *illness*, *operation*. Students work in pairs or groups. Highlight the following points:

- *Happy birthday!* and *Many happy returns!* mean the same.
- We use *Cheers!* and *Good health!* to express good wishes before drinking. *Good health!* is quite formal.

POSSIBLE ANSWERS
New Year: Happy New Year! Good health! Cheers! The best of luck for the New Year.
Birthday: It's lovely, thank you very much. Happy birthday! Many happy returns!
Illness: Thanks for coming. I hope you feel better soon! The best of luck for your operation.
Christmas: It's lovely, thank you very much. Merry Christmas!
Wedding: Thanks for coming. Congratulations! I hope you'll be very happy! Good luck! The best of luck for the future.
Wedding anniversary: Happy anniversary! Thanks for coming. Congratulations! Good health! Cheers!

Pronunciation

See *Teacher's tips: helping students with pronunciation* on pages 6–7.

[T4.8] Play the recording. Pause after each phrase for students to repeat and copy the intonation.

2 [T4.9] Play the recording, pausing for students to write the best phrase. Alternatively, pause the recording and ask students to call out their answers.

ANSWERS
a Happy birthday! Many happy returns!
b Congratulations!
c Cheers! Good health!
d It's lovely, thank you very much.
e Happy New Year!
f Good luck!
g I hope you feel better soon!
h Thanks for coming.

3 Refer students to the tapescript for recording 9 on page 165 of the *Students' Book*, and put them into pairs to practise. Give students a few minutes to invent and practise their own conversations. Invite three or four pairs to act out their conversations.

Writing (PAGE 40)

Write an invitation

1 Word to check: *engagement*. Students read the e-mail and decide what the invitation is for. Get students to tell you where they found the relevant information in the e-mail.

ANSWER
The invitation is for an engagement party. The relevant information is in the second paragraph.

2 Students work in pairs to order the different parts.

ANSWERS
1 Greeting
2 Personal news
3 When the event is happening
4 Where it is and how to get there
5 Arrangements to meet
6 Contact details
7 Signing off

3 Highlight any useful words/phrases from Marianne's e-mail in exercise 1, for example, *Actually, / Anyway, / the reason I'm sending you this is to tell you about / We'd love to see you! / just let me know / I really hope you can come!*

Put students into groups to think of an imaginary occasion and to write their e-mails to people in other groups. Students who have access to e-mail could send their invitations to each other for homework.

ADDITIONAL PRACTICE

Workbook: Improve your writing, exercise 11, page 29

Study ... (PAGE 40)

Remembering verb + noun combinations

Give students a few minutes to read about the different approaches to recording verb + noun combinations. Students work in pairs or small groups to discuss the advantages and disadvantages of each approach.

Practise ... (PAGE 41)

1 Present continuous

Students work individually before checking answers with the whole class. Refer students to *Language summary A* on page 150 of the *Students' Book* if they have problems with the spelling. There is also additional spelling practice in the *Workbook* on page 29.

ANSWERS
a We're travelling first class.
b It's beginning to rain.
c My brother is the one who is lying on the sofa!
d This train's stopping at every station.
e They're making a lot of noise.

2 Present continuous and Present simple

Students could do this activity orally in pairs, taking turns to say the correct forms aloud, in complete sentences. Then they write the answers for homework as consolidation.

ANSWERS
a is cooking b Do you know c come d don't like
e is coming f 're having g Do you want
h take; 'm walking

3 Dates and special occasions

Students work in pairs before checking answers as a class.

ANSWERS
a relatives b a meal c a ceremony d a party
e cards to people f a meal

4 *day*

Give students a few minutes to reorder the phrases individually before checking their answers in pairs. Then, ask students to write sentences using six of the phrases with *day*.

ANSWERS
a the day before yesterday b the day after tomorrow
c my day off d Have a good day e twice a day
f a bad day g open all day h one day
i every day at ten o'clock / at ten o'clock every day
j go out for the day on k the other day
l six days a week

5 Phrases for special occasions

This could be done orally as a class.

ANSWERS
a Happy b Happy c Merry d Good e Happy
f for g better h happy i Good j best
k happy

Pronunciation spot

The sounds /θ/ and /ð/

See *Teacher's tips: helping students with pronunciation* on pages 6–7.

1 [T4.10] Play the recording, showing students how the sound is unvoiced in a (they can feel no vibration in their throats), but voiced in b (there is vibration).
2 Students work in pairs, saying the words aloud to each other to decide which sound is used in each word.
3 [T4.11] Students listen and check. Pause the recording after each word to check answers and to give students the opportunity to repeat each word.

ANSWERS

/θ/	/ð/
month	they
thought	together
third	father
thirty	whether
health	
thanks	

Remember! (PAGE 41)

Students do the *Mini-check* on page 159 of the *Students' Book*. Check answers with the whole class, and ask students to tell you their scores out of 20.

ANSWERS
1 Are you enjoying 2 has 3 don't work
4 are you reading 5 is spending 6 are coming
7 Having 8 Congratulations! 9 returns 10 send
11 Happy 12 off 13 out 14 for 15 out 16 up
17 the 18 fl 19 a 20 the

module 5

Appearances

Reading and vocabulary

(PAGES 42–43)

Physical appearance

See *Teacher's tips: working with lexical phrases* on pages 8–9 and *Making the most of the* mini-dictionary on pages 9–10.

1 If possible, bring in some photos of famous men and women to prompt students for this discussion. Start by telling students who you think is the most attractive man/woman, and why. Students discuss in pairs or groups, then report back briefly on how similar/different their ideas are.

2 Draw students' attention to the summaries. Give students a few minutes to read individually, matching headings to paragraphs. Students check ideas in pairs and then as a class.

ANSWERS

Ideas of beauty 200–300 years ago	3
The bigger the better	7
Pale is beautiful!	2
The importance of a long neck	4
The perfect modern woman	1
Showing your emotions	6
The world's most handsome men	5

3 Go through the example, getting students to find the relevant part of the text and to explain why the answer is true. Tell students to put a question mark if there is nothing in the text to suggest that the answer is true. Students work individually or in pairs before checking with the whole class.

ANSWERS

a True (*Until the 1920s …*)
b True (*lead is poisonous!*) c ?
d True (*they would have to spend …*) e ?
f True (*a true gentleman showed …*)
g True (*'big is beautiful'*)

4 **a** Students work in pairs to find words in the text. Check answers with the whole class.

ANSWERS AND LANGUAGE NOTE

2 *attractive** 3 *tanned* 4 *tall* 5 *pale*
6 *athletic-looking* 7 *manly* 8 *slim* 9 *brave*
10 *blue-eyed*

* *Beautiful*, although stronger in meaning than *attractive*, is also a possible answer. *Gorgeous*, however, is too strong here. It means 'very beautiful or attractive'.

b Students work individually or in pairs, using their mini-dictionaries if necessary. Check answers with the whole class.

ANSWERS

cowardly	brave
dark-haired	blond
fair-skinned	tanned
fat	slim
short	tall
ugly	attractive/beautiful

5 Elicit one or two more examples for different sections of the diagram, for example, *hair: long*. Put students into pairs or small groups to find more examples in the text. Copy the diagram onto the board for feedback.

ANSWERS

a **general appearance:** *Gorgeous* (in the title), *beautiful* (paragraphs 1 and 7), *beauty* (paragraphs 2 and 4), *fashionable* (paragraph 2), *beauties* (paragraph 3), *attractive* (paragraph 5), *make-up* (paragraph 6)
b **height:** *tall* (paragraphs 1 and 5), *a long neck* (paragraph 4)
c **build:** *slim* (paragraph 1), *athletic-looking* (paragraph 1), *strong* (paragraph 5), *big* (paragraph 7), *fat* (paragraph 7), the fattest (paragraph 7)
d **skin:** *tanned* (paragraph 1), *suntans* (paragraph 2), *pale* (paragraph 2), *whiter* (paragraph 2)
e **eyes:** *blue-eyed* (paragraph 1)
f **hair:** *long* (paragraph 1), *blond* (paragraph 1), *wigs* (paragraphs 3 and 6)

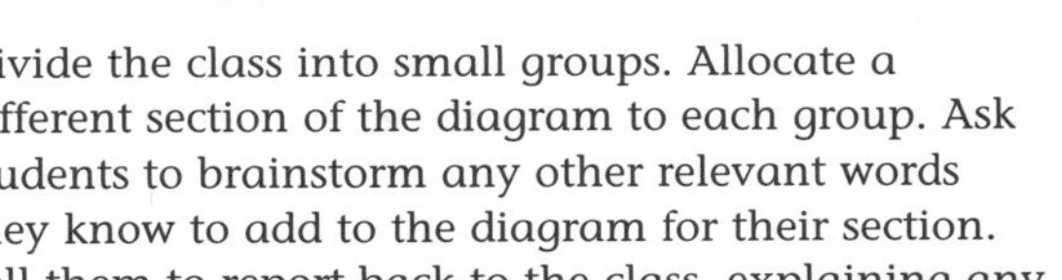

***Reading and vocabulary*, exercise 5: additional suggestions**

- Divide the class into small groups. Allocate a different section of the diagram to each group. Ask students to brainstorm any other relevant words they know to add to the diagram for their section. Tell them to report back to the class, explaining any unfamiliar words.
- Ask each group to make a poster of the diagram, including the words from the text and any others they have thought of for each section. Put the posters on the walls of the classroom, and give students time to walk around and look at them. Students ask the people who made the poster about any words that are unfamiliar.

Pronunciation

See *Teacher's tips: helping students with pronunciation* on pages 6–7.

1 [T5.1] Use a couple of examples to show students that a syllable is a part of a word with a pronounced vowel sound in it. For example, *supermodel* has four syllables, *su-per-mo-del*. Demonstrate that in English words of more than one syllable, one of the syllables is stressed – it is longer and louder, with slightly higher pitch. Model the word *supermodel* to demonstrate this,

exaggerating the stress slightly to help students hear it. Play the recording or model the words yourself, pausing after each word for students to discuss in pairs where the stress is. Check answers with the whole class.

ANSWERS
See tapescript for recording 1 on page 165 of the *Students' Book.*

2 [T5.1] Play the recording again for students to repeat, or drill the words yourself. Students work in pairs to practise.

ADDITIONAL PRACTICE

Workbook: Vocabulary, exercises 10–11, page 33

Language focus 1 (PAGES 44–45)

Comparative and superlative adjectives

1 Words to check: *elegant, mature, sophisticated*. Students work in pairs or small groups to discuss the pictures and to choose adjectives that describe them. Emphasise that they should use their mini-dictionaries if necessary.

2 [T5.2] Explain that students will hear a fashion expert describe the same pictures. They should decide if they agree with her or not. Remind students that they do not need to understand everything. Play the recording. Students compare their ideas in small groups before discussing them as a whole class.

3 **a** Give students a few minutes to think about the correct form for each gap. Suggest that they write in pencil, so that they can change any answers when they listen to the recording.

b [T5.3] Play the recording and check answers with the whole class.

ANSWERS
See tapescript for recording 3 on page 165 of the *Students' Book.*

Grammar

1 Give students a few minutes individually or in pairs to find the comparative and superlative forms of the adjectives. Direct them to the examples of comparatives and superlatives in exercise 3. Write the table on the board. As you check the answers, elicit one or two more examples for each rule, and highlight:
- the spelling rules for 1-syllable adjectives
- the different rules for 2-syllable adjectives ending in *-y* and for adjectives with 2/3 or more syllables
- the use of *the* with all superlatives.

Refer students to *Language summary A* on pages 150–151 of the *Students' Book* for more information.

ANSWERS

	adjective	comparative	superlative
1 syllable	young tall	younger taller	the youngest the tallest
2 syllables ending in *-y*	heavy pretty	heavier prettier	the heaviest the prettiest
2/3 or more syllables	sophisticated elegant	more sophisticated more elegant	the most sophisticated the most elegant
irregular forms	good bad	better worse	the best the worst

2 Students work in pairs to discuss rules of form before checking answers as a class or in *Language summary A*.

3 Give students a minute or two to match the beginnings and endings of the sentences. Write the complete sentences on the board. Give students time to read and remember them. Rub out the prepositions and get students to test each other in pairs.

ANSWERS
a She's **older than** me.
b **The best in** the world.
c It's **the same as** mine.
d It's **similar to** this one.
e They're **different from** the others.
f She **looks like** me.

PRACTICE

1 Focus students' attention on the examples. Students work individually on their sentences, then compare answers in pairs or small groups.

***Practice*, exercise 1: alternative suggestion**

Students write their sentences with *This person* at the beginning, instead of the student's name. Then they read out their sentences in groups, and the other students guess who they are talking about in each case.

2 Go through the example with the students, showing them other alternatives. For example, *My brother is the tallest person in my family. My grandmother is the oldest person in my family.* Students work individually on their sentences.

3 Demonstrate this by talking about the differences between you and your own family, then asking students what they can remember. If possible, bring in some family photos to pass round while you are talking, and ask students to do the same.

Pronunciation

See *Teacher's tips: helping students with pronunciation* on pages 6–7.

1 [T5.4] Emphasise that students only need to listen for the number of comparative and superlative adjectives. Students check answers in pairs and then with the whole class.

ANSWERS
There are three comparative and superlative adjectives. See tapescript for recording 4 on page 165 of the *Students' Book*. The forms are underlined.

2 [T5.4] Play the recording again or say the sentences yourself, rather than asking students to read from the page, as this will affect their rhythm. Highlight the schwa sound /ə/ in *than, from, to* and *as*.

ADDITIONAL PRACTICE

RB **Resource bank:** 5A Put these in order (Comparatives and superlatives), page 130

Workbook: Comparative and superlative adjectives, exercises 1–5, pages 30–31

Language focus 2 (PAGES 46–47)

Describing people

Before you start the activity, get students to brainstorm any questions they already know for asking about appearance. Do not correct any mistakes at this point, but simply answer the questions for a famous person you think the students will know. Students guess who you are describing.

Words to check: *clean-shaven* /kliːnˈʃeɪvən/, average /ˈævərɪdʒ/. Do an example first, then students work individually or in pairs before checking with the whole class.
Note: differences in meaning and form are covered in the *Grammar* box.

ANSWERS
1 What does he look like? He's tall, dark and handsome.
2 How is he? He's fine.
3 What's he like? He seems very nice.
4 How old is he? About 22.
5 How tall is he? About average height.
6 What colour are his eyes? Brown.
7 Has he got a beard? No. He's clean-shaven.

Grammar

Give students a few minutes individually or in pairs to match questions to topics. As you check the answers, highlight:

- the questions which use *be* (*How is he? What's he like? How old is he? How tall is he? What colour are his eyes?*) and the question which uses *have got* (*Has he got a beard?*)
- the word order in the questions *What colour are …?* and *Has he got …?* (not ~~*What are colour …?*~~ and ~~*He has got …?*~~)
- the plural form of the question about eye colour (*What colour are his eyes?*), compared with the singular form of a question about hair colour, for example, *What colour is her hair?*
- the difference in meaning and form between *look like* (appearance) and *be like* (opinion), in the questions *What does he look like?* and *What's he like?*
- the fact that it is unusual to give the exact age of someone when describing them. Usually, people mention an approximate age, as in the answer *About 22.* Another way of saying this is *He's in his early* (or, for a slightly older man, *mid/late*) *twenties.* Note the use of the possessive adjective.

Drill any questions/answers which your students find difficult, for example, *What … look like?* versus *What … like?* Refer them to *Language summary B* on page 151 of the *Students' Book* for more information.

ANSWERS
a What does he look like? b How tall is he?
c How is he? d Has he got a beard?
e What's he like? f What colour are his eyes?

PRACTICE

1 Students work individually or in pairs before checking with the whole class.

ANSWERS
a What is you new dress like?
b What colour are her eyes?
c Has he got long hair?
d Is her hair fair or dark?
e Is he in his thirties?
f Does she wear glasses?
g Is she shorter or taller than me?

2 **a** [T5.5] Draw students' attention to the picture on page 46. Explain that students will hear descriptions of the different players and must decide who the speaker is talking about in each case. Pause the recording after each description. Students call out the name of the person being described. Point out to students that not all the players are described.

ANSWERS
1 c 2 a 3 f 4 e 5 g 6 i

b Direct students to the tapescript for recording 5 on page 165 of the *Students' Book*. They read the descriptions and work in pairs to decide on the questions asked and to underline words and phrases for describing people. Emphasise that for some of the answers, more than one question is possible. As you check the answers, highlight:

- the use of an adjective + *-ish* (*longish dark hair* = quite long dark hair)
- the adjectives *shaved* and *dyed* to describe hair
- *well-built* and *average build* to describe body shape.

POSSIBLE ANSWERS

1 What does he look like?
he's quite tall; he's got fair hair; a bit longer than the others; he's quite good-looking
2 Has he got a beard? / Is he clean-shaven?
He's got a little beard; a little moustache
3 What does he look like?
He's got a shaved head; He's very well-built
4 What's his hair like? / What colour is his hair?
he must have dyed hair; it's dyed blond; It's very, very short
5 What does he look like? / Is he well-built?
He's black; He's about average height and build
6 What does he look like? / How old is he?
he's in his mid to late twenties; longish dark hair; he's wearing a scarf

***Practice*, exercise 2b: additional suggestion**

Students use the diagrams they made for recording words and phrases to describe appearance in *Reading and vocabulary*, exercise 5, on page 43, and add the words and phrases from *Practice*, exercise 2b.

3 If possible, bring in a selection of photos of famous people for this activity, in case students choose not to describe one of their classmates. Put students into pairs. Student A thinks of someone (a classmate, someone in the picture on page 46 or a famous person). Student B asks questions to help them guess who it is.

Set up the following scoring system. Student B scores points according to how many questions are asked before getting the right answer – 10 points after one question, 9 points after two questions and so on, down to 1 point after ten questions. If Student B fails to guess after ten questions, Student A gets 3 points.

Demonstrate the activity with a strong student. Circulate as students work, helping with vocabulary and noting down examples of good language use and/or errors to focus on later.

4 Get each student to choose a photo of someone in Modules 1–5. Emphasise that they should not write who the person is or where they found the picture. Set a time limit of ten minutes for students to write a description. Circulate as students write, helping with vocabulary.

Put students into pairs to show each other their descriptions. Each student must decide which photo is being described.

***Practice*, exercise 4: alternative suggestion**

Arrange the written descriptions around the classroom. Students mingle, reading the descriptions, and write under the description the page number they think the photo is on.

ADDITIONAL PRACTICE

RB **Resource bank:** 5B An alien family (Vocabulary: describing people's appearance), pages 131–132

Workbook: Describing people, exercises 6–8, pages 31–32

Wordspot (PAGE 47)

look

See *Teacher's tips: working with lexical phrases* on pages 8–9.

1 Students work in pairs to fill the gaps. Check answers with the whole class.

ANSWERS

a look up b look after c strange-looking
d looking forward e have a look f look good
g look out h look for i look at j look round
k good-looking l look like

2 Do the first phrase with the class. Students then work individually or in pairs. Check with the whole class.

ANSWERS

a **see:** have a look, look at, look out, look round
b **describing people:** good-looking, look good, look like, strange-looking
c **try to find:** look for, look up
d **other phrasal verbs:** look after, look forward to

3 Do an example with the class and give students a few minutes to complete the questions individually, before comparing answers in pairs.

ADDITIONAL PRACTICE

Workbook: Wordspot, exercise 13, page 35

Task: Describe a suspect to the police (PAGES 48–49)

See *Teacher's tips: making tasks work* on pages 10–11 and *Responding to learners' individual language needs* on pages 12–13.

Preparation: reading

1 Direct students' attention to the pictures and explain that together the pictures make a story. Students check the meaning of any unknown words in the box in their mini-dictionaries. Discuss the questions with the class.

***Preparation: reading*, exercise 1: additional suggestion**

If you have read any crime stories of interest in the news: bring in the newspaper pictures/headlines for discussion and vocabulary.

2 Set the scene, telling students that thieves have stolen diamonds from an apartment building. Check the words *description*, *suspect* and *lift*, then put students into Groups A and B. Within each group, students work in smaller groups of two to four. Refer Group A to page 142, and Group B to page 145. Give them time to read their role cards, and check that they understand what they have to do. Make sure that As look at the picture on page 140 for only two minutes. Bs must not look at the picture!

Tell As to look at *Useful language a*, and Bs to look at *Useful language b*. Circulate and help with vocabulary. Encourage students to make a note of their description/questions, to help them with *Task: speaking* later.

Task: speaking

1 Put students into pairs, A and B, and check that they understand what to do. Make it clear that B (the police officer) can choose whether to make written notes about the suspect or to draw a picture of the suspect. Demonstrate how B can use questions to check the accuracy of the drawing. Circulate and collect examples of good language use and/or errors to focus on later.

2 As students finish the interview, direct them to the pictures of suspects on page 147. Make it clear that B (the police officer) has a maximum of two chances to choose the right picture. If the first guess is wrong, A can explain why, but not point to the correct picture until B has had a second guess.

3 Have some brief class feedback on how many guesses the police officers needed. Ask two or three students to comment on the accuracy of the witnesses' descriptions. This leads naturally into analysis and correction of the language used during *Task: speaking*. Put the language you collected onto the board or an overhead transparency. Give students time in pairs to decide which are examples of good language use, and which are errors for correction.

***Task: speaking*: alternative suggestion**

If your students enjoy roleplaying: give the police officers and the witnesses role cards with different characteristics, so they can act out the interview 'in character'. Examples for the police officer: *It is late in the day. You are tired and you want to go home. / You are a new officer and you don't want to make any mistakes.* Examples for the witness: *You don't remember the man very well, but you want to help the police officer as much as possible. / You have a very good memory and you want to know if there is a reward for helping the police to catch the thief.*

Optional writing

Remind students to follow the guideline information for this, writing a paragraph for each point. As students write, circulate to provide help with vocabulary, and note down examples of good language use and/or errors to focus on later.

Write the examples on the board and focus students' attention on both the good language use and/or errors before students proofread their newspaper reports. *If you are short of time*: ask students to write up their newspaper reports for homework.

ADDITIONAL PRACTICE

Workbook: Vocabulary booster: parts of the face and body, exercise 12, page 34; Improve your writing, exercise 15, page 35

Song (PAGE 49)

His Latest Flame

1 Words to check: *flame*, *'cause*. Students work individually to read the song, checking any unknown words in their mini-dictionaries. Students answer the questions individually before checking their answers in pairs and then with the whole class.

ANSWERS

The three people in the song: a man, his friend and Marie
The relationship between them: both men are in love with the same woman, Marie. Until yesterday, Marie was the girlfriend of the man who sings the song, but now she is the *latest flame* of his friend.
How they are feeling: the man who sings the song is very sad, but his friend is very happy. We don't know about Marie.

2 [T5.6] Draw students' attention to the first line of the song, as an example. There is a choice of words. Play the recording. Students decide which is the correct word. Check answers with the whole class.

ANSWERS

today love say green smiled gone yesterday mine

3 Students work in pairs to complete the synopsis of the story. Check answers with the whole class.

ANSWERS

b his friend, the singer c his friend, Marie
d the singer, his friend e his friend
f the singer, his friend, Marie g the singer

4 This activity could be written or spoken. Students work in small groups and tell the story from the three different perspectives. Encourage them to imagine details such as how the friend and Marie met, how long the singer has known Marie, etc. Circulate and help with vocabulary. Ask representatives from a few different groups to report back one story each to the class.

***Song*, exercise 4: alternative suggestion**

Divide the class into Groups A, B and C. Further divide the groups so that students work in groups of three or four. Give students five to ten minutes to create stories: Group A from the point of view of the singer, Group B, his friend, and Group C, Marie. Regroup students into groups of three, with a representative from A, B and C, to hear each other's stories.

Consolidation modules 1–5 (PAGES 50–51)

A Present tenses, *should*, *can*

Before students fill the gaps, ask them to read the text individually for two minutes and to answer the following question: *Do the police have a lot of information about how this incident happened?* Check the answer with the whole class. (Answer: *No, they don't.*) Give students five minutes to fill the gaps individually. Students check their answers in pairs before checking with the whole class.

ANSWERS
1 are looking for 2 sees 3 shouldn't 4 should
5 want 6 think 7 can't 8 can 9 live
10 are asking 11 should 12 don't feel 13 can't
14 is visiting

B Vocabulary: Revision

Set this up as a race. Students work in pairs. The winning pair is the first to complete the race correctly. Check answers with the whole class.

ANSWERS
2 excited 3 dentist 4 turn off 5 fall asleep
6 presents 7 scared 8 dream 9 mixture
10 engineer 11 relatives 12 slim

C Comparative and superlative adjectives

Students work in pairs to complete the news article before checking answers with the whole class.

ANSWERS
1 the biggest 2 taller 3 heavier 4 larger
5 the most important 6 more accurate 7 tall
8 long

D Vocabulary: Pairs

Students work in pairs, A and B. Student A begins by naming one pair. Students then take turns to find pairs of words. When they have found eight pairs, they check answers with another pair. The group then tries to think of the opposites of the remaining words, or to think of a definition for them.

ANSWERS

terrific	awful
stay up late	go to bed early
excited	disappointed
attractive	ugly
fall asleep	wake up
angry	in a good mood
tanned	pale
expensive	cheap

E Real life

Students work in pairs before checking answers with the whole class. Give students ten minutes to choose one of the situations and to write a six- or eight-line dialogue to perform for the rest of the class.

ANSWERS
1 Sorry, could you repeat that, please?
2 Thanks for coming.
3 Can we have the bill, please?
4 Is it OK if I leave early today?
5 Happy anniversary!
6 Good luck!
7 Can I borrow your mobile phone, please?
8 How much does this cost?
9 Could you turn the sound/music down, please?
10 Happy New Year!

F Listening and grammar: Present simple and Past simple

1 Students predict the type of song they think it is in small groups. Have some brief class feedback.

2 Emphasise that students should not look at the song. In pairs, they match words to make phrases.

ANSWERS
a see your face b feel ashamed c look like you
d turn the corner e call out your name
f bring back memories

3 [C1] Remind students not to look at the song. Play the recording. Students check answers in pairs and then as a class.

ANSWERS

see your face	5
feel ashamed	4
look like you	1
turn the corner	2
call out your name	3
bring back memories	6

4 Play the recording again. Students decide which verb form they hear. Check answers with the whole class.

ANSWERS
1 saw 2 looked 3 walked 4 thought 5 was
6 turned 7 called 8 felt 9 wasn't 10 can
11 see 12 Brings 13 can't 14 're

5 Students discuss the questions in small groups. Have some brief class feedback.

ADDITIONAL PRACTICE

RB **Resource bank:** Learner-training worksheet D (Recording new vocabulary), page 133

module 6

Time off

Language focus 1 (PAGES 52–53)

Intentions and wishes

1 Check that students understand the questions and put them into pairs or small groups for the discussion.

2 **a** Ask students to comment on the differences between the two people, and to guess what a *couch potato* and a *live wire* are.

ANSWERS
A *couch potato* is someone who spends a lot of time sitting and watching television; a *live wire* is someone who is very active and has a lot of energy.

b Get students to predict which of these types their partner is. Students do the quiz in pairs, taking turns to read out the statements and making a note of each other's answers.

3 **a** Students compare the sentences they ticked.

b Pairs report back to the class to find out how many live wires and how many couch potatoes there are.

Grammar

1 Write sentences a–d on the board and elicit another example of each verb form from the quiz, for example, *I'm going to walk for more than half an hour today. I'm not planning to get up before ten tomorrow. I'd like to go on a cycling holiday or climb a mountain one day. I'd rather play sport than watch it.* Students discuss the best alternatives in pairs. As you check the answers, highlight the following points.

- In both sentences a and b, the person has thought about the plan, but in sentence b, they have thought more about the plan, including how to do things, for example, where to buy the computer.
- We generally use *I'm going to* (*the cinema*) instead of *I'm going to go to* (*the cinema*), because it sounds less awkward.
- We use *would like to* as a less direct, and therefore more polite, way of saying *want to*.
- We use *would rather* to mean that we want one thing more than another thing.
- The negative forms are *I'm not going to*, *I'm not planning to* and *I wouldn't like to*.

Refer students to *Language summary A* on page 151 of the *Students' Book* for more information.

ANSWERS
a I intend to buy a new computer.
b I have thought carefully about buying a new computer.
c I want to buy a new computer.
d I like new computers more than second-hand ones.

2 Elicit the form of the verb used in each case.

ANSWERS
We use the infinitive (for example, *to buy*) after *I'm going*, *I'm planning* and *I'd like*.
We use the infinitive without *to* (for example, *buy*) after *I'd rather*.

3 Elicit the meaning of *I'd* in each case.

ANSWER
I'd means *I would* in *I'd like* and *I'd rather*.

4 Students work in pairs to create questions. Check answers with the whole class, and highlight the question forms *(What) are you going to …? (What) are you planning to …? Would you like to …? Would you rather …?*

ANSWERS
a Are you going to see it?
b Are you planning to do it?
c Would you like to see it?
d Would you rather go home?

PRACTICE

1 Go through the examples with the class. Check the meaning of *resolution* by eliciting an example or giving one of your own. Point out that resolutions can be positive and negative. Give students time to look through the list of phrases. Words to check: *spend time* + verb *-ing*; *keep in touch with*; *stop* + verb *-ing*. Put students into pairs to compare and discuss their resolutions. Have some class feedback on some of the more unusual resolutions.

2 Do the first question with the class, then give students a few minutes to prepare the others. Put students into groups of three to ask their questions.

Pronunciation

See *Teacher's tips: helping students with pronunciation* on pages 6–7.

1 [T6.1] Play the recording, pausing after each sentence, or model the sentences yourself. Highlight the contracted forms and show students that the stress falls on the main verbs, for example, *planning … have* or *going … see*, and that *to* is therefore weak. Drill the phrases.

2 [T6.2] Play the recording, or say the sentences yourself, for students to repeat. Make sure that students are using the contracted forms. Refer them to these in the tapescript for recording 2 on page 165 of the *Students' Book*. Extend this pronunciation work by drilling the questions made in *Practice*, exercise 2.

ADDITIONAL PRACTICE

RB **Resource bank:** 6A Talk about the future (*going to*, *would like to*, *would rather*, *will/won't*), page 134

Workbook: Intentions and wishes: *going to*, *planning to*, *would like to*, *would rather*, exercises 1–3, pages 36–37

Vocabulary and speaking (PAGE 54)

Holidays

See *Teacher's tips: working with lexical phrases* on pages 8–9 and *Making the most of the* mini-dictionary on pages 9–10.

1 a Before you start the activity, elicit one or two examples of the important features of a holiday. Put students into pairs or small groups to discuss their (four) most important features. Ask a few groups to report back on their ideas.

b Students describe what they can see in each picture, saying whether they think they are positive or negative aspects of holidays.

2 Do an example with the class, then give students a few minutes to decide where the extracts come from.

ANSWERS
B P P P B B P P B P B

3 Students work individually to put the words and phrases into categories. Then put students into pairs or small groups to compare their answers. As you check the answers, drill the phrases if necessary.

POSSIBLE ANSWERS

Ideal holiday	Awful holiday	Not sure/Either
luxurious	queue	no nightlife
swimming pool	flight … delayed	self-catering accommodation
peaceful	crowded	excursions
relaxing		go on a cruise
		book online

4 a Tell students about a holiday of your own as an example. Ask if any of them have had a similar experience.

b Students tell their stories in pairs or small groups, and see how many experiences they have in common.

ADDITIONAL PRACTICE

Workbook: Vocabulary, exercise 8, page 39

Listening and speaking (PAGE 55)

The holiday from hell

1 Give students time to read the information from the website, and ask them why it is a 'dream' holiday.

2 Put students into pairs. Give them time to prepare what they are going to say. Get one or two pairs to act out their conversations for the class.

3 a [T6.3] Establish that Mark and Rosa have now come back from the holiday, and are talking about how terrible it was. Explain that students will hear the story in two parts. Write the headings *At the airport* and *During the flight* on the board. Words to check: *Caribbean*, *hurricane*. Students listen and briefly list the problems Mark and Rosa had under the two headings. Write their answers in two columns on the board, and have some class feedback.

ANSWERS

At the airport	During the flight
The flight was delayed because of bad weather.	They were told that there was a hurricane at their destination.
Mark and Rosa had to spend the night at the airport, sleeping on the floor.	They had to fly to the capital city instead.

b [T6.4] Students predict the second part of the story. Get students to write the six headings in their notebooks, leaving space to make notes. Words to check: *frog*, *ant*. Play the recording straight through. Students compare answers in pairs.

ANSWERS
When they arrived in the Caribbean: they had to go to the capital city. Mark and Rosa were told it was for just one night, but because of the hurricane there were no flights to San Antonio, so they had to stay there for another three nights.
At the hotel itself: it was awful, noisy and dirty. There was nothing to do.
With the hotel swimming pool: it was a greeny-black colour, and it was full of frogs.
With the weather: the hurricane arrived, and so it was very windy and rainy. Mark and Rosa were terrified by the sound of the windows banging and the trees crashing in the wind.
With the food at the hotel: instead of a typical breakfast, they had vegetables and salad. There were hundreds of ants in the bowl of lettuce. Mark and Rosa didn't eat at the hotel again.
With the sea: there wasn't a beach, just some rocks. Because there were big ships travelling past, the sea was polluted and brown. It was too dirty to swim in.

4 [T6.3] [T6.4] Students work in pairs to fill the gaps before listening again. Check answers with the whole class.

ANSWERS
Part 1
1 £1000 2 two 3 May 4 beautiful 5 delayed
6 the next morning 7 twelve 8 hurricane
9 five-star 10 sea
Part 2
11 beach 12 dirty 13 frogs 14 vegetables
15 ants 16 hurricane 17 terrified 18 three days
19 nothing 20 five 21 perfect

5 a Before you start the activity, elicit or give some language for the friend to use while they are listening to Mark or Rosa's story, for example, *Oh no, really? You're joking!* Suggest that the friend could give advice about what to do next, for example, *I think you should ...*

b Students discuss the question as a class.

ADDITIONAL PRACTICE

RB **Resource bank:** 6B Holiday crossword (Holiday vocabulary), page 135

Language focus 2 (PAGE 56)

Predictions: *will* and *won't*

Check that students understand the context, and emphasise that they need only choose the statements which are true of their capital city in August. Students compare their ideas.

Grammar

1 Go through the three options concerning sentences a–h. Elicit/explain that these sentences are all *predictions*.

ANSWER
The correct answer is b.

2 Students discuss questions a–c in pairs. Highlight:
- the use of the contraction *'ll*, particularly after personal pronouns, *it* and *there*
- the use of *will* in a positive sentence, and *won't* (*will not*) in a negative sentence
- the question form *Will I ...?*
- the use of the infinitive without *to* after *will/won't*
- the use of *be able*, not *can*, after *will/won't*.

Consolidate by getting students to change the form of the other sentences: change sentence e into the positive, sentence f into the negative, sentence g into a question. Refer students to *Language summary B* on page 152 of the *Students' Book* for more information.

ANSWERS
a *'ll* means *will*. b *Won't* means *will not*.
c *Will there be lots of tourists?*

PRACTICE

1 Put students into pairs. Focus students on the example, and suggest some other topics, for example, *accommodation, clothes to take*. Students act out the conversation in pairs. Feed back briefly on any errors you heard in the use of *will/won't* during this activity.

2 a Establish that if Matt stays longer in the country, he may want to do some of the things in the box. Students match the parts of the questions individually or in pairs.

b [T6.5] Play the recording, pausing briefly after each question for students to check their answers.

ANSWERS
2 Will I have to give a tip?
3 Will I have to pay immediately?
4 Will I need to book a seat?
5 Will it be very crowded?
6 About how much will it cost?
7 Will the people be able to speak English?
8 How long will the journey take?
9 What documents will I need?
10 Will there be anywhere to sleep?

c Students choose questions for two of the situations, for example, *open a bank account: Will I have to make an appointment? What documents will I need?* Put students into pairs to act out their conversations.

Pronunciation

See *Teacher's tips: helping students with pronunciation* on pages 6–7.

1 [T6.6] Play the recording, pausing after each sentence for students to write *will, 'll, would* or *'d*. Students check answers in pairs.

2 [T6.6] Refer students to the tapescript to check their answers. Then play the recording again.

ANSWERS
See tapescript for recording 6 on page 166 of the *Students' Book.*

ADDITIONAL PRACTICE

Workbook: Predictions, exercises 4–5, pages 37–38; Pronunciation, exercise 6, page 38

Real life (PAGE 57)

Social chit-chat

1 Students read the definition of *chit-chat*. Ask students if the people in the first picture know each other, whether they are friends and what topic(s) from the box they might talk about. Students then discuss the other pictures in pairs.

2 [T6.7] Students tick the topics in the box when they hear them. Students check answers as a whole class.

ANSWERS
a the weather; plans for the day; family
b holidays; reasons for your visit; family; health; the weather
c reasons for your visit; holidays; where you're from; family
d what you did at the weekend; sport

3 [T6.8] Look at the first answer with the class, and elicit some possible questions: *It's a nice day, isn't it? It's lovely weather today, isn't it?* Students predict the other questions. They then write the actual questions in their books as they listen to the recording.

ANSWERS
See tapescript for recording 8 on page 167 of the *Students' Book*.

Pronunciation

See *Teacher's tips: helping students with pronunciation* on pages 6–7.

[T6.9] Play the recording or say the questions yourself. Point out that the speakers use a higher pitch at the beginning of the question, which makes them sound interested. Demonstrate this by giving an example of a question with very flat intonation, then contrasting it with the same question asked with interest. Play the recording again for students to repeat.

4 **a** Put students into pairs to prepare their conversations. Suggest that they practise the conversation first, so that they can act it out without reading from a script.

b *Either*: tell the students listening to each pair, as they act out their conversations, to think about the three questions in exercise 4a. For each conversation they listen to, students can then answer the questions when the conversation is finished. *Or*: arrange the written dialogues around the room. Students circulate and read them, answering the three questions for each dialogue they read.

Task: Plan your dream holiday

(PAGES 58–59)

See *Teacher's tips: making tasks work* on pages 10–11 and *Responding to learners' individual language needs* on pages 12–13.

Preparation: listening

1 [T6.10] Emphasise that students should make brief notes on Andy and Fiona's answers. Play the recording.

ANSWERS
a the last week in June; next week
b a week
c somewhere hot and not too far away, like Spain or Greece; maybe somewhere more exotic and exciting, like Thailand
d want to be near a beach
e fairly quiet, but with somewhere to go in the evening
f two
g £500 per person
h self-catering

2 Check that students know where the places are. Words to check: *villa*, *apartment*, *theme park*, *resort*. Students work in pairs to decide on three possible holidays for Andy and Fiona. Have some class feedback on students' ideas.

Task: speaking

1 Divide students into Groups A and B. Within each group, students work in smaller groups of two to four.

As prepare questions to ask Bs about the kind of holiday they would like, and practise asking the questions. Refer them to *Useful language a*. Bs decide what sort of last-minute holiday they would like to go on. Refer them to *Useful language b*.

Put students into pairs, A and B, and check that they understand what to do. Point out language for suggestions, for example, *How about* + verb *-ing …? You/we could* + verb Student A interviews Student B, and together they plan a dream holiday. Circulate and collect examples of good language use and/or errors to focus on later.

2 Regroup students to report back on the holidays they have planned. Refer them to *Useful language c*, and point out that *going to* is used because they are talking about plans. Have some brief class feedback on the most interesting holidays from each group.

Writing (PAGE 60)

Write a postcard

1 **a** Do the first pair of phrases as an example. Students then work on the rest in pairs before checking with the whole class.

ANSWERS
The following phrases are suitable for a postcard to a friend:
a Hi Tim! b when I get home!
c There are loads of places to go …
d The food's not too expensive and really tasty …
e I'm staying in … f Bye for now!
g It's lovely and sunny, h Well, here I am in …
The other phrases are not suitable because they are too formal. Some are more appropriate to a formal letter, and some are in the style of a holiday brochure.

b Students copy the phrases onto the postcard, then compare answers in pairs before checking with the whole class.

ANSWERS
1 Hi Tim! 2 Well, here I am in 3 I'm staying in
4 It's lovely and sunny,
5 The food's not too expensive and really tasty
6 when I get home! 7 There are loads of places to go
8 Bye for now!

2 Give students a moment or two to read the list of things to include in their postcard. They then work individually or in pairs to write it. Put the postcards up on the classroom walls for everyone to read.

ADDITIONAL PRACTICE

Workbook: Improve your writing, exercise 11, page 41

Study ... (PAGE 60)

Increasing your vocabulary (1): Word families

1 Discuss questions a–e with the class, but do not let students read the dictionary entries yet. Students should be familiar with most of the words, but may not have made the connection that they are all members of the same word family.

2 Students check their answers to exercise 1.

ANSWERS
a sunny b sunrise, sunset c sunbathe
d sunglasses e suntanned

3 Put students into small groups to discuss the different ways of remembering word families.

Practise ... (PAGE 61)

1 Intentions and wishes: *going to*, *planning to*, *would like to*, *would rather*

Students work individually before checking answers with the whole class.

ANSWERS
a visit b take c going d planning e Would
f to invite g to come h 'd (would)

2 *will/won't*

Do this exercise orally. Students work in pairs, A and B. Student A says the first sentence as it appears, Student B transforms it into a sentence with future meaning using *will* or *won't*. Then they change and Student B reads the next sentence.

ANSWERS
a It'll be difficult to find a parking space.
b She won't be at home on Tuesday.
c Will your cousin be at home?
d Will you be able to find your way without a map?
e The last bus has gone: we'll have to walk.

3 Holidays

Put the individual items onto two sets of cards. Students match the cards in pairs. Check answers with the whole class.

ANSWERS
a to book online b go on a cruise c nightlife
d sightseeing e self-catering f swimming pool

4 Holidays

Do this as a race. The winner is the first student to check and correctly spell all the words.

ANSWERS
a flight b *correct* c delayed d accommodation
e *correct* f peaceful g relaxing

5 Social chit-chat

Students work individually before checking answers as a class.

ANSWERS
a Is this your first time in Australia?
b Is she feeling better now?
c Are you here on holiday?
d Did you have a good weekend?
e Have you got any plans for today?
f Did you see the football on Saturday?
g Nice day, isn't it?
h Did you get nice weather?

6 Write a postcard

Students work in pairs before checking answers as a class.

ANSWERS
a Here b staying c home d It's e for

Pronunciation spot

The /ŋ/ and /n/ sounds

See *Teacher's tips: helping students with pronunciation* on pages 6–7.

1 [T6.11] Highlight the pronunciation of the two sounds. Play the recording or model the words yourself.

2 [T6.12] Play the recording, for students to hear the differences in ending.

3 [T6.13] Students listen and write the words they hear.

ANSWERS
wing been sun thing bang being win ran
sung ban rang thin

4 Students work in pairs, taking turns to say one of the words. Their partner decides which word they have said.

Remember! (PAGE 61)

Students do the *Mini-check* on page 159 of the *Students' Book*. Check answers with the whole class, and ask students to tell you their scores.

ANSWERS
1 home 2 we are 3 to visit 4 Will 5 feeling
6 will 7 flight 8 peaceful 9 relaxing
10 luxurious 11 to 12 on 13 in 14 for
15 Is 16 Are 17 Did 18 Have 19 Would
20 Would

module 7

Ambitions and dreams

Vocabulary and speaking (PAGE 62)

Ambitions and dreams

See *Teacher's tips: working with lexical phrases* on pages 8–9 and *Making the most of the* mini-dictionary on pages 9–10.

1 Focus students' attention on the pictures and the example. Elicit one or two more examples of ambitions. To personalise the topic, tell students about your ambitions when you were young. Put students into pairs or small groups to discuss the questions. Ask one or two students to feed back from their pair or group to the class.

2 Remind students of the importance of remembering word combinations, and of how to record them systematically, for example, in word locusts (see *Vocabulary and speaking*, exercise 4, on page 7 of the *Students' Book*). Give students a few minutes individually to match the verbs and phrases. Encourage students to use their mini-dictionaries. Check answers with the whole class. Pronunciation to check: *earn* /ɜːn/, *novel* /ˈnɒvəl/.

ANSWERS

1 learn how to drive 2 become famous
3 earn 1 million 4 start your own business
5 go abroad 6 get married
7 buy a house or flat 8 appear on television
9 go to university 10 write a novel
11 go round the world 12 have children

3 Do an example with the class. Give students a few minutes individually to put the ambitions into three lists. Students then work in pairs or small groups to compare and explain their answers. Note that the third list (*Things that you think are easy/difficult to do*) will depend entirely on students' views.

POSSIBLE ANSWERS

Things that most people do	Things that very few people do	Things that you think are easy/ difficult to do
learn how to drive	become famous	
go abroad	earn 1 million	
get married	start your own business	
buy a house or flat	appear on TV	
go to university	write a novel	
have children	go round the world	

ADDITIONAL PRACTICE

RB **Resource bank:** 7A Ambition dominoes (Verb/noun collocations), page 136

Workbook: Vocabulary, exercise 9, page 45

Listening (PAGES 62–63)

Before they were famous

1 Students discuss as a class which people they have seen in films, on TV or in magazines, and what they know about them (where they are from, what films they have been in, information about their private lives, etc.).

2 Refer students to page 141 of the *Students' Book*, where they can read a brief profile of each famous person. Check as a class that students understand who the people are.

3 **a** Check briefly that students understand what all the jobs in the box are. Then ask them, as a class or in pairs, to guess which person did which job. Tell students that one of the famous people did some jobs that aren't mentioned in the box. Ask them to guess who this was and what they did.

b [T7.1] Students listen to see if their guesses were correct. Words to check: *advert*, *monastery*, *tips*.

ANSWERS

a **Tom Hanks:** bellman
b **Catherine Zeta-Jones:** child actress
c **Colin Farrell:** footballer
d **Keanu Reeves:** worked in an ice rink and a pasta restaurant
e **Renée Zellweger:** gymnast
f **Kate Winslet:** child actress
g **Tom Cruise:** priest
h **Sting:** teacher

4 Students work in pairs to complete the sentences, and to match them to the famous people. Check answers with the whole class.

ANSWERS

a taught; Sting b spent; Tom Cruise
c made; Kate Winslet d dropped; Keanu Reeves
e laughed; Colin Farrell f worked; Tom Hanks
g dreamt; Renée Zellweger
h asked; Catherine Zeta-Jones

5 Students work in pairs to discuss the questions. Have some brief class feedback on any interesting points.

***Listening*, exercise 5: alternative suggestion**

In pairs, students think of other jobs which would provide useful experience for becoming an actor, singer, TV presenter, etc. They then justify their choices to the rest of the class.

Language focus 1 (PAGES 63–64)

Present perfect and Past simple with *for*

Note: rather than dividing the Present perfect into several different uses, as is customary in many teaching materials, our approach is to show that the Present perfect has essentially one meaning: it connects the past to the present. The past action or state is still part of the present in some way. Therefore, in both *Language focus 1* and *2*, students are shown that the Present perfect refers to a period of time that continues from the past to the present, which we believe is more useful for students than distinguishing between different uses.

1 Check the meaning of *pop star*. Focus students on the picture of Sting. See if they remember that he was a teacher before he was a singer. Direct students to the two sentences in exercise 1a, and give them a minute or two, individually or in pairs, to consider the questions in exercise 1b before checking with the whole class.

ANSWERS
The finished action is *became famous*; the action that continues up to the present is *has been a famous pop star*.

2 Students discuss the tenses in pairs. Check answers with the whole class.

ANSWERS
The Present perfect is used in sentence 1; the Past simple is used in sentence 2.

Grammar

1 Give students a few minutes in pairs to decide on the sentence endings. As you check the answers, highlight the following points.
- Sentence a refers to a period of time which began in the past and continues to the present.
- Sentence b refers to a finished period of time in the past.

ANSWERS AND LANGUAGE NOTE
a *and I'm very happy here* b *as a child**
* This means the same as *when I was a child.*

2 Elicit the Past simple and Present perfect forms of the verbs onto the board. As you do so, highlight the following points.
- *Have* and *has* are often shortened to *'ve* and *'s*.
- For regular verbs, the past participle is formed from the verb + *-ed*; for irregular verbs, the past participles have to be learnt individually. Refer students to the list on page 157 of the *Students' Book*.

ANSWERS
a worked; have/has worked b knew; have/has known

3 Elicit the negative and question forms. As you do so, highlight the following points.
- Negatives are formed with *haven't* and *hasn't*.
- In questions, *have/has* and the pronoun are inverted.

Refer students to *Language summaries A* and *B* on page 152 of the *Students' Book* for more information.

ANSWERS
You haven't known him for a long time.
Have you known him for a long time?

PRACTICE

Note: you may wish to do the *Pronunciation* box at this point, if your students would benefit from hearing some examples before the *Practice* activities.

1 Focus students on the examples. Establish that they can complete the sentences with either the Past simple or the Present perfect, depending on what is true for them. As students write their sentences, circulate to help with vocabulary.

***Practice*, exercise 1: alternative suggestion**

If you have a strong class: ask students to do the exercise orally, without writing out their sentences first. This also gives more opportunity for student–student correction.

Pronunciation

See *Teacher's tips: helping students with pronunciation* on pages 6–7.

1 [T7.2] Play the recording, stopping after each sentence to give students time to write. Point out that *for* is weak because it is not stressed. Show students that the *r* in *for* links to the next word if it begins with a vowel, for example, *for about*.

ANSWERS
See tapescript for recording 2 on page 167 of the *Students' Book*.

2 [T7.2] Play the recording again, or say the sentences yourself, for students to repeat.

2 Put students into pairs and do this exercise as a race: the first pair to find six verbs that are the same in all forms, then the first pair to find twelve verbs that have the same past tense and past participle, and so on. Refer students to the list of irregular verbs on page 157 of the *Students' Book*.

3 Direct students to the tapescript for recording 1 on page 167 of the *Students' Book*. Students work individually to find the past tense forms before checking answers in pairs. Then they work together to list the past participles, if necessary checking the list of irregular verbs on page 157.

ANSWERS

Past tense forms	Past participles
knew	known
wanted	wanted
made	made
asked	asked
replied	replied
was	been
laughed	laughed
told	told
had	had
dreamt (dreamed)	dreamt (dreamed)
trained	trained
spent	spent
taught	taught
dropped	dropped
worked	worked
helped	helped

***Practice*, exercise 3: additional suggestion**

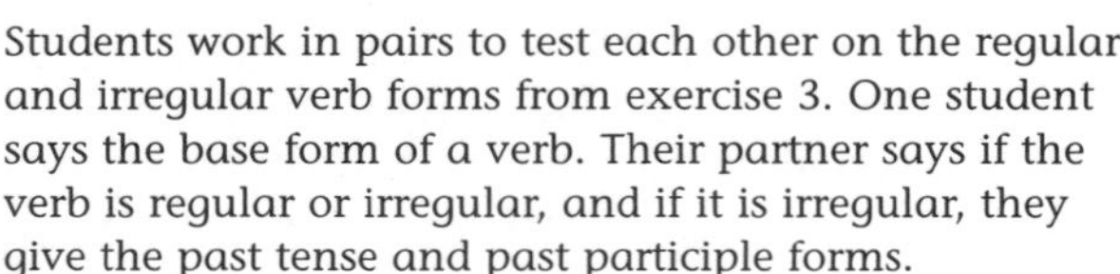
Students work in pairs to test each other on the regular and irregular verb forms from exercise 3. One student says the base form of a verb. Their partner says if the verb is regular or irregular, and if it is irregular, they give the past tense and past participle forms.

ADDITIONAL PRACTICE

RB Resource bank: 7B Life circles (Present perfect and Past simple), page 137; 7C Happy verb families (Irregular past tenses and past participles), pages 138–139; Learner-training worksheet E (Using the *mini-dictionary*: irregular verbs – part 2), page 140

Workbook: Present perfect, exercises 1–3, page 42

Language focus 2 (PAGES 64–65)

Present perfect and Past simple with other time words

1 Students look at the picture. Ask them briefly what they think each of Robbie's friends is like, from their appearance. Students complete the sentences individually or in pairs.

2 [T7.3] Students listen to check their answers.

ANSWERS
1 had 2 was 3 went 4 wanted 5 didn't go 6 spent 7 studied 8 decided 9 didn't enjoy 10 liked

3 Encourage students to predict what has happened to each of Robbie's friends before they read the text to see if their predictions were correct. To make this stage more structured, write the predictions on the board and ask students to underline any information in the text which is the same. Then check answers with the whole class.

4 **a** Put students into pairs or small groups to discuss the questions.

POSSIBLE ANSWERS
Ameet **has** had ten different jobs, **has** started his own company, **hasn't** made £1 million.
Edward **has** moved to the United States, **has** made a lot of money, **hasn't** had a girlfriend.
Lucy **has** appeared in plays and commercials, **hasn't** been to Hollywood.
Kate **has** worked for Greenpeace, **has** had a baby.
Hannah **has** been married three times, **has** lived in four different countries.

b This depends on students' ideas. For example, they might find it surprising that Edward is the one who has made a lot of money.

Grammar

1 Give students a few minutes, individually or in pairs, to underline the verbs and to answer the questions.

ANSWERS
The Past simple refers to a past time that is finished (as described in exercise 1).
The Present perfect refers to a period of time that continues to the present (as described in exercise 3).

2 Write the sentence heads on the board, and elicit which time words can be used with each, so that there are three lists. Demonstrate how the time words which say when something happened cannot be used with the Present perfect by writing one or two sentences on the board, for example, ~~I've seen him last week~~. ~~I haven't seen him five years ago~~. Ask students to correct them.

Tell students to find examples of the Present perfect with time phrases in exercise 3, for example, *She's just had her first baby*; *His most popular game … has already sold over ten million copies*; *he's never had a girlfriend*; *He hasn't made £1 million yet*.

Check that students understand the meaning of the time words. Ask questions like: *Which time word means 'not at any time'? Which one means 'a short time before now'? Which one means 'before now, maybe sooner than you expected'? Which one means 'not until now'?* Elicit the answers: *never*, *just*, *already*, *yet*. Point out that these time words do not have a fixed time. Refer students to *Language summary C* on page 152 of the *Students' Book* for more information.

ANSWERS

a I saw him …	b I've … seen him	c I haven't seen him …
five years ago	already	yet
in 2002	just	
last year	never	
when I was six years old		

PRACTICE

1 **a** If necessary, highlight the difference between *been* and *gone* before starting this exercise. Put two examples on the board: *1 He's been to the hospital. 2 He's gone to the hospital.* Ask students in each case: *Where is he now?* Elicit the answers: *1 He's not at the hospital: he's either at home again, or somewhere else. 2 He's either at the hospital or on his way there.*

Go through the example in the book with the class. Emphasise that students need to put the words in the correct order, and to change the verbs into the Present perfect.

ANSWERS

1 I haven't finished school yet.
2 I've just had lunch.
3 I've already been on holiday this year.
4 I've never broken an arm or a leg.
5 I haven't been to the dentist's yet this year.
6 I haven't done anything exciting this week.
7 I've never met anyone famous.
8 I haven't travelled on a plane this year.
9 I haven't done any sport this week.
10 I've never stolen anything.

b Demonstrate what students have to do, either with the example or by doing one of the sentences yourself. Students discuss answers in pairs or small groups.

2 If necessary, give students time to think about their answers to these questions and to ask you for any vocabulary they need, before discussing their answers with a partner. After the discussion, feed back on any interesting points that you overheard.

***Practice*, exercise 2: alternative suggestion**

Set up the exercise as a survey. In groups of four to six, students find out who has visited the most cities / foreign countries, changed school/job the most times, etc. Groups then compare their findings.

3 Give students time to think of three or four people that they knew and to make some notes about them. They could also tell a partner about the people, to help them clarify what they are going to write. Refer students back to the text about Robbie's old friends on page 65 of the *Students'* Book before they start writing.

ADDITIONAL PRACTICE

Workbook: Present perfect, exercises 4–8, pages 43–44; Improve your writing, exercise 13, page 47

Reading and speaking (PAGE 66)

1 Focus students' attention on the pictures and the brief introduction to Ewan McGregor, and find out if they have seen any of his films. Words to check: *theatre* /θɪətə/, *starring role*. Establish the idea of an audience asking a famous actor questions about his life. Students read the questions and check any unknown vocabulary in their mini-dictionaries.

2 Give students a few minutes to match the answers to the questions. Words to check: *supportive, mime, to shut down on something* (= to give up on something). Students compare answers in pairs before checking with the whole class.

ANSWERS

a 1 b 5 c 3 d 2 e 4 f 7 g 6

3 Students reread Ewan's answers. Emphasise that they should find reasons for their answers. Students check answers in pairs before checking with the whole class.

ANSWERS

a False (answer 1: *I love the theatre … I'd like to do more …*)
b True (answer 5: *I've really enjoyed them all.*)
c False (answer 7: *Imagine that! … It's unbelievable.*)
d False (answer 4: *they all do …*)
e True (answer 2: *we took her out of school … I feel it's important to be together, so we do the best we can.*)
f False (answer 2: *it was difficult because she missed her friends …*)
g False (answer 6: *I hated mime classes …*)

4 Demonstrate the idea of the activity by telling students about somebody you would like to interview, and listing some of the questions you would ask them. Put students into pairs. Give them a few minutes to think of a famous person. Refer them to the questions in exercise 1 as an example. As students prepare questions, circulate and help with vocabulary.

5 *Either*: select some students to act out their interviews in front of the class. The other students guess who the famous person is. *Or*: ask students to write an imaginary interview. Put the interviews around the classroom. Students circulate to read them. *If you have a large class*: you can save time with the first option if you put students into groups of six or eight to act out their interviews.

Task: Talk about your dreams, ambitions and achievements

(PAGE 67)

See *Teacher's tips: making tasks work* on pages 10–11 and *Responding to learners' individual language needs* on pages 12–13.

Preparation: listening

1 Discuss the three definitions, and elicit an example of each.

ANSWERS

an achievement = something you have done which you are proud of
an ambition = something you want to do one day

a dream = something you would like to do, but probably won't

2 [T7.4] Draw students' attention to the pictures and check that students understand what each one shows. Play the recording. Students check answers in pairs before checking with the whole class.

ANSWERS
Bill: d **Ralph:** c, e **Deb:** a **Ian:** b **Swati:** f

3 [T7.4] Students listen again and make brief notes. Check answers in pairs and then with the whole class.

ANSWERS
Bill: his family went to the United States from Ireland. His ambition/dream is to go to Ireland, rediscover his family roots and meet his Irish relatives.
Ralph: his greatest achievement was scoring three goals for his local football team. His ambition/dream is to visit the Taj Mahal in India.
Deb: her ambition/dream is to own a red Ferrari (even though she can't drive yet).
Ian: his ambition/dream is to own a big house in the mountains, so that he can invite friends and family for a party, and also enjoy the peace and quiet.
Swati: her greatest achievement was getting a place at university to study medicine. Her ambition is to make a medical discovery that helps people.

Task: speaking

1 Before students work individually to decide on four or five dreams, ambitions and achievements, go through the list of suggestions and elicit some examples. Circulate to provide help with vocabulary.

2 Give students five to ten minutes to plan what they will say about each thing. Draw their attention to *Useful language a* and *b*. Emphasise that students should only make notes, not write out what they want to say, as this will sound stilted.

3 Regroup students to tell each other about their dreams, ambitions and achievements. Circulate and collect examples of good language use and/or errors to focus on later. Ask each group to report back on the most interesting/unusual ideas.

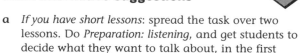

Task: alternative suggestions

a *If you have short lessons*: spread the task over two lessons. Do *Preparation: listening*, and get students to decide what they want to talk about, in the first lesson. Do *Task: speaking* in the second lesson.

b *If you want to personalise* Preparation: listening: tell students about some of your own dreams, ambitions and achievements instead of using the recording. If possible, bring pictures or realia to make your talk interesting, and try to use some of the phrases from the *Useful language* box in your model.

Wordspot (PAGE 68)

for

See *Teacher's tips: working with lexical phrases* on pages 8–9.

1 Students work in pairs to match the phrases/sentences.

2 [T7.5] Play the recording, pausing after each example to give students time to check their answers. Then check with the whole class.

ANSWERS
- a How long have you been in London? For about three months.
- b Are you waiting for someone? Yes, I am. My brother will be here soon.
- c What do you want for your birthday? Well, there's a new computer game I'd like.
- d I'm looking for somewhere to live. Do you know of any apartments to rent?
- e It's one o'clock. Time for lunch!
- f Eating so many chips and burgers is really bad for you.
- g The bus didn't arrive so I was late for class.
- h 'This coffee's cold.' 'Why don't you ask for another one?'
- i (Phone rings) 'Hello? Just a moment. Peter? It's for you!'
- j It's a beautiful morning. Let's go for a walk!
- k What's for dinner? Chicken and chips!
- l Eating vegetables and fruit is good for you.

3 Students work in pairs or small groups to complete the diagram. Check answers with the whole class.

ANSWERS
- a **verb + for:** ask for, waiting for, looking for, go for a walk
- b **for + time:** for three hours, For about three months
- c **health and exercise:** good for you, bad for you
- d **other phrases:** for your birthday, for dinner, Time for, It's for you!
- e **adjective + for:** late for

4 **a** [T7.6] Play the recording, pausing after each question to give students time to write. Repeat the recording if necessary.

b Refer students to the tapescript to check their answers. Drill the questions to help familiarise students with them. Put students into pairs to ask and answer the questions. Encourage them to try to ask the questions from memory rather than by reading them, which will result in flat intonation.

ANSWERS
See tapescript for recording 6 on page 168 of the *Students' Book.*

Study ... (PAGE 68)

Learning irregular past tenses and past participles

Give students a few minutes to look at the ideas and to comment on them with a partner. Discuss briefly which methods students are interested in. Set students the task of trying the ideas for the next week or two. Ask them to be ready to report back at the end of that time.

Practise ... (PAGE 69)

1 Present perfect: irregular verbs

Students work in pairs. Ask them to do this orally first. One student says the infinitive, the other says the Past simple and past participle forms, and they take turns. Emphasise that, at the end, they should look up any forms they are unsure of. Students write the activity for homework as consolidation.

ANSWERS
a became, become b could; been able to
c dreamt/dreamed; dreamt/dreamed
d had, had e knew, known f made, made
g said, said h spent, spent i took, taken
j taught, taught k told, told

2 Present perfect or Past simple?

Students work individually or in pairs before checking answers with the class.

ANSWERS
a stayed b have lived c started d we've saved
e studied

3 Present perfect and Past simple with time words

Give students a few minutes to discuss their answers in pairs before checking with the whole class.

ANSWERS
a 2 b 2 c 2 d 1 e 2 f 2

4 Ambitions and dreams

Do this as a team game. Write the verbs on the board, and read out each of the other items one at a time. A member from each group runs to the board and writes the item under a particular verb, as told by their team. The first team to write under the correct verb is awarded a point. Students copy the completed table at the end.

ANSWERS
a buy b become c learn d go e write
f make g have h earn

5 Phrases with *for*

Students work individually or in pairs before checking answers as a whole class.

ANSWERS
a He'd like to speak b thinking c Did you have
d healthy e I'm going to eat f They're too late

Pronunciation spot

The sounds /æ/ and /ʌ/

See *Teacher's tips: helping students with pronunciation* on pages 6–7.

1 [T7.7] Play the recording or model the pairs of words, highlighting the difference between the two sounds. Point out that for the first word in each pair, the jaw is much lower, and it moves up to produce the second sound.

2 [T7.8] Students work in pairs, saying the phrases aloud to try to identify the /æ/ and /ʌ/ sounds. Play the recording or model the phrases for students to check. *If your students find this difficult*: tell them how many of the two sounds there are in each phrase. This may help to motivate them.

3 Drill the phrases. Students work in pairs to practise saying them.

***Pronunciation spot*, exercise 1: additional suggestion**

Students use the pairs of words, and take turns to say each word. Their partner says *One* if they think the word contains the /æ/ sound, and *Two* if they think it contains the /ʌ/ sound. In this way, students give each other feedback on their pronunciation of the sounds.

Remember! (PAGE 69)

After looking back at the areas they have practised, students do the *Mini-check* on page 159 of the *Students' Book*. Check answers with the whole class, and ask students to tell you their scores out of 20.

ANSWERS
1 've never been 2 's already visited 3 began
4 hasn't come 5 moved 6 's always been 7 the
8 fl 9 a 10 fl 11 become 12 written 13 spent
14 dreamt/dreamed 15 buy 16 go 17 become
18 earn 19 want 20 waiting

module 8

Countries and cultures

Language focus 1 (PAGES 70–71)

Using articles

1 Students look at the pictures and discuss briefly what they can see. Use the pictures to check the meaning of *kilt* and *bow* /baʊ/. Other words to check: *myth*, *bullfight*, *barbecue*, *camel*. Put students into pairs or small groups to discuss the statements. Have some brief class feedback on some of their ideas. *If you have a multi-nationality class*: ask students from the countries mentioned to comment on the statements relating to them.

2 [T8.1] Ask students to listen, and to note whether the speaker says the statement is true or not, and why. Put students into the same pairs or groups as before to compare their answers. If students from one of the countries mentioned disagree with the speaker, the discussion will be livelier!

ANSWERS

a False (only true if you are at home at that time)
b True (at least in the speaker's family and region)
c False (it can be very hot in the summer)
d False (perhaps true in the south, but most people aren't interested)
e True (they like to behave well in public)
f True (football is a passion for them)
g False (they eat a whole range of different things)
h True (because they always have good weather)
i True (in the desert) / False (in the cities)
j False (they only wear them for special occasions)

Grammar

1 Give students a few minutes individually or in pairs to look at the example sentences and to think about the rules. If students are struggling, prompt them. Write the first example on the board with articles in front of the nouns, and ask students to correct the mistakes, for example, *The English people drink the tea every day at five o'clock*. Then ask students to reread the text on page 70 and to find more examples of talking about people or things in general, for example, *Italian people*, *Men in Scotland*, *pasta*, *camels*. Point out that the nouns are often in the plural form and that no articles are used. (Avoid discussing uncountable nouns at this stage.) Then tell students to find all the names of cities and countries in the text, and elicit the fact that there are usually no articles. Explain that *the United States* is an exception.

Students might ask you about other exceptions they know of, for example, *the United Kingdom*. If they do, highlight that we use the definite article (*the*) with certain place names, including:

- seas and oceans (*the Mediterranean*, *the Atlantic*)
- rivers (*the Amazon*, *the Nile*)
- ranges of mountains (*the Andes*, *the Himalayas*)
- countries when they are referred to as a group of states or different parts (*the United Kingdom*, *the United States*, *the Netherlands* – but *Britain*, *America*, *Holland*).

However, only focus on these exceptions if students ask.

ANSWERS

When we talk about people or things in general, we usually use no article.
With the names of people and countries, we usually use no article.

2 Go through the phrases with the students or put them into pairs to fill the gaps. Then refer them to *Language summary A* on pages 152–153 of the *Students' Book* to check their answers. In feedback, point out that these phrases, like irregular verbs, need to be learnt. Remind students of the word locusts they created in Module 1 (see *Vocabulary and speaking*, exercise 4, on page 7 of the Students' Book). They could do the same with article use in phrases with the prepositions *at*, *in* and *on*.

ANSWERS AND LANGUAGE NOTE

at home at night at **the** top
in **the** afternoon in **the** south in **the** world
on holiday on **the** left on **the** coast

Language summary A covers more uses of articles: *a/an* and *the* for first and second mention; using *the* when something is seen as unique; using *the* with superlative forms. Some of these uses may be familiar or straightforward for students with a similar article system to English. If your students do not use articles in their first language, you may prefer not to overload them with all these uses at this stage.

PRACTICE

1 Go through the example with the class. Demonstrate that students need phrases from b, c and e to make complete sentences, and that phrases from a and d are optional. Check the meaning of *general statements* (= things we say or write when we talk about people or things in general, as in the first rule in the *Grammar* box). Students work in pairs to create sentences.

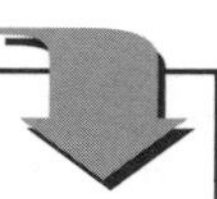

Practice, exercise 1: additional suggestion

After students have worked together to create sentences, put pairs together into groups of four or six to read out some of their sentences and to agree/disagree. Encourage them to give reasons if they disagree, to introduce an element of discussion.

2 a Do the first sentence as an example with the class. Point out that students have to put in *the* where necessary, and also decide whether the content of the

statements is true or not. They do not need to correct the false statements at this stage. Students work in pairs or small groups to help each other with the answers. Check for the correct use of *the* before playing the recording.

ANSWERS
1 Asia, Europe
2 New York, **the** biggest city, **the** world
3 Mount Fuji, Japan, **the** highest mountain, **the** world
4 **The** Queen of England, Downing Street
5 **The** Mediterranean Sea, the Pacific Ocean
6 **The** Sun, **the** Moon
7 **The** Himalayas, Asia
8 **The** Moon, **the** sky, night
9 **The** Mississippi River, **the** United States

b [T8.2] Students listen and check. You can run this as a competition, pausing the recording before each answer to ask what different pairs/groups think. Then play the correct answer and award points accordingly.

ANSWERS
See tapescript for recording 2 on page 168 of the *Students' Book*.

In order for students to change the sentences, play the recording again and stop after each sentence. Students can help each other in pairs before checking with the whole class.

ANSWERS
2 New York is the biggest city in the United States. Tokyo, Mexico City and São Paulo are bigger than New York.
3 Mount Everest is the highest mountain in the world. Mount Fuji is the highest mountain in Japan.
4 The Queen lives in Buckingham Palace. The British Prime Minister lives in Downing Street.
5 The Pacific Ocean is bigger than the Mediterranean Sea.
6 The Sun is bigger than the Moon.
8 You can't always see the Moon in the sky at night.

***Practice*, exercise 2: additional suggestion**

Students work in small groups to make posters with maps and pictures to illustrate some of the facts in exercise 2. They can label them, for example, *the river Nile: the longest river in Africa*. This helps to make some of the rules about the use and non-use of *the* more memorable.

3 Students need a loose piece of paper to do this exercise. Demonstrate by writing two or three sentences about yourself on the board. Circulate as students write, noting examples of good use of articles and/or errors to focus on later.

4 Students exchange pieces of paper. Emphasise that students should not say the name of the person whose paper they now have. Students read the sentences aloud. The others guess who wrote the sentences. Feed back on any problems with article use you noted. *If you have a large class*: ask students to do exercise 4 in groups of four to six, to ensure that pace is maintained.

ADDITIONAL PRACTICE

RB **Resource bank:** 8A Article snakes and ladders (Use and non-use of articles), pages 141–143

Workbook: Using articles, exercises 1–5, pages 48–49

Language focus 2 (PAGES 72–73)

Quantifiers with countable and uncountable nouns

1 Provide prompts if necessary, for example, *location*, *nightlife*, *architecture*, *climate*. As a class, discuss which students think is 'the world's best city'.

2 Focus students' attention on the pictures and text about Zürich. Explain that they will hear somebody called Stuart talking about what it is like to live there. As a class, students predict what he might say. To make this stage more concrete, write students' predictions on the board.

3 [T8.3] Play the recording. Students tick the topics that Stuart mentions. Check answers with the whole class.

ANSWERS
scenery traffic banks skyscrapers nightlife restaurants

4 [T8.4] Students work in pairs to order the sentences before listening to check their answers.

ANSWERS
See tapescript for recording 4 on page 169 of the *Students' Book*.

Grammar

1–2 Some of this should be revision for students at this level, so give them time to discuss their answers to the questions in pairs before going through the answers with the class. As you feed back, highlight the following points.

- Countable nouns have a plural form, for example, *banks*; uncountable nouns have no plural form.
- *Many* is used with countable nouns; *much* is used with uncountable nouns.
- *Some* and *a few* are used in positive sentences.
- Any is used in negative sentences. It is also used in questions where the answer could be *yes/no*, for example, *Are there any nice restaurants near here?*
- *A lot of* is used in positive sentences; *much/many* is used in negative sentences.
- *Too much/many* means that the speaker is unhappy about the large amount or number of something.

Refer students to *Language summary B* on page 153 of the *Students' Book* for more information.

ANSWERS

1 **Countable nouns:** bank, hotel, museum, restaurant, shop, skyscraper
Uncountable nouns: nightlife, pollution, scenery, traffic

2 a ✘ *A* in the first sentence means 'one'; *some* in the second sentence means 'an indefinite number of'.
b ✔
c ✘ *A few* in the first sentence means 'a small number of'; *a lot of* in the second sentence means 'a large number of'.
d ✘ *A lot of* in the first sentence means 'a large amount of'
(a neutral remark); *too much* in the second sentence means 'more than enough' (a criticism).
e ✘ *Many* in the first (negative) sentence means that there are a few parks; *any* in the second (negative) sentence means that there are no parks at all.

PRACTICE

1 If necessary do the first one with the class, getting students to explain why two or three of the quantifiers are not correct. Students then work individually or in pairs before checking with the whole class.

ANSWERS
a a lot of b enough c many d any e some
f a lot of g any h a few

Practice, exercise 1: additional suggestion

Students make true sentences about their home town, using some of the ideas in the exercise, for example, *traffic* or *parks*. To structure their work, ask them for three positive and three negative points.

2 Tell students to think of a place they know something about which they would recommend to a foreign visitor. Direct students to the prompts listed in *Language focus 2*, exercise 3, and give them a few minutes to prepare reasons for their recommendation.

Go through the examples with the class. Students work in pairs or small groups. Emphasise that students should try to persuade their partners to visit the place they recommend.

ADDITIONAL PRACTICE

RB **Resource bank:** 8B The Hungry Hippo café (Quantifiers – *some*, *any*, *much*, *not enough*, etc.), pages 144–145

Workbook: Quantifiers with countable and uncountable nouns: *some*, *any* and *no*, exercises 6–8, pages 50–51

Vocabulary and reading
(PAGES 74–75)

Geographical features

See *Teacher's tips: working with lexical phrases* on pages 8–9 and *Making the most of the* mini-dictionary on pages 9–10.

1 Focus students' attention on the questions in blue. Emphasise that they should not read the text yet. Students spend a few minutes in pairs trying to answer the questions. Discuss ideas as a class. To make the next activity more concrete, write students' ideas on the board. Words to check: *salty*, *coastline*, *extreme*, *canal*.

2 Students read the text quickly, to see which of their answers is right. Set a time limit of three minutes to ensure that they read quickly. Have some brief class feedback.

3 Go through an example with the whole class before students work in pairs to find the geographical words in the text. Each person in the pair agrees to find different words. They then teach each other. The pronunciation of several of these words will be difficult for students to anticipate. Check answers with the whole class, drilling the following words: *ice* /aɪs/, *desert* /ˈdezət/, *island* /ˈaɪlənd/, *climate* /ˈklaɪmət/, *canal* /kəˈnæl/.

ANSWERS
See solution to puzzle on page 147 of the *Students' Book*.

Pronunciation

See *Teacher's tips: helping students with pronunciation* on pages 6–7.

1 [T8.5] Play the recording or model the words to demonstrate the two different ways the letter 'i' is pronounced.
2 Give students a minute or two in pairs to try saying the words and to put them into two columns, /ɪ/ and /aɪ/.
3 [T8.6] Play the recording for students to check their answers. Play it again for students to repeat.

ANSWERS

/ɪ/	/aɪ/
mineral	white
fill	climate
single	island
historical	coastline
	size
	ice

Task: Complete a map of New Zealand (PAGE 76)

See *Teacher's tips: making tasks work* on pages 10–11 and *Responding to learners' individual language needs* on pages 12–13.

Preparation: listening

1 Students look at the pictures of New Zealand and discuss briefly what they know about the country. Put students into pairs and give them a few minutes to read the quiz. Encourage them to guess the answers if they are not sure, and to use their mini-dictionaries for unfamiliar vocabulary. If your students really know nothing about New Zealand, do not spend long on predicting the answers. Check the meaning of *fjord*, *glacier* and *sheep*, then move quickly on to the listening.

2 [T8.7] Play the recording and ask students to circle the correct answers. Students compare answers in pairs before checking with the whole class, and comment on anything they found surprising/interesting.

ANSWERS
1 c 2 a 3 b 4 b
5 a–h (*sheep* are not mentioned in the recording, but New Zealand is still famous for them!)

***Preparation: listening*: alternative suggestion**

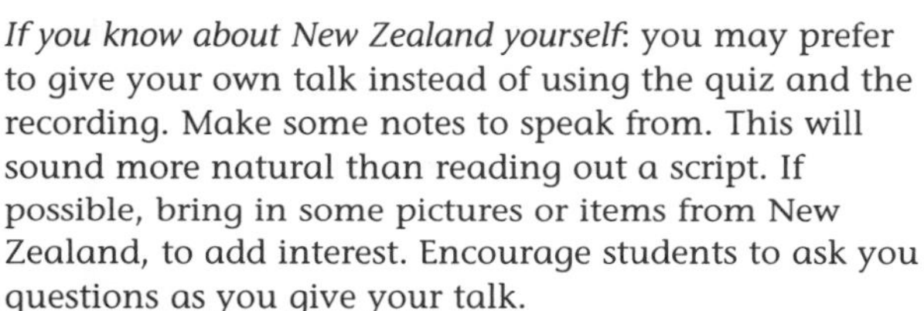

If you know about New Zealand yourself: you may prefer to give your own talk instead of using the quiz and the recording. Make some notes to speak from. This will sound more natural than reading out a script. If possible, bring in some pictures or items from New Zealand, to add interest. Encourage students to ask you questions as you give your talk.

Task: speaking

Put students into Groups A and B. Direct Group A to page 142, and Group B to page 144, and make it clear that each group should not look at the other's map. Establish that each group will be finding out about places on the other's map. Together As prepare what to say, as do Bs.

Give students five to ten minutes, individually or in their groups, to think about their explanations and, if necessary, to make notes. Draw their attention to *Useful language a* and *b*. Circulate and help with vocabulary and the wording of the explanations.

Regroup to form pairs, A and B. Make sure that both Student A and Student B know which places they have to ask about before they start. If possible, arrange the seating so that students cannot easily see each other's maps. Students add the new information to their own map as they listen to each other. As students exchange information, note down examples of good language use and/or errors to focus on later.

When they have finished, students compare maps and check how many places they marked correctly. Encourage them to work out why they marked any places inaccurately, and to review what they should have said to be more accurate.

Real life (PAGE 77)

Asking for and giving directions

1 [T8.8] Emphasise that students only need to note down the place each person is looking for and how they are going to get there. Play the recording. Students discuss answers in pairs before checking with the whole class.

ANSWERS
1 Church Street; by car 2 The Factory; on foot
3 Central Station; by bus

2 a Students work in pairs to fill the gaps. Emphasise that only one word is needed for each.

b [T8.9] Play the recording. Students check their answers.

ANSWERS
See tapescript for recording 9 on page 169 of the *Students' Book.*

Pronunciation

See *Teacher's tips: helping students with pronunciation* on pages 6–7.

[T8.9] Play the recording or model the questions yourself. Highlight for students the difference between polite intonation and flatter intonation, which can make the person asking for directions sound abrupt or rude.

3 Draw students' attention to the pictures and do the first picture as an example with the class. Give students a few minutes in pairs to match the pictures and phrases before checking answers with the whole class. As you feed back, highlight:

- the difference between *turn left* (showing movement) and *on your left* (showing position)
- the difference between *cross the road* (showing movement) and *on the other side of the road* (showing position)
- that *go down to the end* does not indicate that there is a hill
- that *the second right* describes the second opportunity to turn right
- that *past* is a preposition of movement
- that *the lights* mean 'traffic lights'.

ANSWERS
a Turn left at the traffic lights.
b Go down to the end of the road.
c It's on the corner.
d Go past the cinema.
e It's on your left.
f Cross the road.
g Go straight on at the lights.
h It's on the other side of the road.
i Take the next right.
j It's the second right.

4 Refer students to the tapescript for recording 8 on page 169 of the *Students' Book*. Give them a few minutes to read and underline useful phrases. Students discuss answers in pairs before checking with the whole class. As you check the answers, highlight that *get a bus* and *take a bus* have the same meaning.

5 Put students into pairs, A and B, and explain that they will practise asking for and giving directions. Ask them to decide where they are. Direct students to pages 143 and 146 of the *Students' Book*, and make it clear that they should not look at their partner's map. Give them a minute or two to familiarise themselves with their maps and to find the station. Emphasise that students should imagine that they are at the station. Students work in pairs asking for directions using relevant phrases from exercises 2–4, and marking the places they are directed to on their own maps. Circulate, noting down examples of good language use and/or errors to focus on later. When they have finished, students compare maps and discuss any problems which arose.

Writing (PAGE 78)

Giving written directions

1 Check that students understand why Patrick has written the directions. Give them a few minutes to read through the directions and to complete the gaps. Students compare answers in pairs before checking with the whole class. As you check the answers, highlight:

- the difference between *take the train/bus* (meaning 'catch the train/bus') and *it takes ... minutes* (meaning 'the journey lasts ... minutes')
- the meaning of *along* and *towards* – demonstrate these prepositions of movement via drawings on the board or by using suitable objects (pen, ruler, book, etc.) to represent streets and buildings
- the difference between *as far as* (followed by a place) and *until* (followed by a phrase such as *you come to* ...).

ANSWERS
1 From 2 as far as 3 outside 4 Get off
5 Keep walking 6 on your 7 cross 8 until
9 you will see 10 your 11 by 12 get lost

2 Students work individually to match verbs with the words and phrases. They compare answers in pairs before checking with the whole class.

ANSWERS
a take a 71 bus b come to a set of traffic lights
c cross the road d turn left e keep walking
f follow the signs for Colby g get lost
h get off at the next stop

3 First, ask students to decide where to write directions to. Refer them to the model text in exercise 1, and set a time limit of fifteen minutes to write two or three paragraphs of directions. Circulate to provide help with vocabulary, and note down examples of good language use and/or errors to focus on later. *If you are short of time*: ask students to write the directions for homework.

***Writing*, exercise 3: alternative suggestion**

Tell students not to write the name of the place they are writing directions to. When students have finished writing, collect their descriptions and display them around the class. Students circulate, reading each other's work and guessing where the directions are to.

ADDITIONAL PRACTICE

RB **Resource bank:** 8C Where's the nearest bank? (Language for giving directions), page 146; Learner-training worksheet F (Noticing and remembering prepositions and articles in phrases) page 147

Workbook: Improve your writing, exercise 14, page 53

Study ... (PAGE 79)

Using the *mini-dictionary* (3): Additional information

1 Before looking at the dictionary entry, discuss as a class anything students can think of in terms of information about a word which can be found in their mini-dictionaries. Remind students of any areas they have not mentioned, and then refer students to the dictionary entry. Students discuss the questions in pairs before checking answers as a class.

2 Students work in small groups to discuss the questions. Encourage them to guess if they are unsure.

3 Students check answers in their mini-dictionaries.

ANSWERS
a on the first syllable b /kɔːt/
c uncountable d salty

Pronunciation spot

The sounds /eɪ/ and /aɪ/

See *Teacher's tips: helping students with pronunciation* on pages 6–7.

1 [T8.10] Explain to students that diphthongs are double vowels. Play the recording or model the sounds yourself to show how they are made. If necessary, drill the individual vowel sounds quickly, one after the other, until students are saying each diphthong. For example, /e/, /ɪ/, /eɪ/. Highlight the different words to reinforce the diphthongs.
2 Students work in pairs, saying the words aloud to help them decide which diphthong is in each word.
3 [T8.11] Play the recording. Students listen and check their answers before practising the words in pairs.

ANSWERS

/eɪ/	/aɪ/
way	five
train	mobile
birthday	right
take	sign
plane	light

Practise ... (PAGE 79)

1 Using articles

Students work in pairs to complete the sentences. Before checking answers as a class, tell students that there are eight examples of *the*. Students re-check their work before checking answers with the whole class.

ANSWERS
a I'm usually at home in **the** evening.
b Go past the cinema, and Station Road is on **the** left.
c It's a small town in **the** south of Turkey: it's on **the** coast, so it's very popular with tourists.
d While we were on holiday in Egypt, we decided to go on a cruise along **the** River Nile.
e Is Mont Blanc **the** highest mountain in Europe?

2 Quantifiers with countable and uncountable nouns

Students work individually or in pairs before checking answers with the whole class.

ANSWERS
a too much b A lot of c some d enough
e some

3 Geographical features

Do this as a race. Students work in pairs. The winning pair is the first to spell the words correctly.

ANSWERS
a ice b canals c border d desert e island

4 Asking for and giving directions

Students work in pairs and do this orally. They take turns to read the sentences aloud, saying *Beep* where there is a gap. Their partner tries to supply the missing word. Students can then write the answers as consolidation.

ANSWERS
a on b Turn c give d on e is

5 Giving written directions

Students work individually or in pairs before checking answers with the whole class.

ANSWERS
a Keep walking until you come to the hospital.
b Leave the station and cross the road.
c Follow the road for about 500 metres.
d Get off the bus at the next stop.

Remember! (PAGE 79)

After looking back at the areas they have practised, students do the *Mini-check* on page 160 of the *Students' Book*. Check answers with the whole class, and ask students to tell you their scores out of 20.

ANSWERS
1 the 2 the 3 the 4 fl 5 the 6 no 7 a few
8 some 9 Any 10 too much 11 desert
12 border 13 island 14 climate 15 looking
16 get 17 Turn 18 cross 19 Keep 20 Get

module 9

Old and new

Vocabulary and speaking (PAGE 80)

Modern and traditional

See *Teacher's tips: working with lexical phrases* on pages 8–9 and *Making the most of the* mini-dictionary on pages 9–10.

1 Ask students to name some of the objects/actions they can see in the pictures. Then direct them to columns A and B and give them a few minutes, individually or in pairs, to match the items, using their mini-dictionaries if necessary.

ANSWERS

a	air conditioning	electric fans
b	booking online	queuing up for tickets
c	central heating	coal fires
d	charge and credit cards	cash
e	computer games	board games
f	a dishwasher	doing the washing-up
g	downloading sound files	buying a CD or cassette
h	a microwave oven	a cooker/stove
i	renting a DVD	going to the cinema
j	sending text messages	sending letters and faxes
k	shopping malls	street markets
l	a washing machine	washing clothes by hand

2 Go through an example with the class. Then give students a few moments individually to choose four pairs of items and to think about the advantages/ disadvantages, before putting them into pairs or small groups to compare their ideas. If necessary, give a personal example of an item which you have problems with. The question can then be discussed in groups or as a class.

Pronunciation

See *Teacher's tips: helping students with pronunciation* on pages 6–7.

1 [T9.1] Use the recording, or model the compound nouns yourself, to demonstrate the stress patterns.

2 [T9.2] Students work in pairs to decide where the main stress falls before listening to the recording to check their answers. Drill the compound nouns with the whole class.

ANSWERS

See tapescript for recording 2 on page 169 of the *Students' Book*.

ADDITIONAL PRACTICE

Workbook: Vocabulary, exercise 8, page 57; Vocabulary booster: technology, exercise 10, page 58

Reading and speaking (PAGES 80–81)

1 Ask students to rank the importance of the different things to them. Demonstrate this by showing how you would rank them, giving reasons for your choices. Students discuss their ideas in small groups. Ask a student from one or two groups to report back to the class.

2 Check the meaning of *reality TV show*. Make sure that students understand that the Bowler family lived exactly as they would have done 100 years ago. Discuss possible differences as a class, and list students' ideas on the board.

3 Students read the text to see how many of their ideas are mentioned before comparing ideas in pairs. Have some brief class feedback.

4 Students read the text again before checking answers in pairs and then with the whole class. Emphasise that they should be able to explain their answers.

ANSWERS

a The children, Kathryn, Hilary and Joseph – they changed their clothes on the way to and from school.
b Joyce – she became a typical 1900 housewife.
c Hilary – she says it was really weird having so much contact with the family, and that it was hard being nice to each other all the time.
d Kathryn – she says that she missed the telephone.
e Joyce – she says that life was simpler in 1900.

5 Demonstrate the activity with the whole class. Students work individually and then in pairs. Check answers with the whole class.

ANSWERS

a people could buy b has an easier life
c really difficult d problems e difficult f strange

6 Ask students if they would like to take part in an experiment like this. Draw their attention to the example, or demonstrate the activity by telling the class one or two things you would miss. Give students a few minutes to make their own lists, then put them into groups to discuss their ideas. Ask a student from one or two groups to report back to the class.

Language focus 1 (PAGE 82)

may, *might*, *will*, *definitely*, etc.

Note: it is not necessary for students to have read the text on page 81 in order to do *Language focus 1*. The context of future changes links back equally well to *Vocabulary and speaking* on page 80. You will need briefly to explain to students that the Bowler family took part in an experiment to see what life was like in 1900, if they have not read the text on page 81.

1 Establish the context of changes in the future, perhaps by referring back to the reading text on page 81 of the *Students' Book*. Put students into small groups to discuss their opinions.

2 [T9.3] Tell students that they will hear some predictions on the same topics that they discussed in exercise 1. Give students a minute or two to read the sentences, and to predict the kind of language that goes in the gaps. Play the recording for students to complete the gaps. If you think your students will have difficulty hearing the words, or will need help with spelling, write the following prompts on the board first: *probably*, *definitely*, *may*, *might*. Avoid spending time on these words when checking answers as these are covered in the *Grammar* box. Ask students to comment on whether the people's opinions are the same as theirs.

ANSWERS
See tapescript for recording 3 on page 169 of the *Students' Book*.

Grammar

1 Give students a few minutes in pairs to reorder the sentences. As you check the answers, write the sentences on the board in order of probability, and highlight:
- the use of the infinitive without *to* in all the forms
- the pronunciation of *definitely* /defɪnətli/ and *probably* /prɒbabli/
- the pronunciation of *may* /meɪ/ and *might* /maɪt/
- the negative forms *may not* and *might not*, which are not usually contracted
- the use of *may* and *might* to show uncertainty. They mean it's possible that something will happen, but also possible that it won't. There is not a significant difference in the degree of probability between the two: intonation is more important in showing how certain you are.

ANSWERS
1 We'll definitely buy a new car.
2 We'll probably buy a new car.
3 We might buy a new car.
4 We probably won't buy a new car.
5 We definitely won't buy a new car.

2 Students discuss the questions in pairs. Check answers with the whole class. Refer students to *Language summary A* on page 153 of the *Students' Book* for more information.

ANSWERS
Probably and *definitely* come after *will* (in positive sentences) and before *won't* (in negative sentences).

PRACTICE

1 **a** Go through the example with the class. Give students a few minutes to prepare their sentences.

b Tell students that they need to give reasons for their opinions. Demonstrate with a student. Then put students into pairs to compare answers.

Practice, exercise 1: alternative suggestion

If you want the exercise to be more challenging for your students: ask them to spend a few minutes thinking about their opinions rather than writing them down. Students then pair up and ask each other about their ideas, for example, *What do you think about number 4?*

2 **a** Students work individually on their predictions, adding reasons wherever possible.

b Students compare answers in pairs or small groups. Have some brief class feedback on any surprising answers.

ADDITIONAL PRACTICE

RB **Resource bank:** 9A In the 2020s (*will*, *won't*, *may* and *might* for future possibility), page 148

Workbook: *may*, *might*, *will*, *definitely*, etc., exercises 1–4, pages 54–55

Language focus 2 (PAGES 83–84)

Present tense after *if*, *when*, *before* and other time words

1 Words to check: *power station*, *demolish*. Draw students' attention to the pictures showing four different plans to replace an old power station. Students discuss briefly if there are any such developments in or near their own town, why they would/wouldn't need to use them, etc. Give them a few minutes, in pairs, to discuss the good/bad points of each. Have some brief class feedback. Be careful to avoid overlap with exercise 2.

2 **a** [T9.4] Play the recording. Students listen to find out which plan each person talks about, and whether they think it is a good or bad idea. Have some feedback in pairs and then as a whole class.

ANSWERS
1 d (new flats); a good idea
2 c (a new hotel); a good idea
3 a (a new shopping centre); a bad idea
4 b (a new cinema); a bad idea

b Students work in small groups to discuss the four plans. Encourage students to justify their answers. Have some brief class feedback to find out which plans are the most/least popular.

3 [T9.5] Give students a minute or two to read the sentences, and to predict the kind of language that goes in the gaps. Play the recording for students to complete the gaps. Check answers with the whole class.

ANSWERS
See tapescript for recording 5 on page 170 of the *Students' Book*.

Grammar

1–2 Refer students to the phrases in **bold** and give them a few minutes, individually or in pairs, to think about the questions. As you check the answers, highlight the following points.

- Although we are talking about the future in the sentences, we use a present verb form after *if*, *when*, *before* and *after*. This may well be different in the students' own language. Give students an incorrect sentence, for example, ~~If they will build a new hotel on the site, there will definitely be more jobs~~, and invite them to correct it.
- The two clauses can be reversed, as in *Language focus 2*, exercise 3, sentence d. There is no comma between the clauses in this case.
- There is a difference in meaning between *if*, *when* and *as soon as*. Refer students to *Language summary B* on pages 153–154 of the *Students' Book* for more information.
- *Will* and *won't* are most commonly used in the main clause, but other verb forms are also possible, for example, *going to* (exercise 3, sentence b) and *might* (exercise 3, sentence c).

ANSWERS
1 the future
2 a present tense verb form, in this case the Present simple

PRACTICE

1 Students work individually or in pairs before checking with the whole class.

ANSWERS
a will suffer; opens b opens; will be
c will get; decide d hear; 'll tell
e continues; will change f start; will need
g 'll be; see h doesn't give; will fall

2 When students have completed the conversations, encourage them to practise reading them aloud a few times in their pairs. They can then act them out for the class without referring to their books too much, and will therefore sound more natural. *If you have a large class*: put students into groups to act out their dialogues.

3 [T9.6] As students listen, they decide which conversations were most similar to the recorded examples.

Practice, exercise 3: additional suggestion

The recorded conversations can be used as models for work on intonation. Students listen and repeat, trying to copy the intonation. They then act out the conversations in their pairs.

ADDITIONAL PRACTICE

RB **Resource bank:** 9B Worried parents (Present tense after *if*, *when*, *as soon as* and other time words), page 149

Workbook: Present tense after *if*, *when*, *before* and other time words, exercises 5–6, page 56; Word order, exercise 7, page 57

Task: Facelift! (PAGES 84–85)

See *Teacher's tips: making tasks work* on pages 10–11 and *Responding to learners' individual language needs* on pages 12–13.

Preparation: reading

Introduce students to the Paradiso Coffee Bar and draw students' attention to the picture. Briefly elicit one or two descriptions. Words to check: *lively*, *attentive*. Refer students to the example before they read the text to find differences. Students compare their lists in pairs and then as a whole class.

POSSIBLE ANSWERS
The description says there is a wide selection of drinks and cocktails, but in the picture the only drink available is tea.
The description says the surroundings are clean, but in the picture the washing-up hasn't been done.
The description says the surroundings are modern, but in the picture the furniture is old.
The description refers to the bar's attractive colours, but in the picture the colours are horrible.
The description says there are tropical plants, but in the picture there is just one old pot plant.
The description says there are works of original art, but in the picture there is just an ordinary poster on the wall.
The description says that delicious food is available, but in the picture the only food available is a sandwich, and it doesn't look delicious.
The description says that the staff are polite and attentive, but in the picture the waiter looks bored.

Task: speaking

1 Explain the meaning of *facelift* if necessary. Establish that students must work together to produce a plan for improving the Paradiso Coffee Bar. Refer them to the menu and the blank plan, and also to the list of questions. Words to check: *equipment*, *stools*.

Before putting students into small groups to discuss their ideas, direct them to the *Useful language* box. *Either*: go through the *Useful language* box with the class. Point out the use of the modal verbs *should*, *will*, *shall* and *could*, and check that students understand what they mean. *Or*: simply let students refer to the *Useful language* box as necessary. Set a time limit of fifteen minutes.

While students are discussing their ideas, circulate to help with vocabulary, and note down examples of good language use and/or errors to focus on later.

2 Give students a few minutes to summarise their ideas before asking each group to report back to the class. Ask for votes (a show of hands) for each idea; the group with the highest number of votes wins.

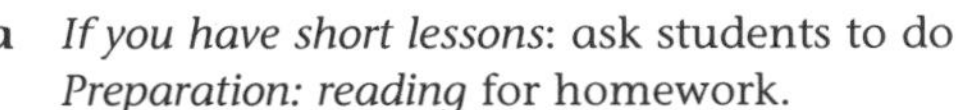

Task: alternative suggestions

a *If you have short lessons*: ask students to do *Preparation: reading* for homework.

b *If you think your students need to see a model of* Task: speaking: demonstrate by giving a presentation of some of your ideas for improving the Paradiso Coffee Bar. If possible, draw a plan and bring some visual aids to show, for example, new furniture. Make notes rather than reading out your talk, as this will sound more natural.

c *If you have a large class*: put students into groups of six to eight for *Task: speaking*, to ensure that pace is maintained.

Wordspot (PAGE 86)

if

See *Teacher's tips: working with lexical phrases* on pages 8–9.

1 **a** Demonstrate the matching activity by doing the first example with the class. Students then work individually or in pairs.

b [T9.7] Play the recording for students to check their answers. Check with the whole class if necessary.

ANSWERS

1 I don't know if I can help you.
2 I'd like a table for two if possible.
3 Do you mind if I sit here?
4 We can stop here for lunch if you like.
5 I wouldn't buy that if I were you.
6 I'll wait here all day if necessary!
7 I wonder if he still remembers me?
8 I asked her if she was married.
9 What if nobody comes to the show?
10 Do you know if Barbara's arrived yet?

2 Give students a few minutes to look at the diagram and to discuss their ideas with a partner. Check answers with the whole class.

ANSWERS

(answers in **bold**)

a I **asked** her if … / I **don't** know if … / I wonder if …?
b if necessary / if **possible**
c What if …? / Do you **know** if …?
d If **I were** you …
e Do you **mind** if I …? / if **you** like

3 Put students into pairs, A and B. Refer Student A to page 143, and Student B to the box at the bottom of page 86. Feed back on any problems students have.

ANSWERS

1 Do you know if Wasim is coming tonight? I don't know if he's coming or not. / I think so – I'll ask him if he's ready.
2 Do you mind if I open the window? Sure, go ahead.
3 Do you think I should tell Cristina what happened? No, I wouldn't tell her if I were you.
4 Do you want to have your lunch now? If possible, yes – I'm hungry.
5 You can go now if you like. Thanks. I'll see you tomorrow. / Thank you.
6 Is Mark upstairs? I think so – I'll ask him if he's ready.
7 I wonder if Carla would like a lift home. I'm not sure … let's ask her.
8 Will you drive me home later? Yes, I will … if necessary.

Study … (PAGE 86)

Guessing meaning from context

1 Write example a on the board, and ask students to tell you what part of speech *fleece* is, and what you do with it. (Answers: *a noun*; *put it on*.) From these questions, they should be able to guess that it's an item of clothing to keep you warm. As a class, discuss the importance of being able to guess what unknown words mean, for example, in exams, when reading without access to a dictionary, when reading quickly, when listening outside class. Students read through example b.

2 Give students a few minutes individually to read through the text and to make notes/guesses about the words in **bold**. Students check their answers in pairs before discussing them with the whole class.

ADDITIONAL PRACTICE

RB **Resource bank:** Learner-training worksheet G (Deducing meaning from context – part 1), page 150

Practise … (PAGE 87)

1 *may*, *might*, *will*, *definitely*, etc.

If you do this activity in class time, put the sentences onto pieces of cut-up card. Students work in pairs or small groups to order the pieces of card. When they have completed a sentence, they write it down and swap their cut-up sentence with another pair/group.

ANSWERS

a We definitely won't arrive before ten o'clock.
b There might not be enough food for everyone.
c We will probably spend Christmas at home this year.
d I might take the children swimming later.
e There may not be enough time.
f I probably won't see you tomorrow.
g The weather may get better tomorrow.
h It will definitely be a difficult game.

2 Present tense after *if*, *when*, *before* and other time words

Students work individually to choose the correct form before checking answers in pairs and with the whole class.

ANSWERS
a 'll tell; happens b 'll cook; get
c might come; come d 'll give; go e passes; 'll be

3 Modern and traditional

Do this as a race. The first student to write the words correctly is the winner.

ANSWERS
a washing machine b hot water c vacuum cleaner
d computer games e fridge f central heating
g Internet

***Practise** ..., exercise 3: additional suggestion*

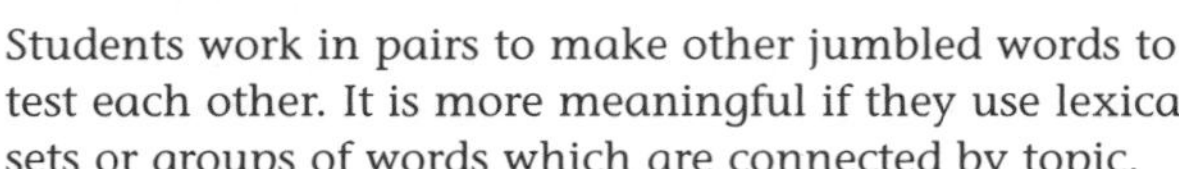

Students work in pairs to make other jumbled words to test each other. It is more meaningful if they use lexical sets or groups of words which are connected by topic.

4 Modern and traditional

Students work in pairs to match the words. Remind them that one of the compound nouns is written as one word.

ANSWERS
a shopping mall b air conditioning c dishwasher
d board game e credit card f microwave oven

5 *if*

Students work individually or in pairs to insert *if* in the appropriate place before checking with the whole class.

ANSWERS
a What **if** he can't pay?
b **If** I were you, I'd look for another job.
c Do you know **if** David is coming or not?
d Do you mind **if** I borrow your pen?
e I'll take you to the station **if** you like.
f We'll call the police **if** necessary.
g I wonder **if** that new café is open yet.
h I don't know **if** she wants to see me or not.
i Paul asked me **if** I wanted to see his new motorbike.
j I'd like you to send it to me tomorrow, **if** possible.

Pronunciation spot

The sounds /əʊ/ and /ɒ/

See *Teacher's tips: helping students with pronunciation* on pages 6–7.

1 [T9.8] Play the recording, or model the sounds yourself to show how they are made. Point out that /əʊ/ is a diphthong (a double vowel), and so it takes longer to say than /ɒ/. Highlight the different words to reinforce the sounds.

2 Students work in pairs, saying the words aloud to help them decide which sound is in each word.

3 [T9.9] Play the recording. Students listen and check their answers before practising the words in pairs.

ANSWERS

/əʊ/	/ɒ/
clothes	hot
go	long
home	lots
mobile	modern
old	online
telephone	shopping

Remember! (PAGE 87)

After looking back at the areas they have practised, students do the *Mini-check* on page 160 of the *Students' Book*. Check answers with the whole class, and ask students to tell you their scores out of 20.

ANSWERS
1 text 2 heating 3 conditioning 4 market
5 washing
6 My friends probably won't be here before six o'clock.
7 I definitely **won't** go out with her again.
8 It'll probably **be** sunny again tomorrow.
9 I **may** not be able to come tomorrow.
10 We **will** know the answer when they telephone.
11 be 12 stops 13 get 14 were 15 leave
16 card 17 like 18 mind 19 message 20 if

module 10

Take care!

Vocabulary (PAGES 88–89)

Health and accidents

See *Teacher's tips: working with lexical phrases* on pages 8–9 and *Making the most of the* mini-dictionary on pages 9–10.

1 **a** Elicit one or two examples, then put students into pairs to make their lists.

***Vocabulary*, exercise 1a: alternative suggestion**

- Make this activity a race. Give students, in pairs, one minute to write down as many health problems as they can. Alternatively, without setting a time limit, see which pair is the first to write down ten problems.

b Give students a time limit to scan the quiz (for example, thirty seconds) so that they only look at the problems, not the choices. Have some brief class feedback on the problems mentioned, and answer any questions about vocabulary.

2 Establish that more than one answer to each question may be correct. Put students into pairs to work through the quiz together. Students use their mini-dictionaries to check unfamiliar vocabulary. Give them a limit of three words each to look up, to encourage them to use their mini-dictionaries only for those words which they cannot guess from context.

3 [T10.1] Tell students to circle the correct answer(s) as they listen, and to make brief notes on other information the nurse gives. If students find the listening challenging, play it again, stopping after each question to check the answers. Students discuss the question in pairs.

ANSWERS

1 c (five or ten minutes under the tap)
2 b (take aspirin or paracetamol; lie down and have a rest if you feel bad)
3 b (even if you feel better)
4 b
5 a and c (ice or cold water will take the sting away)
6 c (if the rash gets worse, speak to a doctor)

***Vocabulary*, exercise 3: alternative suggestion**

Do the listening as a jigsaw. One group listens to questions 1–3, while the other group (if possible in another room) listens to questions 4–6. Then students from the two groups pair up and exchange information.

4 Go through the examples with the class. Refer students back to the quiz to find more word combinations. Students work individually or in pairs before checking with the whole class.

ANSWERS

I've got + a temperature
to take + an aspirin / a course of antibiotics / the pills
to keep + warm/cool
have + a rest
feel + dizzy
put + a plaster / butter or oil / some ice / some cream (on something); the burn under cold water

Listening and speaking (PAGE 89)

1 Check that students understand that the Health Helpline is for people who need advice about an illness or accident, but do not think that the situation is serious enough to need to go to hospital. Before students read the website information, ask them to work in pairs to predict what sort of information people are asked to have ready when they phone, for example, what medicine they take. Make a list of students' predictions on the board. Word to check: *symptoms*. Students read quickly to see if they were right.

2 [T10.2] Emphasise that students only need to answer the three questions. Play the recording. Students check their answers in pairs and then with the whole class. Ask students how they would feel if they were the nurse talking to this man. Word to check: *stomach* /stʌmək/.

ANSWERS

a He feels generally unwell, and has a pain in his stomach.
b He ate too much junk food for lunch (three burgers, large french fries, two milkshakes, two ice creams and two large colas).
c The nurse advises him to lie down for a couple of hours, and to phone again if he still feels unwell.

3 Refer students to the tapescript on page 170 of the *Students' Book*, and give them five minutes to underline any useful words or phrases. Students work in pairs to prepare their conversations, using the diagram to help them. While students act out their conversations, note down examples of good language use and/or errors to focus on later.

ADDITIONAL PRACTICE

RB **Resource bank:** 10A What can I do for you? (vocabulary: health problems), page 151

Workbook: Vocabulary, exercises 8–9, page 62; Vocabulary booster: at the doctor's, exercise 10, page 63

Reading (PAGES 90–91)

1 Introduce the idea of life 200 or 300 years ago. *Either*: elicit ideas from the whole class. *Or*: put students into small groups to discuss their ideas first.

2 Focus students on the pictures. Ask them what they show about life in those times, for example, very large families or bad teeth. Students read the paragraphs quickly and match them to the pictures. Emphasise that students should not use their mini-dictionaries at this stage.

ANSWERS
a 1 b 4 c 2 d 5 e 3

3 Students work individually using their mini-dictionaries before reading the text again. Check answers with the whole class. Pronunciation to check: *average* /ˈævərɪdʒ/, *life expectancy* /laɪf ɪkˈspektənsi/, *diseases* /dɪˈziːzɪz/, *hygiene* /haɪdʒiːn/.

ANSWERS
- a False (the average life expectancy is more than eighty)
- b True
- c False (one in every nine – approximately 10%)
- d False (everybody had poor hygiene)
- e True
- f True

4 Demonstrate this activity by telling students something from the text which you already knew, and something which surprised you. Give students a few minutes individually to reread the text and to think about their answers. Students work in small groups to discuss their ideas and reactions to the text. Have some brief class feedback on any interesting points.

Language focus 1 (PAGE 91)

used to

Discuss the question with the class.

ANSWER
Use is the main verb in example 3.

Grammar

1–2 Write examples 1 and 2 on the board. Give students time to decide which explanation is right and to find another example in the text. Students discuss answers in pairs before checking with the class. As you check the answers, highlight the use of the auxiliary *did* and the word order in negative and question forms, as with other Past simple forms. Refer students to *Language summary A* on page 154 of the *Students' Book* for more information.

ANSWERS
1 We use *used / didn't use to* + verb to talk about habits (and states) in the past.
2 Other examples in the text include *women used to have many more children than they do today* (paragraph 2); *even rich people didn't use to wash much* (paragraph 3); *He not only cut hair, but also used to take out teeth* (paragraph 4).

PRACTICE

1 Go through the example. Students work individually or in pairs before checking with the whole class.

ANSWERS
- b Families used to be much larger than they are now.
- c Doctors often used to kill their patients instead of curing them.
- d Barbers used to pull out teeth as well as cutting people's hair.
- e People didn't use to go to the dentist's when they had toothache.
- f Many people used to die in hospital instead of getting better.
- g Many women used to die in childbirth.
- h People didn't use to brush their teeth very much.
- i People used to think that baths were dangerous.

***Practice*, exercise 1: alternative suggestion**

To make this a speaking activity, students work in pairs. They look at either column A or column B, and cover up the other column. One student reads out a beginning, and the other student responds with a suitable ending. They then change over.

Pronunciation

See *Teacher's tips: helping students with pronunciation* on pages 6–7.

1 [T10.3] Play the recording once for students to listen to the rhythm of the sentences. Highlight the fact that *to* is weak /tə/, and that the *s* in *use(d) to* is pronounced /s/, not /z/ as in the main verb *use(d)*.

2 [T10.4] Play the recording, or model the sentences yourself, for students to repeat.

2 Give students a few minutes individually to complete the sentences. Put students into pairs to compare sentences, encouraging them to ask follow-up questions if appropriate, for example, *Why? / Why not?*

ADDITIONAL PRACTICE

RB **Resource bank:** 10B The Ghost (*used to* and Past simple), page 152

Workbook: *used to*, exercises 1–3, page 60

Language focus 2 (PAGES 92–93)

Past continuous

1 [T10.5] Focus students' attention on the photo of Frane Selak, and play the recording. Discuss the questions as a class and ask students to predict what has happened to Frane.

ANSWER
He has had at least seven lucky escapes.

2 a Students work individually to check meaning and pronunciation in their mini-dictionaries. Pronunciation to check: *bruises* /bru:zɪz/, *injuries* /ˈɪndʒəri:z/, *lose* /lu:z/.

b [T10.6] Play the recording. Students complete the table as they listen. Repeat the recording if necessary. Students compare answers in pairs before checking with the whole class.

ANSWERS

	Type of accident (car, train, etc.)	Injuries
1	train	broken arm
2	aeroplane	cuts and bruises
3	bus	
4	car	
5	car	lost most of his hair
6	bus	
7	car	

Grammar

1–5 Students work individually and then in pairs to look at the examples and answer the questions. Copy the example sentences onto the board to highlight the different verb forms while checking the answers. You may also find it useful to draw a timeline to contrast the Past simple and Past continuous. See *Language summary B* on page 154 of the *Students' Book* for examples of timelines. As you check the answers, highlight:

- the fact that the Past continuous describes an action already in progress when another event (described in the Past simple) occurs
- the Past continuous form, if necessary by eliciting a table of positive, negative and question forms onto the board (alternatively, refer students to the table in *Language summary B* on page 154)
- the contractions *wasn't/weren't* in the negative form
- the inversion of the subject and *was/were* in the question form.

ANSWERS
1 An example of the Past simple is *fell*; an example of the Past continuous is *was travelling*.
We form the Past continuous with *was/were* + verb *-ing*.
2 The action of travelling on the train started first.
3 The Past continuous *was travelling* describes the situation; the Past simple *fell* describes the main events.
4 The action *his car … caught fire* happened first; the action *he lost most of his hair* happened second.
5 Two other time words are *as* and *while*.

PRACTICE

1 a Ask students to read the sentences through once, to familiarise themselves with them, before attempting to fill in the gaps. Students work individually before comparing answers in pairs.

b [T10.6] Play the recording again or refer students to the tapescript to check their answers. Have some brief class feedback.

Note: if your students find it very difficult to pick out the verb forms used in Frane's story, you may wish to do the *Pronunciation* box, and then come back to this listening/reading activity.

ANSWERS
See tapescript for recording 6 on pages 170–171 of the *Students' Book*.

Pronunciation

See *Teacher's tips: helping students with pronunciation* on pages 6–7.

1 [T10.7] Play the example phrases. Highlight the fact that the weak form *was* /wəz/ occurs in positive sentences, but not in negative sentences.

2 [T10.7] Play the phrases again, or say them yourself at natural speed, for students to repeat. Drill the sentences. Help students to make *was* weak by stressing the present participle: *was travelling, was driving, was watching*.

2 Use the cartoons to check the following vocabulary: *traffic jam*, *fly*, *telephone pole*, *mobile phone*, *mother-in-law*. Establish that each picture shows the scene just before the accident. Elicit the story of what happened in the first cartoon from the whole class. Then put students into pairs to explain the other three stories. Have some brief class feedback on their ideas, noting any errors with the Past continuous to focus on later.

ANSWERS
A traffic jam: a
A fly: c
A telephone pole: c
Someone speaking on a mobile phone: d
Someone giving a lift to their mother-in-law: b

3 Check that students understand the idea of filling in a claim form to send to an insurance company. Students read the texts and match each one to a cartoon. Students discuss whose fault the accident was in pairs, before reporting back to the whole class.

ANSWERS
1 a 2 c 3 d 4 b

4 **a** Give students a few minutes to finish the sentences, then put them into pairs to compare answers.

b Students test each other by asking about the sentences at random, for example, *What was I doing at seven o'clock this morning? – You were …*

ADDITIONAL PRACTICE

RB **Resource bank:** 10C Bob's night out (Past continuous and Past simple), pages 153–154

Workbook: Past continuous, exercises 4–7, pages 60–62

Task: Choose the Hero of the Year

(PAGES 94–95)

See *Teacher's tips: making tasks work* on pages 10–11 and *Responding to learners' individual language needs* on pages 12–13.

Preparation: reading

1 Check students understand that each person is a 'hero' because they rescued someone. Establish that these three people are finalists, and the newspaper will give the winner £10,000. Put students into pairs to look at the pictures and to guess what the three people did.

2 Direct students to the questions. They should be able to answer the first three questions.

ANSWERS

	Kathy	Shirley	Simon
a Age?	32	67	10
b Where?	At a bus stop	On a ship at sea	By the sea
c Who?	An old lady	Passengers from the ship	A man

3 Students work in pairs to put the pictures in order. They should tell the story to each other as they do so. Circulate and supply vocabulary as necessary, for example, *cigarette lighter, to threaten, to tie up*. Then ask students to read the story to check their answers. Words to check: *to set fire to, shoelace*.

ANSWERS
The picture order is d, b, a, c.

4 Students work individually or in pairs to answer the remaining questions from exercise 2 about Kathy Reynolds. Check answers with the whole class. Ask students to comment briefly on Kathy's story, for example, on how brave she was.

ANSWERS
d The old lady needed help because a mugger was threatening her with a knife.
e The 'hero' was walking home; she was lighting a cigarette.
f She set fire to the mugger's trousers with her cigarette lighter, knocked him down and tied him up with a shoelace. She then called the police.
g She was much shorter than the mugger.

Task: speaking

1 **a** Put students into Groups A and B. Direct Group A to page 144, and Group B to page 143, of the *Students' Book*. Students read the relevant texts.

b Put students into groups of two or three within Groups A and B. Tell them to help each other to answer the questions from *Preparation: reading*, exercise 2, using the pictures and words provided. Give students ten minutes to do this. Circulate, helping with vocabulary and making sure that weaker students manage to fill in all the information.

2 Establish clearly that Groups A and B have been working on different stories. Put students into pairs, A and B. Students ask each other the questions from *Preparation: reading*, exercise 2, to find out about the other two finalists. While students are doing this, collect any examples of good language use and/or errors to focus on later.

3 Put pairs of students together into groups of four or six to decide on the prizes. Draw their attention to the *Useful language* box. Tell students to be prepared to explain their decisions to the rest of the class. Nominate one confident student in each group to do this.

***Task*: alternative suggestions**

a *If you have short lessons*: do *Preparation: reading* in the first lesson, then *Task: speaking* in the second lesson. Divide students into As and Bs at the end of the first lesson, and give them the relevant story at the back of the book to look at for the next lesson.

b *If your students enjoy roleplaying*: ask them in *Task: speaking*, exercise 2, to take on the role of the 'hero' in their story. Their partner interviews them about their experience, with questions such as *Who did you rescue? Why were you there and what were you doing?* Students answer the relevant questions.

c *If you have a large class or if you want to get all students speaking*: regroup students in *Task: speaking*, exercise 3, so that they report back to each other in small groups, instead of having one student from each group reporting back to the class.

Writing (PAGE 95)

Time words in narrative

1 Tell students to read the story through once before attempting to fill the gaps. Students work individually or in pairs before checking with the whole class.

ANSWERS
1 At the age of sixty-seven 2 until 3 as
4 Immediately 5 Then 6 soon
7 as quickly as possible 8 Eventually 9 Later
10 always

2 Tell students to choose an option and to spend five to ten minutes writing the main facts of the story. Tell them not to worry about time phrases for the moment. Students then write a final draft for homework, inserting time phrases from the box.

***Writing*, exercise 2: alternative suggestion**

If you have a weak class: elicit the story of Simon Roland, using the pictures and vocabulary on page 143, and write it on the board. Guide students to use time phrases and past tenses accurately. Rub out some words/phrases from the story, and ask students to write the story in their notebooks, supplying the missing words/phrases as they do so.

Consolidation modules 6–10 (PAGES 96–97)

A Past continuous, articles

Encourage students to read the text through once without writing anything. Then give students five minutes to fill the gaps individually. Students check their answers in pairs before checking with the whole class.

ANSWERS
2 saw 3 was sitting 4 the 5 was crying 6 asked
7 stopped 8 said 9 gave 10 fl 11 fl 12 fl
13 said 14 fl 15 fl 16 fl 17 were you crying

B Vocabulary: Three things

Set this up as a race. Students work in pairs. The winning pair is the first to complete the race correctly. Check answers with the whole class.

ANSWERS
1 **have:** an accident, a rest, a serious illness
2 **go on:** a cruise, a coach tour, a cycling holiday
3 **rent:** a DVD, a computer game, accommodation
4 **send:** a letter, a fax, a text message
5 **take:** pills, medicine, a 71 bus

C Grammar and listening: Present perfect, future forms, *used to*

1 Draw students' attention to the pictures of the three people. Elicit one or two ideas as a class to demonstrate the activity. Students work in pairs to make predictions about the three people. Words to check: *retire*, *earn*.

2 [C1] Play the recording. Students listen to see how many of their predictions were correct.

ANSWERS
Philip used to have more money than he has now.
Carla will probably retire soon.
Philip would rather spend time with his family than go out to work.
Eliza has lived in Los Angeles for nearly forty years.
Eliza has been married four times.
Eliza used to be a famous film star.
Eliza might go abroad next year.
Carla has already earned over $1 million.

3 [C1] Play the recording again, pausing after each extract to allow students time to make notes. Check answers with the whole class.

ANSWERS
See tapescript for recording 1 on page 171 of the *Students' Book*.

D Vocabulary: Revision

Students work in pairs. Encourage them to work through the list, completing any words they can easily remember before looking at the individual modules. Brief feedback as a class. Find out which words students found it most difficult to remember.

ANSWERS
1 abroad 2 bee 3 crowded 4 dizzy 5 eventually
6 fridge 7 hairdresser 8 ice 9 lift
10 mother-in-law 11 nightmare 12 outdoor
13 plaster 14 queue 15 run 16 skyscraper
17 traffic jam 18 unbelievable 19 volunteer
20 weird

E Speaking: Real life

1 Put students into pairs. Use the pictures to help you establish the different relationships. Give students a few minutes to choose one of the relationships.

2 Give students ten minutes to choose one of the situations and to write a six- or eight-line dialogue to perform for the rest of the class. Remind students to use two phrases from the box. As students perform their conversations, the other students guess what the situation is. Note down examples of good language use and/or errors to focus on later.

module 11

The best things in life

Reading and vocabulary

(PAGES 98–99)

Hobbies and interests

See *Teacher's tips: working with lexical phrases* on pages 8–9 and *Making the most of the* mini-dictionary on pages 9–10.

1 You could start by telling students about a hobby or interest of your own. If possible, bring in pictures/objects to illustrate it. Then put students into small groups to discuss the questions. Have some brief class feedback.

2 Focus students on the box and elicit one or two examples to demonstrate the activity. Encourage students to record the collocations using word locusts as they learnt to do in Module 1 (see *Vocabulary and speaking*, exercise 4, on page 7 of the *Students' Book*).

ANSWERS
collect: coins, trading cards, stamps, dolls, memorabilia
play: backgammon, chess
make: jewellery, models
go to see: a musical, a rock concert, your favourite football team

3 Words to check: *interest*, *obsession*. Ask students to read the article quickly. Set a time limit of just one minute to ensure that students do read quickly. They should underline any of the hobbies/collections mentioned, and identify them in the pictures.

ANSWERS
Hobbies/Collections: supporting your favourite football team; shopping; going to musicals (*Cats*); eating fast food; collecting coins, dolls, trading cards, stamps, Beatles memorabilia (books, posters and models), *Star Wars* memorabilia, free gifts with breakfast cereals (plastic figures of US presidents)

4 Go through the statements with the class. Give students a couple of minutes to try to answer the question without reading the text again. Students then check their answers in the text. Encourage them to give reasons in their own words. Check answers with the whole class.

ANSWERS
a **Jason Joiner:** he has 20,000 items relating to *Star Wars* films.
b **Bob Martin:** he used to watch the musical *Cats* once a week, but the show has now closed.
c **Peter Holden:** although he eats two McDonald's meals a day, he doesn't eat the french fries.
d **John Weintraub:** he broke into a breakfast cereal factory because he was desperate to get the final plastic model in a series he was collecting.
e **Rodolfo Renato Vazquez:** he organises a Beatles event, and people travel from all over the world to see his memorabilia.
f **Bob Martin:** he spent £20,000 on going to see the musical *Cats*, but says that he could just about afford it because he doesn't drink, smoke or have a car.

5 Put students into pairs or small groups to discuss the questions. Have some brief class feedback.

6 Focus students on the example in the puzzle, pointing out that they need to look back at the text and that the words are not in the same order as they appear in the text. Students work individually before checking answers with the class.

ANSWERS
See solution to puzzle on page 147 of the *Students' Book*.

Pronunciation

See *Teacher's tips: helping students with pronunciation* on pages 6–7.

1 [T11.1] Use the example words to highlight the pronunciation of the /ŋ/ sound and its occurrence in the *-ing* form. Students work in pairs to underline all the /ŋ/ sounds in the text. Play the recording. Students check their answers.

ANSWERS
collecting supporting shopping spending looking coming dining something trading nothing belonging
Students may also have underlined the /ŋ/ sounds in the following words: *thing, Washington, collecting* (second occurrence).

2 Play the recording. Students repeat the words and then practise saying them in pairs.

Language focus 1 (PAGE 100)

Gerunds (*-ing* forms) after verbs of liking and disliking

Note: the scope of *Language focus 1* does not extend to the use of gerunds in general, but is confined to the use of gerunds with phrases for expressing likes and dislikes. Encourage students to see these as whole phrases, for example, *like* + verb *-ing*.

Students may ask about present participles, which are also *-ing* forms. If they do, show them that present participles are verb forms, and are often used to make verbs continuous, for example, *She's travelling in Europe. He was staying with his friends. We've been waiting for hours.*

1 Demonstrate the activity by telling students about some of your likes and dislikes, and by highlighting the phrases *I love it/them! I hate it/them! It's OK. / I don't mind it/them.* Make sure that students know when to say *it* or *them*. Word to check: *tattoo*. Students discuss which of the things they like/dislike in pairs or small groups. Encourage them to give reasons.

If students ask about the difference between *like* and *enjoy*, explain that *like* (= think X is nice or good) can be used to talk about any of the things in the box, while *enjoy* is used to talk about things that you do/experience, for example, *enjoy buying presents / sunbathing*.

2 [T11.2] Ask students to listen, and to answer the questions for each of the five people. Students compare answers in pairs and then with the whole class. Ask students if any of the opinions are surprising, and if they (or any people they know) have similar feelings.

ANSWERS
1 chocolate, especially white chocolate (likes)
2 buying presents, especially for the family (dislikes)
3 watching sport on TV, especially Formula One (likes), football (dislikes) and tennis (dislikes)
4 sunbathing, especially lying down and reading (likes)
5 long car journeys (dislikes); travelling by train (likes)

Grammar

1 Students work in pairs to answer the questions. Check answers with the whole class and highlight the following points.
- Gerunds (*-ing* forms) are like nouns or pronouns.
- Gerunds can be the subject or object of a sentence, and often come after prepositions.

ANSWERS
a The *-ing* form *buying presents* is the object of the sentence.
b The *-ing* form *Sunbathing* is the subject of the sentence.
c The *-ing* form *reading* is the object of the sentence. It comes after a preposition.

2 Students work individually, finding phrases for expressing likes/dislikes in the tapescript for recording 2 on page 171 of the *Students' Book*. As you check the answers, highlight that gerunds can follow all of the phrases for expressing likes/dislikes, with the exception of *it's OK*. Refer students to *Language summary A* on page 154 of the *Students' Book* for more information.

ANSWERS
The phrases used for expressing likes/dislikes are *I love, I specially love, I hate, it's OK, I can't stand, I'm crazy about, I don't like ... very much, I really enjoy, I like, I'm very keen on.*
After verbs such as *like* and *enjoy*, the form of the verb is *-ing*.

PRACTICE

1 Students work individually to fill the gaps in the sentences.

ANSWERS
a loves/likes, on b like/enjoy, stand
c about, much d really, likes, keen e travelling

2 Encourage students to think of unusual likes and dislikes. Give students a minute or two individually to think about their answers before discussing them in pairs. Remind students to get their partner to justify their answers, by asking questions like *Why? / Why not?* Have some brief class feedback on any interesting/amusing answers.

3 Students can use ideas from *Language focus 1*, exercise 1, to complete the sentences. Alternatively, give them these prompts on the board: *smoking, going to the gym, cooking, walking, politics*. Students can also use their own ideas. Put students into pairs or small groups to compare answers.

***Practice*, exercise 3: alternative suggestions**

- Students complete the sentences, then stand up and mingle. They compare answers with as many different people as possible.
- Students write out their sentences on a piece of paper. Then, working in groups of four to six, they shuffle the pieces of paper so that they each have someone else's sentences. They take turns to read out the sentences. The rest of the group guesses who wrote them.

ADDITIONAL PRACTICE

RB **Resource bank:** 11A The Lovebug Dating Agency (Gerunds; expressions for liking and disliking), pages 155–156

Workbook: Gerunds (*-ing* forms) after verbs of liking and disliking, exercises 1–3, pages 66–67; Vocabulary booster: *-ed* and *-ing* adjectives, exercise 8, page 69

Language focus 2 (PAGES 101–102)

like doing and *would like to do*

Elicit briefly some ideas as to what the pictures show. Each pair of pictures shows a person doing something they like, and dreaming/thinking about something they want. Give students a few minutes, individually or in pairs, to match the sentences with the pictures, before checking with the whole class.

ANSWERS
1 c 2 h 3 e 4 d 5 f 6 a 7 b 8 g

Grammar

1 Do an example with the class. Then give students a few minutes, individually or in pairs, to underline the verbs followed by an *-ing* form, and to circle the verbs followed by an infinitive.

ANSWERS
Verbs followed by an *-ing* form: *likes* (sentence 3), *loves* (sentences 6 and 8)
Verbs followed by an infinitive: *plans* (sentence 2), *love* (sentence 4), *like* (sentence 5), *hopes* (sentence 7)

2 Students look at rules a and b. As you check the answers, highlight that:
- *like* and *love* are followed by a gerund
- *would like* and *would love* are followed by an infinitive (as are *plan* and *hope*)
- the question forms are *Would you like to …?* and *Do you like …-ing?*

ANSWERS
a *She likes* means she enjoys.
b *She'd like* means she wants to.

3 Students discuss the questions in pairs and then as a whole class. As you check the answers, highlight that:
- *love* is more emphatic than *like*
- *Would/Do you love …?* is not so common as *Would/Do you like …?*

Refer students to *Language summary B* on pages 154–155 of the *Students' Book* for more information.

ANSWERS
We use *like/love* to talk about how we feel about something generally.
We use *would like/love* to talk about something we want to do in the future.

PRACTICE

1 a Students work individually to complete the questions. As you check the answers, drill the questions chorally.

ANSWERS AND LANGUAGE NOTES
1 ***Would*** *you like* ***to live*** *abroad one day? In which country?*
2 ***Would*** *you like* ***to have*** *a pet? What kind?*
3 ***Would*** *you like* ***to learn*** *any other languages apart from English? Which one(s)?* (The use of *any* in the first question makes the question form *Do you like …?* wrong, as it would suggest that the questioner expects a negative response.)
4 ***Do*** *you like* ***getting up*** *early? Why (not)?*
5 *Which city* ***would*** *you most like* ***to visit*** *one day?*
6 ***Do*** *you like* ***listening*** *to music? What kind?* (*Would you like …?* is possible, but unlikely, here. In the context in which this question might be asked, a more informal question would be used, for example, *Shall I put some music on?*)
7 ***Do*** *you like* ***cooking****? Do you have a speciality? What is it?*
8 *Which famous person* ***would*** *you most like* ***to meet****? Why?*

b Students ask and answer the questions in pairs. Have some brief class feedback on any interesting answers.

***Practice*, exercise 1b: alternative suggestion**

Students mingle to ask and answer questions, asking a different person for each question to ensure that they speak to as many different people as possible.

2 a Elicit the first line of each dialogue with the class to demonstrate the activity. Students work individually before comparing their answers in pairs.

b [T11.3] Play the recording for students to check their answers.

ANSWERS
See tapescript for recording 3 on page 171 of the *Students' Book*.

3 Students work in pairs to prepare a similar four-line dialogue. Give them a few minutes to rehearse before performing their dialogues for the class.

Pronunciation

See *Teacher's tips: helping students with pronunciation* on pages 6–7.

1 [T11.4] Play the recording, asking students to notice the polite intonation. Point out that flat intonation makes the invitation sound reluctant.

2 [T11.4] Refer students to the tapescript for recording 4 on page 171 of the *Students' Book*. Replay the recording or model the invitations yourself, pausing after each one to give students time to repeat. Students practise the invitations in pairs.

ADDITIONAL PRACTICE

RB **Resource bank:** Learner-training worksheet H (Using the *mini-dictionary* to find constructions that follow verbs), page 157

Workbook: *like doing* and *would like to do*, exercises 4–6, pages 67–68, Improve your writing, exercise 12, page 71

Task: Survey about the most important things in life

(PAGES 102–103)

See *Teacher's tips: making tasks work* on pages 10–11 and *Responding to learners' individual language needs* on pages 12–13.

Preparation: reading

Elicit some things that students think are important in life and/or give some ideas of your own. Students look at the statements and see which things were mentioned by the class.

Establish what a survey is, and explain that students will be conducting a survey of their own. Students work individually with their mini-dictionaries to decide which statements they agree/disagree with.

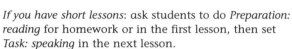

Preparation: reading: alternative suggestion

If you have short lessons: ask students to do *Preparation: reading* for homework or in the first lesson, then set *Task: speaking* in the next lesson.

Task: speaking

1 Put students into small groups to discuss their answers. Do a brief model yourself, explaining your choices and incorporating some of the phrases from *Useful language a*. Encourage students to ask each other to explain their answers, by asking *Why do you think that …?* Circulate and help with vocabulary, noting down examples of good language use and/or errors to focus on later.

2 Focus students on *Useful language b* and explain that they will prepare a summary of the results of their survey to present to the rest of the class. They should nominate one member of their group to present the summary, and make brief notes as a group. Allow a few minutes for students to practise what they will say before each group presents their findings. As a class, discuss any interesting similarities or differences.

Task: speaking: alternative suggestions

a *If you want to maximise individual speaking opportunities*: regroup students after they have prepared their summary, so that they work with students from different groups. In this way, each student presents a summary.

b *If your students enjoy roleplaying*: ask them to act out survey interviews. One person takes the role of a famous person answering questions, and the other is the interviewer.

c *If you want to provide extra listening practice*: make a tape of you and another English speaker discussing your choices for the most important things in life. Students listen and note which things they found predictable/surprising, and/or note the language used to explain and compare choices.

Wordspot (PAGE 104)

like

See *Teacher's tips: working with lexical phrases* on pages 8–9.

1 **a** Establish that this exercise deals with different uses of *like* and that the same word is missing from each phrase. Discuss the example with the class. Students work individually or in pairs to complete the sentences.

b [T11.5] Play the recording before checking answers with the whole class.

ANSWERS AND LANGUAGE NOTE

2 *That sounds **like** David at the door now. I'll go and let him in.*
3 *I'll cook you a meal if you **like**. How about it?*
4 *I'd really **like** to meet Gwyneth Paltrow one day. She's such a fantastic actress.*
5 *What's the weather **like** today?*
6 *'Just pull the handle and turn.' '**Like** this?' 'No, the other way.'*
7 *I've never eaten frogs' legs, but they say they taste **like** chicken.*
8 *You can sit where you **like**. There are plenty of chairs.*
9 *I don't feel **like** cooking tonight. Shall we order a pizza?*
10 *What would everyone **like** to drink?*

In sentences 3, 4, 8 and 10, *like* is a verb. In the other sentences, it is a preposition, and the meaning is quite different.

2 Give students a few minutes to complete the diagram. Check answers with the whole class.

ANSWERS

a **asking for a description:** What's … like?
b **similar to someone/something:** looks like, sounds like, taste like
c **in this way:** Like this?
d **want:** if you like, I'd really like, where you like, I don't feel like, What would … like …?

3 Elicit ideas for sentence a, then tell students to complete the remaining sentences. Students discuss their ideas in pairs, then feed back to the rest of the class. Circulate as students work to help with vocabulary.

ADDITIONAL PRACTICE

Workbook: Wordspot, exercise 9, page 70

Study … (PAGE 104)

Increasing your vocabulary (2): Remembering new words

1 As a class, discuss the first piece of advice and ask students for their views on it. Students work in pairs. Each student reads about two more of the techniques before explaining what they have read to their partner. Then students discuss any advantages and disadvantages of each that they can think of. Discuss ideas as a whole class.

2 Students choose a technique to experiment with for a week or two. Set a date when you will ask them to feed back on their experiment.

Practise … (PAGE 105)

1 Verbs of liking and disliking

Students write a large *L* on one side of a blank piece of paper, and a large *D* on the other side. Explain that *L* means 'like', and *D* means 'dislike'. Say each sentence aloud once. Students must hold up their paper showing *L* or *D* depending on what they think each phrase means.

ANSWERS
a L b L c L d D e D

2 Gerunds (*-ing* forms)

Students work individually to change one of the verbs in each sentence, before checking answers in pairs and then with the whole class.

ANSWERS
a watching b sitting c Going d cooking
e buying f listening g listening h driving
i playing

3 *like doing* and *would like to do*

Students work individually and then in pairs before checking their answers with the whole class. To further check understanding, ask students which sentence is an invitation (d), a polite request (a and e), an ambition (b), an expression of a general like or dislike (c, f and h), a question about a present (g).

ANSWERS
a 'd like to have b would like to be
c don't like driving d Would e would like to speak
f Do g would h like being

4 Hobbies and interests

Students work in pairs, saying the collocations aloud to each other to help them 'hear' which are right and wrong. Check answers with the whole class.

ANSWERS
a sport b chess c jewellery d a TV programme

5 When an interest becomes an obsession

Do this as a race. *Either*: tell the class that the first student to unjumble the words correctly wins. *Or*: set a thirty-second time limit for students to try to unjumble the words. Offer one point for each correct word, and minus one point for any misspelt words. Students swap notebooks to mark each other's words. See which students have the most points.

ANSWERS
a obsession b gifts c weight d desperate
e cereal f collect g afford

6 *like*

Students work in pairs and do this exercise orally first, writing their answers for homework. Check answers with the whole class.

ANSWERS
a I feel like going to bed early tonight.
b She looks like her sister.
c Would you like to come to the cinema with us?
d What was the weather like on your holiday?
e I'd like to talk to you for a moment.
f I can stay in bed all day if I like.

Pronunciation spot

The sounds /s/ and /ʃ/

See *Teacher's tips: helping students with pronunciation* on pages 6–7.

1 [T11.6] Play the recording or model the three pairs of words yourself. Demonstrate to students how the position of the lips differs between the two sounds (they are much further forward for /ʃ/).

2 [T11.7] Students work in pairs, saying the words aloud to help each other hear which sound is used in each word. Play the recording, or model the words yourself, for students to check the answers.

ANSWERS
show /ʃ/ collection /ʃ/ successful /s/, /s/
satisfaction /s/, /s/, /ʃ/ fashion /ʃ/
obsession /s/, /ʃ/ concert /s/ chess /s/ cereal /s/
special /s/, /ʃ/ receiving /s/ obsessed /s/, /s/

***Pronunciation*, exercise 2: additional suggestion**

Write the following pairs of words on the board: *sort/short, seat/sheet, see/she, sew/show*, with the first word in each pair under number one, and the second word under number two. Demonstrate the activity. Say one of the words. Students decide if it comes from column one (with the /s/ sound) or column two (with the /ʃ/ sound). They say *One* or *Two*. Say another word. Again, students say *One* or *Two*. Students then work in pairs to practise.

Remember! (PAGE 105)

After looking back at the areas they have practised, students do the *Mini-check* on page 160 of the *Students' Book*. Check answers with the whole class, and ask students to tell you their scores out of 20.

ANSWERS
1 obsession 2 weight 3 desperate 4 to collect
5 go to see 6 collect 7 play 8 make 9 Would
10 doesn't 11 sounds 12 Do 13 can't
14 What 15 on 16 about 17 like
18 What was 19 can't 20 really

module 12

Got to have it!

Vocabulary (PAGE 106)

Everyday objects

See *Teacher's tips: working with lexical phrases* on pages 8–9 and *Making the most of the* mini-dictionary on pages 9–10.

1 **a** Refer students to the pictures on page 145 of the *Students' Book*, and ask them to name some of the objects they can see. Students work in pairs to match words and objects. Pronunciation to check: *plaster* /ˈplæstə/, *razor* /ˈreɪzə/, *torch* /tɔːrtʃ/, *towel* /taʊəl/.

ANSWERS
Objects you can't find: identity card, driving licence, sunglasses, toothbrush

b Give students exactly one minute to look at the pictures and to memorise them.

2 **a** [T12.1] Explain that students will hear ten questions about the pictures. Play the recording. Students make notes for the answers they can remember.

b Put students into pairs to compare their answers. Refer them to pages 145 and 171 of the *Students' Book* to check their answers. Have some brief class feedback on how many questions students answered correctly.

3 **a** Elicit a few ideas to demonstrate the activity. You could do this by showing which things you keep in your handbag/wallet/pockets. Then give students a few minutes to answer the questions. Put students into pairs to check their answers.

POSSIBLE ANSWERS
In your bedroom: hairbrush, comb, lipstick
In the kitchen: plasters, torch
In the bathroom: hairbrush, comb, lipstick, plasters, razor, toothbrush, towel, shaving foam
In your pockets: keys, mobile phone, identity card, comb
In your handbag: keys, mobile phone, hairbrush, identity card, comb, lipstick, driving licence, plasters, umbrella, sunglasses, torch
In your wallet/purse: credit card, identity card, driving licence

b Students work in pairs to discuss the question. Ask one or two students to report back to the class on their findings.

ADDITIONAL PRACTICE

RB **Resource bank:** 12A What's this? (Describing everyday objects), page 158

Workbook: Vocabulary, exercise 8, page 76

Reading and vocabulary

(PAGES 106–107)

See *Teacher's tips: working with lexical phrases* on pages 8–9 and *Making the most of the* mini-dictionary on pages 9–10.

1 Draw students' attention to the brand names, and elicit products students associate with them. Word to check: *brand*.

2 Explain that students will read about six internationally famous companies. Write the names of the companies on the board, and ask students to say anything they know about where these companies are and what they make. Give students two minutes to read the text and to find the information (not all of it is there). Students compare answers in pairs before checking with the whole class.

ANSWERS
1 the USA; soft drinks
2 Switzerland, 1908; watches
3 Finland, 1984; mobile phones
4 South Korea, 1938; electronic goods
5 Germany; cars
6 the USA, early 1950s; fast food

3 Go through the example with the class. Students work individually to read the text to find the words and phrases. Check answers with the whole class.

ANSWERS
b soft drink c status symbol
d the world's leading mobile phone company
e giant f wealthy banker g worldwide
h his home-made food

4 Establish that designer labels are those made by well-known and fashionable designers. You could bring in magazine adverts for students to look at for ideas. Students discuss the questions in small groups. Have some brief class feedback on any interesting points.

Language focus 1 (PAGE 108)

Present simple passive

Grammar

1–2 Write the example sentences on the board and go through them with the class, underlining the Present simple passive and eliciting the form. As you do so, highlight the following points.

- The form of *be* changes according to whether the subject is singular/plural (*am/is/are*).
- The verb *be* can be contracted, for example, *It's recognised ...*
- The question form is made by inverting the subject and *be*, for example, *Is it recognised ...?*

ANSWERS
1 (Passive forms are underlined.)
a *Colonel Sanders is also remembered for organising the biggest party in history.*
b *The brand is recognised by 94% of the world's population.*
2 We form the Present simple passive with the subject + *be* (*am/is/are*) + past participle.

3–4 Students discuss the questions in pairs before checking answers with the whole class. As you check the answers, highlight that the passive is used when the person who does the action is not important/known. Write on the board *More than 60,000 products from the Coca-Cola company are drunk around the world every minute.* Then ask students why the passive is used. (Answer: because we are more interested in the number of drinks/products than in who actually drinks them.) Refer them to *Language summary A* on page 155 of the *Students' Book* for more information.

ANSWERS
3 In sentence a, the subject is *Colonel Sanders.* In sentence b, the subject is *The brand.*
4 In sentence a, people in general remember Colonel Sanders. (It is not important who they are.) In sentence b, people in general recognise the brand. (It is not important who they are.)

PRACTICE

1 Demonstrate the activity by writing on the board *It's mainly used by women.* Explain that this sentence refers to one of the objects pictured on page 145 of the *Students' Book*. Students have just one chance to guess what it is. Write the next sentence on the board and give students two more guesses, and so on. If students cannot guess, tell them the answer. Students work in pairs to read about and guess the other two objects.

ANSWERS
a lipstick b razors c credit cards

2 Students work individually. Give them a few minutes to decide on objects and to write three sentences about each using the Present simple passive. Circulate and help with vocabulary as students work. As far as possible, correct any errors you see in the use of the Present simple passive. Students work in pairs to read and guess from each other's sentences.

Pronunciation

See *Teacher's tips: helping students with pronunciation* on pages 6–7.

1 Remind students that there are three possible ways of pronouncing the *-ed* endings on regular verbs in the Past simple or past participle forms. (The forms are the same.) Model the three different endings. Highlight that the *-ed* ending on the past participle of regular verbs is pronounced /ɪd/ only when the infinitive ends in *-t* (*accepted*) or *-d* (*ended*). This will help students to see that verbs like *liked* and *recognised* are not pronounced /laɪkɪd/ and /ˈrekɒgnaɪzɪd/.

Students often find it difficult to distinguish between /d/ and /t/ endings. Highlight that:
- /d/ follows voiced sounds
- /t/ follows unvoiced sounds.

It may be useful to remind students of the difference between voiced and unvoiced sounds. A finger placed gently on the throat should vibrate when a voiced sound is produced, but not with unvoiced sounds. It should be easier for students to hear /ɪd/, as this is different and adds a syllable to the base form of the verb. This is the most important of the three different endings.

2 Refer students to the tapescript for recording 2 on page 171 of the *Students' Book*. Put them into pairs to practise saying the regular past participles, in order to decide how each *-ed* ending is pronounced.

3 [T12.2] Play the recording for students to check their answers. Then play the recording again or model the words yourself, pausing after each word for students to repeat. Emphasise that the /ɪd/ endings are the most important.

ANSWERS
a accepted, connected, avoided
b recognised, manufactured, produced, designed, used
c liked, worked

ADDITIONAL PRACTICE

Workbook: Passive forms, exercise 1, page 72; Present simple passive, exercises 2–4, pages 72–73

Language focus 2 (PAGES 108–109)

Past simple passive

1 **a** Word to check: *invented*. Ask students if they know anything about the invention of dark glasses, jeans, shampoo or Chanel perfume. Briefly discuss any ideas students have. Give students a few minutes in pairs to decide on the best version for each invention.

b [T12.3] Play the recording for students to check their ideas. Have some brief class feedback.

ANSWERS
1 c 2 a 3 c 4 a

Grammar

1–2 Write the example sentences on the board and go through them with the class, underlining the Past simple passive and eliciting the form. As you do so, highlight the following points.
- The form of *be* changes according to whether the subject is singular/plural (*was/were*).

- The verb *be* cannot be contracted.
- The question form is made by inverting the subject and *be*, for example, *Was it introduced ...?*

ANSWERS
1 (Passive forms are underlined.)
 a *Chanel No 5 was introduced by the French fashion designer Coco Chanel in the 1920s.*
 b *Because she considered the number five to be her lucky number, the perfume was first presented on the 5th of May.*
2 We form the Past simple passive with the subject + *be* (*was/were*) + past participle.

3 Students discuss the questions in pairs before checking answers with the whole class. Refer them to *Language summary B* on page 155 of the *Students' Book* for more information.

ANSWERS
Coco Chanel introduced Chanel No 5.
In sentence a, the subject is *Chanel No 5*; in sentence b, the subject is *the perfume*.

PRACTICE

1 Students work individually to complete the sentences before checking answers in pairs. Have some brief class feedback.

ANSWERS
a was invented b invented c was manufactured
d wore; were designed e were sold
f were sent g was voted h started, named

2 **a** Ask students which company is featured in the pictures, what they make and what students think the connection between the pictures is. Then ask them to read the text through quickly (without attempting to complete the gaps) to see if their predictions were correct. Words to check: *manufacturer, to recognise something*. Establish that the verbs need to be in the active or passive, and do the first one with the class. Students work individually.

b [T12.4] Play the recording, pausing if necessary, for students to check their answers.

ANSWERS
See tapescript for recording 4 on page 172 of the *Students' Book.*

ADDITIONAL PRACTICE

RB **Resource bank:** 12B The Handbag Gang (Past simple passive), pages 159–160

Workbook: Past simple passive, exercises 5–6, page 74

Task: Decide what you need for a jungle trip (PAGES 110–111)

See *Teacher's tips: making tasks work* on pages 10–11 and *Responding to learners' individual language needs* on pages 12–13.

Preparation: reading

1 Set the scene by finding out if students have ever seen, or regularly watch, reality TV shows such as *Survival!* Establish that the programmes show how people cope without technology in a harsh environment. Draw students' attention to the information on the island of Bedaira by asking them to describe the photos. Words to check: *rainforest*, *uninhabited*, *mosquito*.

2 Students read the text. Check their understanding by asking them questions about Bedaira, for example, *What's the weather like? Are there any dangerous animals? How many people live there?* Find out if any of the students would like to visit Bedaira, and spend seventy-two hours alone there.

Task: speaking

1 Discuss with the class things which students usually take with them when they go away for a few days, if there is anything they cannot live without, how organised they are about packing, etc. Introduce the idea of taking a survival pack to Bedaira, and elicit one or two items that students think they would take with them. Give students ten minutes to work alone with their mini-dictionaries and to choose twelve items from the box. Check the meaning of *energy bars*. Pronunciation to check: *compass* /ˈkʌmpəs/, *repellent* /rɪˈpelənt/, *magnifying* /ˈmægnɪfaɪjɪŋ/, *purification* /pjʊrɪfɪˈkeɪʃən/.

2 **a** Focus students on *Useful language a*, and give them a minute or two to think about how they will explain their choices to other students. Working in groups of four to six, students explain their choices to each other.

b Students now must reach agreement on the twelve items to take. Set a time limit of fifteen minutes. Encourage them to use phrases from *Useful language b*. As you monitor, make sure students are giving reasons for taking each item. Note down examples of good language use and/or errors to focus on later.

At the end of the time limit, nominate one student to report the group's decisions to the rest of the class. Write their choices on the board so that students can see what the differences are between the groups. If students in a particular group could not agree on twelve items, they tell the class what the disagreement was over.

3 [T12.5] Explain that students will listen to the choices of a survival expert. Play the recording. Students listen and tick the twelve items from the box that he chooses. If necessary, play the recording again so that students have some idea as to why he chose the items he did. Students discuss answers in pairs before checking with the whole class. Find out which group chose the most items from the expert's survival pack.

ANSWERS
The twelve items in the expert's survival pack:
bottled water, water purification tablets, energy bars, a tent, matches, a torch, batteries, insect repellent, a knife, clean clothes, a toothbrush, toilet paper

Task: alternative suggestion

If you are short of time: do *Preparation: reading* in the first lesson, and ask students to think about their twelve items (*Task: speaking*, exercise 1) for homework. Do *Task: speaking*, exercises 2 and 3, in the next lesson.

Real life (PAGE 112)

Making suggestions

1 [T12.6] Give students a minute or two in pairs to discuss what they can see in the pictures. Circulate and help pairs with any words they are not sure of. Check that students understand the two questions, then play the recording. Give students time to compare answers in pairs before checking with the class.

ANSWERS
a a couple; pasta, seafood sauce and ice cream
b a shop assistant and customer; lipstick
c two young male friends; a leather purse
d a mother and son; the cheaper trainers and a backpack

2 **a** [T12.7] Establish that in all the conversations people are making and responding to suggestions. Focus students on the gapped sentences, and give them a minute or two to predict any of the missing language, before playing the recording.

ANSWERS
1 Shall I 2 good idea 3 Why don't we 4 OK
5 ... let's have 6 All 7 ... how about 8 You could
9 I'll do that 10 ... how about 11 What about

b Once students have completed the extracts, put them into pairs to discuss which phrases are used for making suggestions (1, 3, 5, 7, 8, 10, 11) and which for responding to them (2, 4, 6, 9). Check answers with the whole class. Elicit/explain that all the responses are accepting (positive).

Then direct students to the tapescript for recording 6 on page 172 of the *Students' Book*, and ask them to underline the phrases for making suggestions. Point out that there are two examples of underlined phrases in dialogue d. *If you have time*: ask students to underline the phrases for responding to suggestions as well. Tell them to find an example of a reluctant acceptance (*I suppose so* in dialogue d) and of a rejection (*I don't think so* in dialogue b).

Pronunciation

See *Teacher's tips: helping students with pronunciation* on pages 6–7.

[T12.7] Play the phrases on the recording, or say them naturally yourself. Point out how the intonation helps the speaker sound interested/polite. Play or say the phrases again, for students to repeat.

Pronunciation: additional suggestion

If your students need more structured practice before moving on to the roleplay: get them to make some suggestions to you. Provide some prompts, for example, *I want to go away this weekend, but I don't know where to go. I want to celebrate my birthday, but I don't know what to do.* Accept or reject their suggestions. Then give one or two students prompts to get suggestions from the class, for example, *What shall we do after class today? What shall I do this weekend?*

3 Give students five to ten minutes in pairs to prepare their conversations. Suggest that they make notes, rather than writing out the conversations word for word, so that they sound more natural. *If you have a large class*: put students into groups of six (three pairs) to act out their conversations. Note down examples of good language use and/or errors to focus on later.

Study ... (PAGE 113)

English around you

Before students read about the different ways of learning English outside the classroom, brainstorm ideas as a class. Then give students a few minutes individually to read the texts to see if any of their ideas are mentioned, and what additional approaches are suggested. Students work in small groups to discuss the advantages and disadvantages of each approach. For homework, encourage each student to try one way of learning English outside class, and arrange for them to report back in a week or two.

Pronunciation spot

The plural 's': /s/, /z/ or /ɪz/

See *Teacher's tips: helping students with pronunciation* on pages 6–7.

1 [T12.8] Play the recording or model the three words yourself. Demonstrate to students how the position of the jaw differs for the /ɪz/ sound.

2 [T12.9] Students work in pairs saying the words aloud to help each other hear which sound is used in each plural. Play the recording, or model the words yourself, for students to check the answers.

ANSWERS

/s/	/z/	/ɪz/
blankets	credit cards	driving licences
ropes	mirrors	glasses
tablets	towels	matches
tents	umbrellas	torches

3 Model the plural forms for students to repeat. Then put students into pairs. Students take it in turns to say the singular form of one of the words in exercise 2; their partner says the plural form.

Practise ... (PAGE 113)

1 Present simple passive

This can be done orally first. Students work in pairs, taking turns to use the Present simple passive. Students write their answers at the end.

ANSWERS
a Thousands of cars are stolen every year.
b All the tickets are sold over the Internet.
c A lot of the world's gold is produced in South Africa.
d The rooms are cleaned every morning.
e Millions of barrels of oil are exported to Europe.

2 Past simple passive

Tell students to cover the box and to try to guess what the missing words are before uncovering the box and completing the sentences. Check answers with the whole class.

ANSWERS
a were b was c by d stolen e written

3 Everyday objects

Do this as a race. The winner is the first student to name the pictures with no spelling mistakes.

ANSWERS
a hairbrush b comb c sunglasses d lipstick
e toothbrush

4 Making suggestions

Students work individually and then in pairs before checking answers with the whole class.

ANSWERS
a go b playing c don't we d Shall e buy

Remember! (PAGE 113)

After looking back at the areas they have practised, students do the *Mini-check* on page 161 of the *Students' Book*. Check answers with the whole class, and ask students to tell you their scores out of 20.

ANSWERS
1 brush 2 bag 3 glasses 4 stick 5 brush
6 built 7 was 8 written 9 paid 10 were
11 was stolen 12 did 13 are sent 14 were worn
15 lost 16 going 17 go 18 go 19 go 20 go

module 13

Choosing the right person

Vocabulary and speaking

(PAGES 114–115)

Personal characteristics

See *Teacher's tips: working with lexical phrases* on pages 8–9 and *Making the most of the* mini-dictionary on pages 9–10.

1 Focus students' attention on the photos and check the meaning of *do* for talking about jobs, as in *What do you/they do?* Discuss the questions as a class. Pronunciation to check: *carpenter* /kɑːpɪntə/, *doctor* /dɒktə/.

> **ANSWERS**
> **Jobs shown in the pictures (clockwise from top):** football coach, carpenter, doctor, Olympic athlete, writer

2 Give students a few minutes, individually or in pairs, to check the meaning of the vocabulary and to decide which jobs are being described. Pronunciation to check: *sympathetic* /sɪmpəθetɪk/, *experienced* /ekˈspɪərɪənst/, *honest* /ɒnɪst/, *imaginative* /ɪˈmædʒɪnətɪv/, *self-discipline* /self ˈdɪsɪplɪn/.

> **ANSWERS**
> 1 doctor 2 Olympic athlete 3 football coach
> 4 writer

3 **a** Do the first example with the whole class to demonstrate the activity. Students work individually or in pairs to complete the table.

ANSWERS

Verb	Noun	Adjective
imagine	imagination	imaginative
organise	organisation	organised
	discipline	disciplined
	talent	talented
	commitment	committed
	laziness	lazy
experience	experience	experienced
	honesty	honest
motivate	motivation	motivated
sympathise	sympathy	sympathetic

b [T13.1] Check that students know how to mark the stress by drawing their attention to the example *imagine*. Model the word for students so that they can hear where the stress falls. Play the recording, pausing after each group of words to allow students time to mark the stress. As you check the answers, highlight the following points.

- Stress patterns often change within word families.
- The suffixes *-tion* and *-ic* attract the stress, and the syllable before them is always stressed.

> **ANSWERS**
> See tapescript for recording 1 on page 172 of the *Students' Book.*

4 **a** As a class, discuss three qualities from exercise 2 that make a good parent. Then give students a few minutes individually to choose qualities for the other jobs/people on the list.

b Look at the examples with the whole class. Students work in pairs or small groups to talk about the qualities they chose for each job/person. Circulate, noting down examples of good language use and/or errors with vocabulary to focus on later.

Listening (PAGE 115)

Interview with the manager of Vacation Express

1 Focus students on the photos, and discuss with them what the different jobs involve and which of the jobs they would like to do. Find out whether any of the students have done jobs like these.

2 [T13.2] Explain that Vacation Express helps young people find temporary summer jobs. Students listen to the recording and make notes under the four headings. Replay the recording if necessary. Words to check: *CV* (*curriculum vitae*), *cruise ship*.

> **ANSWERS**
> **Type of people who register:** mainly young people; a lot of students
> **Reasons for doing this type of work:** to earn money (though the pay isn't very good); to learn new skills; to see another culture; to meet new people; to put it on their CV
> **Personal qualities they are looking for:** a positive attitude; the ability to get on with other people; languages, especially English
> **Examples of jobs they are offering at the moment:** jungle guides in Peru; a water sports teacher on the Spanish coast; a children's entertainer on a cruise ship; teaching jobs in Asia

3 **a** Students work individually to complete the adjective–noun combinations.

b Refer them to the tapescript for recording 2 on pages 172–173 of the *Students' Book*. Students check answers in pairs and then as a class.

> **ANSWERS**
> 2 a temporary job 3 learn new skills
> 4 a great opportunity 5 a positive attitude
> 6 a big advantage 7 a special talent
> 8 a different culture

4 Ask students if they have any experience of temporary/summer jobs. Put them into small groups to discuss the questions. Have some brief class feedback on any jobs which are especially popular or unpopular.

ADDITIONAL PRACTICE

Workbook: Vocabulary, exercise 7, page 82

Language focus 1 (PAGES 116–117)

Present perfect continuous with *how long*, *for* and *since*

1 Explain that each of the people in the photos is looking for a job with Vacation Express. Students work individually to read the texts and to decide on a suitable job for each person before comparing ideas in pairs or small groups. Have some brief class feedback. Words to check: *babysitting*, *fascinate*, *comedian*.

POSSIBLE ANSWERS
Sandra: au pair
Marc: water sports teacher
Yolanda: English teacher
Sanjiv: children's entertainer

Grammar

1 Focus students on the examples and give them a minute or two to consider the form. While they do this, copy the examples onto the board so that you can refer to them more easily in feedback. As you check the answer, elicit/write a table for the form of the Present perfect continuous on the board. See *Language summary A* on page 155 of the *Students' Book* for the complete table. Highlight:

- the contraction of the subject and the verb *have* (*I've/it's/we've*, etc.)
- the inversion of the subject and the verb *have* in the question form (*Have you been working here ...?*)
- the spelling of the present participle (for the rules, see Module 4, *Language summary A*, on page 150 of the *Students' Book*).

ANSWER
We form the Present perfect continuous with the subject + *have/has* + *been* + present participle.

2 Elicit students' answers to the questions as a whole class. Remind students that the Present perfect always indicates a connection between the past and present, as already shown in Module 7. Demonstrate this, using a timeline if necessary. See *Language summary A* on page 155 for examples of timelines.

ANSWERS
In sentence a, she looks after children now. She started doing this when she was fourteen.
In sentence b, he is trying to get work now. He started doing this about a year ago.

3 Students work in pairs to decide how the phrases in the box are used. As you check the answers, highlight the difference between a period of time (*for forty years / six months / a few days*) and a point in time (*since six o'clock / yesterday / Saturday / two weeks ago*).

ANSWERS

for	since
forty years	1965
five hours	last year
six months	2004
	Tuesday
	six o'clock
	October

PRACTICE

1 Refer students to the example. Check understanding by asking which time phrase they would use with *for* for Sandra. Students work individually before checking answers with the whole class.

ANSWERS AND LANGUAGE NOTE
a *She's been looking after young children* ***since*** *she was about fourteen.*
She's been looking after young children ***for*** *about ten years.*
b *Sanjiv's been looking for work* ***since*** *January last year.*
Sanjiv's been looking for work ***for*** *about a year.**
c *Yolanda's been studying Chinese* ***for*** *two years.*
d *Marc's been sailing* ***since*** *he was about eleven.*
* Students may also express the period of time in months, relative to the time of year when they are doing the exercise.

Pronunciation

See *Teacher's tips: helping students with pronunciation* on pages 6–7.

[T13.3] Say *I have been waiting* and *I've been waiting* to students, and elicit the difference. Remind students that the contracted form is more natural-sounding in spoken English than the full form. Play the recording or model the phrases yourself. Replay the recording, pausing for students to repeat the contracted forms. Students practise in pairs.

2 Focus students' attention on the photos and the profile of Florence. Ask students to read the text, and check their understanding by asking a few questions: *When did Florence come to England? What does she do? What did she do before?* (Answers: *five years ago*; *teaches yoga*; *taught French*.)

3 [T13.4] Emphasise that students should write the answers to the questions they hear, not the questions themselves. Play the recording, pausing after each question for students to write the answer. Students compare answers in pairs before checking with the whole class. Note that their answers using *since* will depend on when they are doing the exercise.

ANSWERS

a *Florence has been living in England* **for** *five years* / **since** + year.
b *She's been working as a teacher* **for** *four years* / **since** + year.
c *She's been studying yoga* **for** *ten years* / **since** + year.
d *She's been teaching yoga* **for** *a year and a half* / **since** + month + year.

4 **a** Give students a few minutes to complete the information about themselves. Circulate and help with vocabulary.

b Refer students to the example. Students work in pairs, asking and answering questions. Circulate, noting down examples of good language use and/or errors to focus on later.

ADDITIONAL PRACTICE

Workbook: Present perfect continuous, exercises 2–4, pages 78–79

Language focus 2 (PAGES 118–119)

Present perfect continuous and Present perfect simple

1 Words to check: *wannabe*, *talent*. Students read the text. As a class, discuss whether students know of similar programmes in their countries, and if anyone likes watching them or would like to compete.

2 Students reread the text before comparing answers with a partner. Have some brief class feedback.

ANSWERS

a True (they wanted to be in a TV talent competition to create a new pop group)
b False (they waited in the rain)
c Not sure (one of the competitors mentions thirty seconds, but the text doesn't actually say how long they had)
d False (he began taking lessons a year ago, when he was seventeen)
e False (she said she hadn't seen anything exciting)

Grammar

1–3 Students work in pairs to answer the questions. As you check the answers, highlight the following points.

- The Present perfect always indicates a connection between the past and present, as already shown in Module 7. Demonstrate, using timelines if necessary (see pages 152 and 155 of the *Students' Book*), that the Present perfect simple and continuous are used in the same way, for actions which started in the past and continue to the present.
- With many verbs, speakers choose to use the continuous form if they want to emphasise how long the action has continued, for example:
  I've waited for an hour. / I've been waiting for an hour.
  I've studied English for three years. / I've been studying English for three years.
- State verbs cannot be used in the continuous form, for example:
  She's had that car for ten years. (Not *She's been having that car for ten years.*)
  I've known my teacher for six months. (Not *I've been knowing my teacher for six months.*)

ANSWERS

2 In sentence a, the form of the verb is the Present perfect continuous.
In sentence b, the form of the verb is the Present perfect simple.
3 Sentence d is incorrect, as *like* is a state verb and cannot be used in the continuous form.

PRACTICE

1 Demonstrate the activity using the examples. Give students a few minutes to think about their questions. *If you have a reasonably strong class*: tell students not to write out their questions, but just to practise saying them to themselves. Circulate and help with the wording and pronunciation of the questions.

ANSWERS

b 1 Do you own a car?
2 How long have you owned a car?
c 1 Do you ride a scooter/motorbike?
2 How long have you been riding a scooter / motorbike?
d 1 Do you wear glasses / contact lenses?
2 How long have you been wearing glasses / contact lenses?
e 1 Do you own a pet?
2 How long have you had your pet?
f 1 Do you play football / tennis / another sport?
2 How long have you been playing football / tennis, etc.?
g 1 Do you play the guitar / the piano / another musical instrument?
2 How long have you been playing the guitar / the piano, etc.?
h 1 Do you like football?
2 How long have you liked football?

2 Ensure that students choose different questions by allocating a–h to different students. Tell students they should try to ask their question of everyone in the class, and that they will report back on their findings. Students stand up and mingle, questioning each other, before they report back to the class.

***Practice*, exercise 2: alternative suggestion**

If it is impractical for your students to stand up and move around the class: put students into groups of four to interview each other.

ADDITIONAL PRACTICE

RB Resource bank: 13A Century People (Present perfect simple and continuous for unfinished past), page 161; 13B Old friends (Present perfect simple and continuous for unfinished past), pages 162–163; Learner-training worksheet I (Deducing meaning from context – part 2), page 164

Workbook: Present perfect continuous, exercise 1, page 78

Wordspot (PAGE 119)

how

See *Teacher's tips: working with lexical phrases* on pages 8–9.

1 **a** Establish that this exercise deals with different uses of *how*, and that there is a word missing after *how* in each phrase. Discuss the example with the class. Students work individually or in pairs to complete the sentences.

b [T13.5] Play the recording before checking answers with the whole class.

ANSWERS
2 about 3 much 4 do 5 long 6 fast 7 are
8 tall 9 do 10 high

2 Give students a few minutes to complete the diagram. Check answers with the whole class.

ANSWERS
- a **to ask about the way to do something:** How do you …
- b **to ask about size, amount, number, etc:** How big, How many, How far, How much, How long, How fast, How tall, How high
- c **phrases used when you meet someone:** How do you do?
- d **to make a suggestion:** How about
- e **to ask about someone's health or feelings:** How are you feeling?

3 **a** Put students into pairs, A and B, and direct them to pages 145 and 146 of the *Students' Book*. Give them a few minutes individually to complete the questions with the correct *how* phrase.

ANSWERS
Student A
1 far 2 many 3 are 4 How 5 old 6 How

Student B
1 do 2 much 3 about 4 long 5 do 6 fast

b Demonstrate that students should read the question and the choice of answers to their partner, who has to choose the correct one. Students score a point for each correct answer. Find out which students have the highest scores.

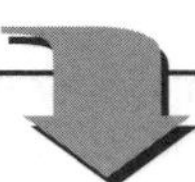

***Wordspot*, exercise 3: additional suggestion**

Students write two or three multiple-choice questions of their own in pairs, using *how*. They then read them out for the rest of the class to guess.

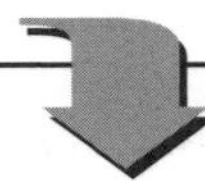

***Wordspot*, exercise 3: additional activity**

Explain to students that we can also use *how* to make an exclamation (for example, *How funny!*) when we want to respond to something someone says or to a situation.

Write the list of adjectives and the situations a–e below on the board. Students work in pairs. Give the pairs a minute or two to match the adjectives with the appropriate situations.

awful kind stupid rude nice strange lovely

- **a** My boss didn't say hello to me this morning.
- **b** Dave's had a terrible accident on his motorbike.
- **c** Mrs Woods has offered to look after the children this evening.
- **d** We're going to the Bahamas for our holiday this year.
- **e** I can't find my wallet anywhere – but I had it two minutes ago.

Feed back with the whole class. Students can act out the conversations, trying to remember the appropriate adjective to use in the response.

ANSWERS
a How rude/strange! b How awful! c How kind!
d How lovely/nice! e How strange/stupid!

Task: Choose a manager for a pop group (PAGES 120–121)

See *Teacher's tips: making tasks work* on pages 10–11 and *Responding to learners' individual language needs* on pages 12–13.

Preparation: reading

1 Use the pictures and short text to elicit as much as possible about SPOTS! For example, they are very popular, they are quite young, they have only been famous for about a year. Remind students that SPOTS! are looking for a new manager. Ask them to think particularly about what the duties of the manager are, for instance, negotiating contracts, managing the band's finances, organising appearances and concerts. Ask students about the advantages and disadvantages of the job, and whether they would like to be manager of a famous band or not.

2 Tell students that they are going to find out about two of the four candidates for the job of SPOTS! manager. Ask them to look at the pictures of Anita and Jack, and to give you their first impressions. For example, they might want to comment on which candidate has the appropriate kind of image for the manager of a pop group. Give students a few minutes to read through the two texts and to complete the table, making notes about the good and bad points to refer back to later. Words to check: *show business*, *soap opera*, *single*, *boy band*. Ask students to compare answers in pairs and then as a class. If students have trouble thinking of points, give them prompts to consider, such as *age*, *experience in the music industry*, *relevant work experience*, *promises*, *image*.

ANSWERS

	Good points	Bad points
Anita Robson	Long background in show business Several hits Wealthy husband in the pop business	Experience was a long time ago No direct experience of management Her age – this may not go with the band's young image
Jack Markus	Lots of management experience Has already managed a famous band His age – he has a young image	Has been in prison – this may affect his reputation Why was he in prison? The last band he managed had financial problems – is he good at financial management?

Task: speaking

1 Words to check: *model*, *hard*. Put students into pairs, A and B. Student A reads the information about the third candidate on page 147, while Student B reads the information about the fourth candidate on page 146.

2 Give students a minute or two to think about the questions they need to ask to complete the missing information in the table. Get one pair to demonstrate. Student A asks a question about the fourth candidate, and Student B writes the answer, in note form, in the table. Then give students time to exchange all the information about the third and fourth candidates. Circulate and, if necessary, help students with summarising the points about the candidates. Collect examples of good language use and/or errors to focus on later.

Task: speaking, exercise 2: additional suggestions

One of the following roleplays can be done after exercise 2.

- Set the scene for a meeting, where all four candidates for SPOTS! manager will be present to speak to the press / an interview panel and to answer questions. Allocate the roles of the four candidates to strong students, who will have the confidence to make a short speech in which they introduce themselves and their ideas. Let them have time to prepare what they will say. Give all the other students in the class different roles as people connected to SPOTS! (for example, band member, music journalist, fan, recording company executive). Ask these people to prepare questions they want to ask at the meeting. Also choose someone to chair the meeting. Circulate and help with language / prompt with ideas. Arrange the seating so that the four candidates and the 'chair' are at the front, then start the meeting. It is probably best not to participate yourself, so that you can give students feedback on their performance afterwards.
- Set up interviews between news reporters and the four candidates. Ask half the class to be reporters, and the other half to be the candidates (it does not matter if there are more students representing one candidate than the others). Give students time to prepare what they will say. Reporters think about their questions and make notes to refer to. Candidates try to anticipate the questions and to think of convincing answers, and make notes to refer to. Put students into pairs to conduct the interviews, then have some brief feedback in which the reporters tell the rest of the class what they found out.

3 Give students time individually to prioritise the candidates from 1 to 4. Direct them to *Useful language a* and *b* to help them explain their choices. *Either*: highlight the language explicitly now. *Or*: leave it until after *Task: speaking*, so as not to distract students. Circulate and help students with the language they need to explain the reasons for their choices.

4 Put students into small groups to explain and compare their choices. Direct them to *Useful language c*. Elicit a few more phrases for agreeing and disagreeing, for example, *That's true. / Exactly! / I see what you mean, but ...* While students are doing this, note down examples of good language use and/or errors to focus on later. *If you have time and motivated students*: ask each group to report back on their opinions, and widen the discussion to the whole class. You can also have a class vote for the new manager of SPOTS!

Task: alternative suggestion

If you have short lessons: do *Preparation: reading* in the first lesson. Divide the class into pairs, A and B, and direct students to the information about the third and fourth candidates, as applicable. Ask them to complete the table with the relevant information for homework. Then, in the second lesson, students exchange their information and do the rest of *Task: speaking*.

Writing (PAGES 121–122)

Completing an application form

1 Divide students into pairs, A and B. Student A reads Ela's e-mail on page 121, while Student B reads the application form on page 122 and plans the questions they will ask. In their pairs, students complete the application form using the information from the e-mail. Circulate so that you can check for accuracy and, if necessary, help students to make corrections. Check answers with the whole class for any sections which students found difficult.

ANSWERS

VACATION EXPRESS

Please complete the entire application.
Remember to tick the job you are applying for.
Mail this application to Vacation Express, PO Box 99, Lichton, L12 8FH, UK.
NAME: (First) Ela
(Last) *Kwasniak*
SEX: MALE / FEMALE
DATE OF BIRTH: 12.7.83 (Month/Day/Year)
ADDRESS: *ul. Rachawickie* 13
Post Code: *20038*
City: *Lublin*
Country: *Poland*
TELEPHONE: (Please include country/city code)
Home: *00 48 81 724105*
Work:
Mobile: *07256 87228*
E-MAIL: *ela@home.pl*
DO YOU HAVE A VALID DRIVER'S LICENCE? *YES* / NO
LANGUAGES SPOKEN: *Polish, English, German and a little Russian*
PRESENT OCCUPATION/STUDIES:
Tennis coach
WHICH OF THESE WORK AREAS MOST INTERESTS YOU?
Hotel/Restaurant ✔
Child Care
Tour Guide
Sports Instructor ✔
Activity Leader
DESCRIBE ANY SPECIAL QUALIFICATIONS OR WORK EXPERIENCE YOU HAVE.
Three years' experience as a tennis coach with young children
HOW DID YOU HEAR ABOUT VACATION EXPRESS?
Newspaper
Website
Personal Recommendation ✔
Other
I certify that the statements on this application are true and complete to the best of my knowledge.
SIGNATURE OF APPLICANT:
Ela Kwasniak
DATE:

2 In the same pairs, students change roles. Student A asks questions to complete the application form about Student B.

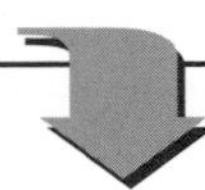

Writing, exercise 2: additional suggestion

If you want to give students letter-writing practice: ask them to write a letter, based on the e-mail from Ela, in which they apply to Vacation Express. Ask students to plan the layout and content of the letter, deciding where the writer's address and the date are, what information is contained in each of the paragraphs and how the letter begins and ends. The letter can then be written for homework.

3 Get students to choose if they would like to roleplay an interview with Ela or with themselves applying for a job. First, put students into Groups A and B. Group A prepares questions to ask, and Group B tries to anticipate the questions it will be asked, and to prepare what answers to give. *If you have a strong class*: suggest that Group A writes hypothetical questions, such as *What would you do if ... (one of the tourists in your group got ill)*?

Then, put students into pairs, A and B, to roleplay the interview. They decide whether the applicant is suited to the job(s) they have applied for. Students then change roles and repeat the process, with Student B acting as interviewer and asking the questions. During the interviews, collect examples of good language use and/or errors to focus on later.

Writing, exercises 2 and 3: alternative suggestion

If the Vacation Express jobs will not appeal to your students: bring in some authentic job adverts for exercise 2. Ask students to write a letter in which they apply for one of the jobs instead of completing the application form. In exercise 3, students exchange letters, prepare questions based on the relevant job advert and interview their partners.

Study ... (PAGE 122)

Revising effectively

Before students read about the different ways of revising the English they have learnt, brainstorm ideas as a class. Then give students a few minutes individually to read the suggestions to see if any of their ideas are mentioned, and to note any additional approaches. Students work in small groups to discuss the advantages and disadvantages of each approach. For homework, encourage each student to spend thirty minutes trying out each technique, and arrange for them to report back in a week or two.

Practise ... (PAGE 123)

1 Present perfect continuous with *how long*, *for* and *since*

Students work individually before checking answers with the whole class.

ANSWERS
a How long b for c since d since e for
f How long

2 Present perfect simple and Present perfect continuous

Students work in pairs, transforming the sentences into the Present perfect continuous and saying them aloud to help them decide if they are right or wrong.

ANSWERS
a cannot change – state verb
b *I've been playing tennis for many years.*
c cannot change – state verb
d *It's been raining since six o'clock this morning.*
e *We've been waiting for nearly an hour.*

3 Personal characteristics

Do this as a race. Write the jumbled words on the board and tell students that they are all personal characteristics. Working in pairs, students have thirty seconds to unjumble any they can for a bonus of five points per correctly spelt word. Then refer students to page 123 of the *Students' Book*, where the meaning of the words is also given. Students work in the same pairs to unjumble the remaining words in a time limit of three minutes. Each correctly spelt word is awarded a point. The winner is the pair with the most points. For homework, students could devise other jumbled words to set each other.

ANSWERS
a committed b experienced c honest d lazy
e imaginative f motivated g sympathetic

4 Adjective-noun combinations

Students cover the box and try to complete the sentences without looking at the options. Then they uncover the box and check/revise their answers. Check answers with the whole class.

ANSWERS
a attitude b talent c skills d advantage
e opportunity

5 *how*

Do this orally. Read out each sentence to students as a prompt. They repeat the sentence back to you, adding a word in the right place. Students write the sentences up for homework as consolidation.

ANSWERS
a How **fast** was he driving?
b How **much** does this cost?
c How **do** you spell your surname?
d How **tall** is Paul?
e How **far** is it from here to the town centre?
f It's very nice to meet you. How do **you** do?
g How **are** you feeling now?
h How **about** another cup of tea?
i How **long** did you have to wait?

Pronunciation spot

See *Teacher's tips: helping students with pronunciation* on pages 6–7.

1 Students work in pairs, saying the words aloud to each other to help them decide in which two the /h/ sound is not pronounced.

2 [T13.6] Play the recording. Students listen and check. Play the recording again, pausing after each word for students to repeat.

ANSWER
The /h/ is not pronounced in *honest* and *hour*.

Remember! (PAGE 123)

After looking back at the areas they have practised, students do the *Mini-check* on page 161 of the *Students' Book*. Check answers with the whole class, and ask students to tell you their scores out of 20.

ANSWERS
1 motivated 2 imaginative 3 lazy 4 sympathetic
5 committed 6 for 7 since 8 since 9 since
10 for 11 has, been 12 has had
13 has it been raining 14 've known
15 've been waiting 16 tall 17 since 18 far
19 opportunity 20 do

module 14

Money, money, money

Vocabulary and speaking

(PAGES 124–125)

Money

See *Teacher's tips: working with lexical phrases* on pages 8–9 and *Making the most of the* Mini-dictionary on pages 9–10.

1 Focus students' attention on the photos and elicit an example. Put students into pairs to discuss the rest of the pictures and to match them to the items in the box.

ANSWER
You can see all of them.

2 Students work in pairs, asking and answering the questions. As you check the answers, elicit full sentences to describe each situation, so that you can highlight the following points.

- You *borrow money* ***from*** someone, and you *lend money* ***to*** someone.
- You *spend money* ***on*** something.
- You *save up* either ***to buy*** something or ***for*** something.

Pronunciation to check: *earn* /ɜːn/, *waste* /weɪst/, *can't afford* /kaːnt əfɔːd/.

ANSWERS
a (Answers will be different for each student.)
b (Answers will be different for each student.)
c *Pocket money* is paid by parents (or grandparents) to children.
A *fine* is paid by someone who has committed an offence or crime, such as parking in the wrong place or speeding. It is paid either to a court or to the police.
A *salary* is paid by an employer to an employee.
A *tip* is paid by a customer to someone who has performed a service, for example, a waiter/waitress, a hairdresser, a taxi driver.

3 **a** Demonstrate the activity by doing an example about yourself. Then give students a few minutes to complete the statements.

b Before students compare answers, remind them of how to agree with / show interest in their partner's answers, for example, *Yes, that's the same for me. / I agree. / Me too. / So do I. / Really? / Why do you think that? / Oh dear. / Why? / Why not?* Students either work in pairs or stand up and mingle, choosing different statements to discuss with each person they talk to. Ask one or two students to report back to the whole class on some of the main differences they found.

ADDITIONAL PRACTICE

Workbook: Vocabulary, exercise 7, page 86

Reading (PAGE 125)

1 Ask students to cover the box and to read the text about money, guessing what the missing numbers might be. Then draw their attention to the numbers in the box, and give them a few minutes to reread the text, filling the gaps with the numbers. Students compare answers in pairs.

2 Refer students to page 142 of the *Students' Book* to check their answers. Students discuss the questions in small groups. Have some brief class feedback.

Pronunciation

See *Teacher's tips: helping students with pronunciation* on pages 6–7.

1 [T14.1] Play the recording, pausing briefly after each number to allow students time to write.

2 Refer students to the tapescript to check their answers. In feedback, highlight:
- plural forms, for example, *two thousand pounds* not ~~two thousands pounds~~
- the use of *and*, for example, *four hundred and fifty* not ~~four hundred fifty~~
- the style for decimals, for example, *nineteen point seven* not ~~nineteen comma seven~~
- (in very small numbers) the use of the plural form for measurements, for example, *nought point seven five kilograms* (= *0.75kg*)
- (in long numbers) the pause between thousands and hundreds, where the comma is often placed, for example, *four thousand* (slight pause) *two hundred and seventy* (= *4,270*).

ANSWERS
See tapescript for recording 1 on page 173 of the *Students' Book*.

3 Students work in pairs to practise saying the numbers in the text about money.

Language focus 1 (PAGE 126)

Past perfect

1 Focus students' attention on the cartoon. As a class, discuss what is happening in the picture. Words to check: *joke*, *mean*, *hiss*, *second-hand*. Students read the jokes and decide which one matches the cartoon. Emphasise that they do not need to complete the texts yet. Then students compare answers in pairs before checking as a whole class. Ask for any ideas for the last line of each joke, but do not comment if the students make right or wrong suggestions.

ANSWER
Joke 2 goes with the picture.

2 [T14.2] Play the recording. Students listen and complete the last line. Elicit/explain the meaning of *punchline*. As a class, decide which joke is the funniest.

ANSWERS
See tapescript for recording 2 on page 173 of the *Students' Book*.

Grammar

1 Copy the example onto the board and elicit the two verb forms used. As you check the answers, highlight the following points.

- The Past perfect is formed with *had* + past participle for all persons. If necessary, elicit a table for the positive, negative and question forms onto the board. Alternatively, refer students to the table in *Language summary A* on page 156 of the *Students' Book*.
- *Had* and the subject are inverted in the question form, for example, *Had I told you ...?*
- The negative form is *had not*, often contracted to *hadn't*, for example, *I hadn't eaten all day.*
- The contracted form is *'d*, for example, *I'd*, *she'd*, *we'd*.

ANSWERS
The verb *was* is in the Past simple; the verb *had been* is in the Past perfect.

2 Students discuss the question. As you check the answer, highlight that the Past perfect is used when it is necessary to show that one action happened before another in the past. Refer students to the timeline in *Language summary A* on page 156.

ANSWER
The action of going to the bank happened first.

3 Refer students back to the jokes to underline more examples of the Past perfect.

ANSWERS
Other examples of the Past perfect include *The young man – who had only worked for ...* (joke 1); *how he had become so rich* (joke 2); *but I had made a profit* (joke 3).

PRACTICE

1 Students work individually or in pairs to match the beginnings and endings, and to change the verbs into the Past perfect. Check answers with the whole class.

ANSWERS
a She couldn't afford the shoes because she had spent all her money on presents for her family.
b By the time George retired, he had earned enough money to buy a holiday home.
c Hilda and Jerry bought a new car with the money they had won in a competition.
d Michael was in a panic because he had lost his wallet.
e When Grandma died, nobody knew that she had saved up thousands of pounds in a box.

Practice, exercise 1: additional suggestions

- Students cover the endings in B and, working in pairs, try to remember the endings.
- Students think of different endings for the beginnings in A, for example, *She couldn't afford the shoes because she had spent a lot of money on a holiday.*

2 a Ask students to read the story quickly to find out what sort of things Arthur Ferguson sold. (Answer: *famous buildings*.) Students then work individually to complete the gaps, before checking answers in pairs.

b [T14.3] Play the recording. Students check their answers.

ANSWERS
See tapescript for recording 3 on page 173 of the *Students' Book*.

ADDITIONAL PRACTICE

Workbook: Past perfect, exercises 1–3, page 84

Language focus 2 (PAGE 127)

Past time words

1 Give students a few minutes in pairs to discuss each headline and to predict what the newspaper story is about. Then give students three minutes to read the newspaper stories and to match them to headlines. Emphasise that one headline is not used.

ANSWERS
a 1 b 3 d 2
Headline c is not used.

Grammar

1–3 As you check the answers, highlight the following points.

- *Just* means that something happened a short time before; *already* means that something happened before a particular time; *never ... before* means that it was the first time that something happened or that someone did something.
- The adverbs *just* and *already* are positioned between the auxiliary *had* and the past participle.
- *Never* comes between the auxiliary *had* and the past participle, while *before* comes after the past participle phrase, for example, *I'd never eaten sushi before.*

Refer students to *Language summary B* on page 156 of the *Students' Book* for more information.

ANSWERS
1 b 2 b 3 b

PRACTICE

Students work individually to complete the sentences before checking answers with the whole class.

ANSWERS
a already b never, before c just d already
e never f never, before g just h never, before

ADDITIONAL PRACTICE

Workbook: Past time words: *already*, *just*, *never ... before*, exercises 4–6, page 85

Task: Tell a story from pictures

(PAGES 128–129)

See *Teacher's tips: making tasks work* on pages 10–11 and *Responding to learners' individual language needs* on pages 12–13.

Preparation: vocabulary

Establish that the pictures are in the right order and that the story they tell is true. Elicit descriptions of the pictures from students, building up the story with the class. Words to check: *floorboards*, *to console someone*, *in tears*, *winnings*, *to tear up*. Pronunciation to check: *tear* (*to tear up*) /teə/ versus *tear* (*in tears*) /tɪə/.

ANSWERS
1 c 2 d 3 b 4 e 5 f 6 a 7 g

Task: speaking

1–2 Students work in pairs to practise telling the story. Circulate as students work, helping with vocabulary and noting down examples of good language use and/or errors with the Past perfect or past time words to focus on later.

3 [T14.4] Ask students to listen and note down five differences. Play the recording twice if necessary.

4 Put students into small groups to compare their answers. Explain that they will report back on the five differences they found. Draw students' attention to *Useful language b*. Give students a few minutes to prepare what they will say. Nominate students to report back on the differences to the class.

ANSWERS
1 He talks about a little girl rather than a little boy.
2 She dropped the coin down the back of the sofa rather than through a hole in the floorboards.
3 He won money in the lottery rather than on horse racing.
4 The money was in his wallet rather than in an envelope.
5 She threw the money out of the window rather than tearing it up.

Task: additional suggestions

a *If your students enjoy roleplaying*: ask them to prepare and act out an interview between a journalist and the father. They can choose which version of the story they use, or they can use another story about a childhood misunderstanding if they know one.

b *If you want to give students writing practice*: ask them to write up one of the versions of the story for homework.

Wordspot (PAGE 129)

make

See *Teacher's tips: working with lexical phrases* on pages 8–9.

1 [T14.5] Students work individually to complete the gaps. They then compare ideas in pairs before listening to the recording.

ANSWERS
a a phone call b profit c dinner d friends
e noise f a cup of tea g cry h angry i a mess
j feel

2 Demonstrate the activity using sentence a as an example. Then give students time, individually or in pairs, to complete the diagram.

ANSWERS
a **produce something:** making dinner, making a very strange noise, make you a cup of tea, make a mess
b **make money:** made a big profit
c **make + adjective:** makes me angry
d **make + verb:** made Lucy cry, makes me feel really ill
e **other phrases:** make a phone call, made lots of friends

3 Give students a few minutes to think about their answers. Then put them into pairs to discuss. Ask one or two pairs to report back on which answers were the same.

POSSIBLE ANSWERS
Things that make you angry: traffic jams; people who are rude; people who are late; problems on public transport
Things that make a lot of noise: babies crying; men repairing the road; thunder; planes flying over your house
Reasons why people make speeches: to celebrate a wedding; to talk about ideas at a political meeting; to say goodbye to someone who is leaving a company
Things that are made in Scotland: whisky, tartan, kilts, shortbread (a kind of biscuit)
Things that you can make with eggs: cakes, omelettes, sauces
Mistakes that you often make in English: forget the third-person *-s*; forget the article

Wordspot: additional activity

Write the following up on the board or on an overhead transparency.

Find someone who:

- *is going to make dinner tonight*
- *makes more than five phone calls a day*
- *has made a difficult decision recently*
- *is wearing something made of wool*
- *likes making beds*
- *has made someone laugh today*
- *would like to make a lot of money*
- *never makes a mess.*

Before you start, remind students of the different question forms they need, for example, *Are you going to …? Do you …? Have you …? Are you …? Would you like to …?* Encourage students to ask follow-up questions, for example, *Do you make more than five phone calls a day? Really? Who do you phone?*

Students then walk around and, if possible, find someone who says yes to each question. Students make a list of the names.

As a round-up, ask students if they found out anything unusual/surprising.

Real life (PAGE 130)

Dealing with money

1 Focus students on the pictures. Elicit where the people are in each case. Working in pairs or as a class, students then discuss in which situation you would do each thing.

ANSWERS

a in a café b in a bank c in a market
d at hotel reception
In a café: pay by credit card, leave a tip, ask if service is included
In a bank: change money, ask about the exchange rate, open a bank account, pay commission
In a market: ask how much something costs
At hotel reception: change money, pay by credit card, ask about the exchange rate, pay commission

2 [T14.6] Tell students to write the number of the picture next to the number of the conversation as they listen to the recording.

ANSWERS

Conversation a: picture d
Conversation b: picture c
Conversation c: picture b
Conversation d: picture a

3 [T14.6] Give students a few minutes to read the sentences. See if they can predict any of the answers before they listen. Play the recording again, stopping after each conversation for students to write their answers. Students then compare answers in pairs before checking with the whole class.

ANSWERS

a The person wants to change **$200** into pesos. The exchange rate is **3.3 pesos** to the dollar. She receives **627 pesos.**
b The woman would like to buy some earrings. The larger ones cost **£20**, and the smaller ones cost **£12.**
c In order to open a bank account, the man needs to bring his **passport** and a **letter** from his **employer or place of study.**
d To drink, the two young women had one **mineral water** and a **fresh orange juice.** They also ordered a club sandwich and a **prawn salad.** This all cost **£11.50**, and they decided to leave **£1** as a tip.

4 **a** Go through the example with the class. Point out that in each case, students have to cross out a word. Emphasise that they don't have to change any of the words. Students work individually before checking their answers in pairs.

b [T14.7] Play the recording. Students listen and check their answers.

ANSWERS

2 of 3 cost 4 one 5 my 6 kind 7 to 8 it 9 to

Pronunciation

See *Teacher's tips: helping students with pronunciation* on pages 6–7.

[T14.7] Play the recording again, stopping after each sentence for students to repeat. Make sure that their intonation sounds polite.

5 **a** Students work individually for a few minutes, underlining useful phrases to do with money. Check answers with the whole class.

b Put students into pairs and give them time to invent three situations (one or two if you are short of time).

ADDITIONAL PRACTICE

RB **Resource bank:** 14A Get rich quick! (Vocabulary: money), pages 165–166; 14B Dealing with money (Vocabulary: banking and money), page 167; Learner-training worksheet J (Using the mini-dictionary to find dependent prepositions), page 168

Study … (PAGE 131)

Test dos and don'ts

Before students read about the different ways of approaching English tests, brainstorm ideas as a class. Then give students a few minutes individually to read the texts to see if any of their ideas are mentioned, and what additional techniques are suggested. Students work in small groups to discuss the advantages and disadvantages of each.

Pronunciation spot

Review

See *Teacher's tips: helping students with pronunciation* on pages 6–7.

1 Give students a few minutes individually to think about how many of the symbols they can remember. Then put students into pairs to decide which words contain which sounds.

2 [T14.8] Play the recording straight through for students to check their answers. Replay the recording, or model the words yourself, pausing after each word for students to repeat.

ANSWERS
a /wɒlɪt/ wallet
b /envələʊp/ envelope
c /θaʊzənd/ thousand
d /ðem/ them
e /nəʊt/ /tɪn/ /θaʊzənd/ note, tin, thousand
f /rɪŋ/ ring
g /sel/ sell
h /kæʃ/ cash
i /bæŋk/ /kæʃ/ bank, cash
j /mʌni:/ money
k /eɪt/ eight
l /faɪn/ fine
m /envələʊp/ /nəʊt/ envelope, note
n /hɒrɪbəl/ /ɒfɪs/ horrible, office
o /hɒrɪbəl/ horrible

Practise ... (PAGE 131)

1 Past simple and Past perfect

Students work individually or in pairs before checking answers as a class.

ANSWERS
a got, stopped b was; had enjoyed c was; had lost
d had been; went

2 Past time words: *already*, *just* and *never ... before*

Write the four sentences on the board. Students work in small groups to discuss where each time word should go in the sentences. Check answers with the whole class.

ANSWERS
a Our friends had **already** left when we arrived at the party.
b Laura had never eaten Thai food **before**.
c He had **just** left the bank when the alarm bell rang.
d She had **already** been married for ten years when she met him.

3 Money

Do this as a race. Students work in pairs. The winner is the first pair to answer each question correctly.

ANSWERS
1 bank notes; change; coins; foreign currency
2 borrow, earn, win
3 a fine; salary; a tip

4 *make*

Students work in pairs before checking answers as a whole class.

ANSWERS
a to laugh b the washing-up c lie
d a bank account e to cry

5 Dealing with money

Give the sentences to students cut up on card. Students work in pairs to order the sentences.

ANSWERS
a Do you think we should leave a tip?
b I'd like to change this into euros, please.
c Can we have the bill, please?
d What's the exchange rate for euros?

Remember! (PAGE 131)

After looking back at the areas they have practised, students do the *Mini-check* on page 161 of the *Students' Book*. Check answers with the whole class, and ask students to tell you their scores out of 20.

ANSWERS
1 win 2 money 3 can't 4 waste 5 fine
6 exchange 7 to change 8 have 9 closed
10 cry 11 'll take
12 How much **does** this pair of shorts cost?
13 felt very annoyed because I **had** just lost all my money.
14 When we arrived at the stadium, the match had **already** started.
15 I was very surprised that I had **never** met him before.
16 on 17 from 18 up 19 to 20 by

module 15

Imagine ...

Reading (PAGES 132–133)

1 Give students a few minutes to think about their favourite song. Then put them into small groups to discuss their answers to the questions. Have some brief class feedback.

2 Focus students' attention on the photos and elicit any information you can from the students about John Lennon and The Beatles. Put students into pairs to discuss the statements. Even if they know very little about John Lennon, they should be able to make educated guesses by looking at the photos and asking their colleagues.

3 Students read the text quickly to check their ideas. Set a time limit of four minutes for this to ensure that students read quickly.

ANSWERS
a False (he was born in Liverpool, England)
b True c True
d False (he wrote it after The Beatles had broken up, when he was a solo artist)
e True
f False (he was shot in New York, outside his home)
g True h True

4 Give students a couple of minutes to read the answers. Demonstrate the activity using the example. Students work individually to reread the text and to write the questions. They compare answers in pairs and then as a class.

ANSWERS
b When did John Lennon meet Paul McCartney? When were The Beatles formed?
c Where did John Lennon write the lyrics to *Imagine*?
d Where was John Lennon shot?
e Where is the special memorial to John Lennon?
f Which song was voted favourite song of the millennium?
g How much did George Michael pay for the Steinway piano John Lennon used when he was writing *Imagine*?
h In the musical *Imagine*, how many different actors played the part of John Lennon?

ADDITIONAL PRACTICE

Workbook: Vocabulary booster: people in politics, religion and public life, exercise 7, page 92

Song (PAGE 133)

Imagine

1 Start by briefly discussing the song *Imagine*. Do students know it, or what it's about? Do any of them have it on CD/tape? Do they like it? Then put students into pairs to decide if the pairs of words have the same meaning or not, looking up any unfamiliar ones in their mini-dictionaries. Go through the answers with the class. Ask students to explain whether the meanings are the same, slightly different or very different.

ANSWERS
All the meanings are different apart from those in c (*it's easy / it isn't hard*).

Song, exercise 1: additional suggestion

Pre-teach the words which are likely to be unfamiliar to your students (*to wonder, greed, to share*) by devising an activity where they match the words to definitions. They then check the answers in their mini-dictionaries. This will mean students have more opportunity for discussion of the different meanings while they are doing exercise 1.

2 [T15.1] Start by giving students a few minutes to look at the song and to predict which words from exercise 1 go in the gaps. (Note that these are not the only words that go in the gaps.) Students then compare their ideas in pairs before listening to the song. Play the song a second time if necessary, or if students want to sing along!

ANSWERS
1 heaven 2 It's easy 3 below us 4 Above us
5 countries 6 It isn't hard 7 die 8 in peace
9 dreamer 10 join 11 possessions 12 wonder
13 greed 14 hunger 15 Sharing 16 dreamer
17 join

3 **a** Remind students that they have found out information about John Lennon both from the song and from the text on pages 132–133. Direct them to the words in the box, and ask them if John Lennon thought that *living in peace* was good. Then put students into pairs or small groups to discuss their ideas about the other things in the box.

ANSWERS

brotherhood ✔	countries ✘
dreamers ✔	greed ✘
heaven ✘	hell ✘
hunger ✘	living for today ✔
living in peace ✔	possessions ✘

b *Either*: discuss the ideas as a class, if you feel you will need to guide the discussion and to help students express their ideas about these issues. *Or*: put students into small groups.

Language focus 1 (PAGE 134)

Conditional sentences with *would*

Point out that the beginnings of the four sentences are ideas expressed in *Imagine*. Give students a few minutes to underline the endings they agree with. They can underline both endings, or neither of the endings if they don't agree with them. Put students into pairs to compare and justify their answers.

Grammar

Refer students to the example sentence and give them time, individually or in pairs, to consider questions a–d. As you check the answers, elicit the negative and question forms of *would*, and write a complete table of positive, negative and question forms on the board. Highlight the following points.

- The conditional with *would* is used to talk about imaginary situations (John Lennon's ideas were seen as dreams).
- The verb after *If* is in the past, even though the sentence refers to the present / a general time. (If students have a subjunctive in their own language, they could compare it to the past form here.)
- *Were* can be used instead of *was* in the first and third person, for example, *If I were president / If she were president*. However, many speakers prefer to use *was*.
- The sentence, which begins with the *if* clause in the example, can also begin with the main clause.

Refer students to *Language summary A* on page 156 of the *Students' Book* for more information.

ANSWERS
a The sentence refers to an imaginary situation.
b In the *if* clause, the verb form is the Past simple.
c In the main clause, the verb form is *would* + infinitive without *to*.
d The sentence refers to no specific time.

***Grammar*: additional suggestion**

Elicit the contracted forms of *would*. Then get students to practise saying the contractions by prompting them with different pronouns, for example:

S: *I'd enjoy life more* T: *we* S: *We'd enjoy life more.*

PRACTICE

1 Students work individually before checking answers with the whole class.

ANSWERS
a were, wouldn't b wouldn't; didn't have
c didn't, wouldn't d would speak; weren't
e were; would need f didn't; wouldn't be
g would be; couldn't h didn't, would

2 **a** Ask students to imagine that they are the president or prime minister of their country, and that they could therefore do things to make it a better place. Direct them to the sentences and ask if they agree with the ideas.

b Put students into pairs. Give each pair a blank piece of paper, and allow a minute or two for them to choose an idea to begin their 'chain' with. Get each pair to write their first sentence, and also their names, on the paper.

c Arrange for each pair to exchange their piece of paper with another pair. Students continue the 'chain' with one more sentence before passing the paper to a different pair. Circulate and, if necessary, provide help with vocabulary. After students have exchanged papers five times, arrange for the papers to be passed to the original pairs (their names should be on the papers). As a class, discuss how the 'chains' have ended up. Have some brief feedback on any problems with form that you noticed.

ADDITIONAL PRACTICE

Workbook: Conditional sentences with *would*, exercises 1–4, pages 90–91

Language focus 2 (PAGE 135)

will and *would*

1 Use the picture to introduce the idea of space travel. Students discuss the questions in pairs. Have some brief class feedback on any interesting ideas.

2 Students read the text and discuss the questions in pairs. Find out which students would volunteer and which would not. Have a brief class discussion about some of the possible advantages and disadvantages.

3 [T15.2] Explain that students will hear three people answering the same question. Play the recording, pausing after each extract to allow students time to write. Students check answers in pairs and then as a whole class.

ANSWERS
See tapescript for recording 2 on page 174 of the *Students' Book*.

Grammar

Students could answer questions a–d individually or in pairs before checking with the class, since the use of *will* and *would* in conditional sentences has already been covered. (See Module 9 for coverage of conditional sentences with *will*.) As you check the answers, elicit the negative and question forms of *will* and *would*, and highlight the following points.

- *If* + present..., *will* (*won't*) + infinitive without *to* is used to talk about a real possibility in the future.
- *If* + past..., *would* (*wouldn't*) + infinitive without *to* is used to talk about an imaginary situation, and therefore refers to the present / a general time.
- The *if* clause and the main clause can be reversed in both sentences.

Refer students to *Language summary B* on page 156 of the *Students' Book* for more information.

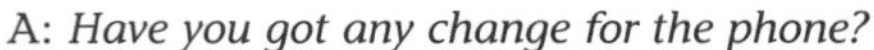

ANSWERS

a **Something that might really happen:** *If we continue to pollute the earth, humanity won't survive.*
b **An imaginary situation:** *If I got the chance, I'd go and live on Saturn.*
c *If I got the chance, ...*
Verb form: *If* + Past simple
If we continue to pollute the earth, ...
Verb form: *If* + Present simple
d *... I'd go and live on Saturn.*
Verb form: *would* + infinitive without *to*
... humanity won't survive.
Verb form: *won't* + infinitive without *to*

PRACTICE

Focus students on the first sentence and elicit one or two possible endings. Point out that this is a real possibility, so *will* (*won't*) is needed in the main clause. Words to check: *change places with a celebrity*; *invisible*. Give students a few minutes to complete the sentences, then put them into pairs to compare answers.

Note: you may wish to do the *Pronunciation* box before the *Practice* activity.

Practice: additional suggestion

If you have a strong class: students could practise asking the appropriate question form, for example, *What would you do if you were invisible?* Their partners then respond with the main clause: *I'd ...*

Pronunciation

See *Teacher's tips: helping students with pronunciation* on pages 6–7.

1 [T15.3] Play the recording or model the sentences yourself at natural speed, pausing after each one to allow students time to write. Students may have trouble hearing the contracted forms, and it may be necessary to play the recording more than once.
2 [T15.3] Refer students to the tapescript to check their answers. Replay the recording, pausing after each sentence for students to repeat.

ANSWERS

See tapescript for recording 3 on page 174 of the *Students' Book*.

Pronunciation: additional suggestion

Put students into pairs, A and B. Ask them to choose four of the sentences to put into conversations, each having two or three lines. Give students a few minutes to prepare the conversations. They then act them out for the class, for example:

A: *Have you got any change for the phone?*
B: *I'll have a look. Yes, here you are!*
A: *Thanks.*
Other students could guess who/where the speakers are.

ADDITIONAL PRACTICE

RB **Resource bank:** 15A Conditional squares (Unreal and real conditionals), page 169, 15B Preposition pelmanism (Revision of prepositions), page 170

Workbook: *will* and *would*, exercises 5–6, page 91

Task: Choose people to start a space colony (PAGES 136–137)

See *Teacher's tips: making tasks work* on pages 10–11 and *Responding to learners' individual language needs* on pages 12–13.

Preparation: reading

1 Use the picture to establish the context of space and space travel. Ask students whether they would like to travel in space, visit another planet, start a space colony, etc. Word to check: *survive*. Then put students into pairs or small groups to discuss what they would need and who they would take with them. Get one or two students to report back to the class.

2 Introduce the idea of a new planet, and give students a few minutes to read the text and to answer questions a–h. Words to check: *spaceship*, *volunteer*. Students compare answers in pairs before checking with the whole class.

ANSWERS

a Because it has water, light and oxygen, and its temperature and air are similar to those on Earth.
b They are not sure, but they haven't found any.
c six people; to start a space colony and a new human society
d never
e not for 100 years or more
f enough food tablets for five years; four guns; blankets; space-tents
g about ten weeks
h ten

3 Elicit one or two ideas about why someone would be suitable/unsuitable, for example, their age, job, experience. Words to check: *divorced* /dɪvɔːst/, *retired* /rɪtaɪəd/, *pregnant* /pregnənt/, *widower* /wɪdəʊə/, *health* /helθ/, *cancer* /kænsə/, *engineer* /endʒɪnɪə/, *agricultural scientist* /ægrɪkʌltʃərəl saɪəntɪst/. Give students plenty of time to read about the candidates and to think carefully about their suitability for the project. Each student chooses six people, and must be ready to explain their choices.

Task: speaking

1 Put students into pairs and ask them to tell each other about their choices before agreeing on a list of the six best candidates. Emphasise that they should make notes on why they have chosen each one, and tell them to be ready to justify their choices to other students. Direct them to *Useful language a*. Circulate and, if necessary, help with vocabulary. As you monitor this exercise and the next, note down examples of good language use and/or errors to focus on later.

2 Put pairs together into groups of four or six, or bring the whole class together to discuss answers and to try to agree on a final list of six people. Direct students to *Useful language a* and *b* for help.

3 Ask a student from each group to report back to the rest of the class.

4 Students discuss the questions as a class or in small groups.

Task: speaking, exercise 4: additional suggestion

Students might also discuss these questions: *What problems might the people have on the journey / on Hero? What would you do if any of these problems happened to you?*

***Task*: alternative suggestions**

a *If you have short lessons*: do *Preparation: reading*, exercises 1 and 2, in one lesson. Then ask students to do exercise 3 for homework. Do *Task: speaking* in the second lesson.

b *If your students enjoy roleplaying*: put them into pairs and, instead of *Task: speaking*, exercises 2–4, ask them to roleplay one of the following situations.

- An interview with one of the chosen volunteers, just before they leave. How are they feeling? Why did they volunteer? What are they hoping/expecting the journey and the planet to be like?
- An interview with a scientist from the control station, following reports of some problems with the mission. What exactly are the problems? Have any of the volunteers been hurt? What are they doing to solve the problems?

Optional writing

Prepare students for this activity by eliciting language under the five headings, as illustrated below.

- **The planet:** *There are lots of beautiful/strange plants/birds/animals/insects. There are (lots of / no) rivers/streams/lakes/forests/mountains. It's (very) warm/cool/quiet/peaceful/isolated/frightening.*
- **The journey there:** *We were excited/worried/bored during the journey. I slept a lot / couldn't sleep. We had some problems with the engines / the fuel supply and we had to … We arrived at night / in the morning.*
- **The other people you are with and what you think of them:** *X seems (very) friendly/shy/bossy/clever/ worried/funny. Y can … / is good at … -ing. I like / don't like Z because …*
- **How you feel at the moment:** *I feel quite/very/really … tired/depressed/anxious/happy because … I hope/want to … I'm glad that …*
- **What you want to say to your friends and family back on Earth:** *I miss you. I wish you were here. This is the best thing I've ever done. If I were you, I'd volunteer for the next trip.*

Also elicit some suggestions of how to start the letter, for example, *Dear … Well, here I am on the planet Hero! We've been here for … days now, and …*

Then ask students to imagine they are one of the volunteers and to plan what to put in the letter. They then swap plans with another student and comment on each other's ideas before writing the letter.

Consolidation modules 11–15 (PAGES 138–139)

A Present perfect simple and Present perfect continuous, Past simple and Past perfect

Draw students' attention to the headline and ask them to guess what has happened to the man. Encourage students to read the text through once without writing anything, to see if their predictions are correct. Then give students five minutes to underline the correct forms. Students check their answers in pairs before checking with the whole class.

ANSWERS
1 failed 2 has been trying 3 hasn't had 4 took
5 failed 6 had been 7 had previously said
8 passed 9 agreed 10 hadn't passed
11 had become 12 decided 13 has been studying
14 has become 15 has stayed

B Vocabulary: Connections

Set this up as a competition, demonstrating the activity with one or two examples. Students work in small groups and take turns to find connections. The winner is the student who continues to find valid connections after the others have run out of ideas. The other students must agree that a connection is valid. Have some brief class feedback on interesting connections.

Note: there are too many possible combinations to suggest answers here. Each group is responsible for deciding if a connection is convincing. Negotiating this is good practice!

C Speaking: Real life

Give students ten minutes to choose one of the situations and to write a six- or eight-line dialogue to perform for the rest of the class. *If you have time*: ask students to create dialogues for each situation.

D Passives

Before students read the text, ask them to guess the answers to the following questions (answers in brackets).

- In which country is the most ice cream eaten? (Australia)
- Where and when was ice cream first made? (China, 4,000 years ago)
- Where was the first ice cream cone made? (USA)
- Which is the most popular flavour? (vanilla)
- On which day of the week is the most ice cream sold? (Sunday)

Students read the text quickly to see if their answers are correct and to familiarise themselves with the text. Then students work in pairs to complete the text before checking answers with the whole class.

ANSWERS
1 is spent 2 is eaten 3 was eaten 4 was made
5 was brought 6 was served 7 was made
8 was given 9 is produced 10 is/are grown
11 is sold

E Speaking and listening

1 Demonstrate the activity by discussing possible answers to the questions for sentence a. Students work in pairs to answer the questions. Emphasise that there is no right or wrong answer at this stage.

2 Give students five minutes to choose one of the sentences and to devise a four- or five-line conversation to perform for the rest of the class. The other students guess who the speakers are, where they are and what the situation is.

3 [C1] Students listen to the conversations and compare them to their own.

ANSWERS
See tapescript for recording 1 on page 174 of the *Students' Book*.

Resource bank

Index of activities

Activity	Language point	When to use	Time (minutes)
1A Get to know the *Students' Book*	None	first day of the course	20–30
Learner-training worksheet A	Using the *mini-dictionary*: introduction	early in the course	20–30
1B Me too!	Present simple and question words	after *Practice*, exercise 2, page 9	15–25
1C Connected lives	Present simple questions with *How often ...?* and adverbs of frequency	after *Practice*, exercise 2, page 12	20–30
Learner-training worksheet B	Using the *mini-dictionary*: irregular verbs – part 1	after *Practice*, exercise 4, page 17	15–25
2A Dead famous	Past simple *yes/no* questions and short answers	after *Practice*, exercise 4, page 17	15–25
2B The millionaire's ball	Past simple and time phrases	after *Practice*, exercise 2, page 18	20–30
2C Invent a story	Past simple and linkers	after *Writing*, exercise 2, page 22	20–45
Learner-training worksheet C	Noticing and recording collocations	after *Vocabulary*, exercise 3, page 24	15–25
3A The secret of successful language learning	Vocabulary extension (word building)	after *Practice*, exercise 2, page 26	20–30
3B Parents and children	*can, can't, have to, don't have to, should, shouldn't*	after *Pronunciation* box, page 27	15–25
4A Party guests	Present continuous and Present simple	after *Practice*, exercise 3, page 35	20–30
4B I'm having lunch with Madonna	Present continuous for future arrangements	after *Practice*, exercise 2, page 37	30–40
5A Put these in order	Comparatives and superlatives	after *Pronunciation* box, page 45	20–30
5B An alien family	Vocabulary: describing people's appearance	after *Practice*, exercise 4, page 47	15–25
Learner-training worksheet D	Recording new vocabulary	after *Consolidation modules* 1–5	20–30
6A Talk about the future	*going to, would like to, would rather, will/won't*	after *Pronunciation* box, page 53	20–30
6B Holiday crossword	Holiday vocabulary	after *Listening and speaking*, exercise 5, page 55	20–30
7A Ambition dominoes	Verb/noun collocations	after *Vocabulary and speaking*, exercise 3, page 62	15–25
7B Life circles	Present perfect and Past simple	after *Practice*, exercise 3, page 64	20–30
7C Happy verb families	Irregular past tenses and past participles	after *Practice*, exercise 3, page 64	15–35
Learner-training worksheet E	Using the *mini-dictionary*: irregular verbs – part 2	after *Practice*, exercise 3, page 64	15–25

Activity	Language point	When to use	Time (minutes)
8A Article snakes and ladders	Use and non-use of articles	after *Practice*, exercise 4, page 71	25–40
8B The Hungry Hippo café	Quantifiers (*some*, *any*, *much*, *not enough*, etc.)	after *Practice*, exercise 2, page 73	25–35
8C Where's the nearest bank?	Language for giving directions	after *Writing*, exercise 3, page 78	20–30
Learner-training worksheet F	Noticing and remembering prepositions and articles in phrases	any time after the end of Module 8	20–35
9A In the 2020s	*will*, *won't*, *may* and *might* for future possibility	after *Practice*, exercise 2, page 82	25–40
9B Worried parents	Present tense after *if*, *when*, *as soon as* and other time words	after *Practice*, exercise 3, page 84	20–30
Learner-training worksheet G	Deducing meaning from context – part 1	after *Study* ..., exercise 2, page 86	20–30
10A What can I do for you?	Vocabulary: health problems	after *Listening and speaking*, exercise 3, page 89	15–25
10B The Ghost	*used to* and Past simple	after *Practice*, exercise 2, page 91	20–30
10C Bob's night out	Past continuous and Past simple	after *Practice*, exercise 4, page 93	25–45
11A The Lovebug Dating Agency	Gerunds; expressions for liking and disliking	after *Practice*, exercise 3, page 100	25–40
Learner-training worksheet H	Using the *mini-dictionary* to find constructions that follow verbs	after *Pronunciation* box, page 102	20–30
12A What's this?	Describing everyday objects	after *Vocabulary*, exercise 3, page 106	15–25
12B The Handbag Gang	Past simple passive	after *Practice*, exercise 2, page 109	24–45
13A Century People	Present perfect simple and continuous for unfinished past	after *Practice*, exercise 2, page 119	20–30
13B Old friends	Present perfect simple and continuous (for unfinished past)	after *Practice*, exercise 2, page 119	20–35
Learner-training worksheet I	Deducing meaning from context – part 2	any time towards the end of the course	25–35
14A Get rich quick!	Vocabulary: money	after *Real life*, exercise 5, page 130	25–35
14B Dealing with money	Vocabulary: banking and money	after *Real life*, exercise 5, page 130	15–25
Learner-training worksheet J	Using the *mini-dictionary* to find dependent prepositions	any time towards the end of the course	15–25
15A Conditional squares	Unreal and real conditionals	after *Pronunciation* box, page 135	20–30
15B Preposition pelmanism	Revision of prepositions	any time towards the end of the course	15–30

Instructions

1A Get to know the *Students' Book*

***You will need:** one set of cards for each pair of students*

- Shuffle each set of cards. Put students into pairs. Place the sets of cards **face down** in piles at the front of the class and allocate one set of cards to each pair.
- One student from each pair comes up to the front of the class, takes **one** card only from the top of their pile and goes back to their partner. Then they write the answer to the question **on their card**.
- When a pair has completed a card, they take it to the teacher to check their answer (see *Resource bank key*). If the answer is correct, they keep the card and take the next card from their pile at the front of the class. If the answer is not correct, they must work out the correct answer.
- The first pair to finish all the cards are the winners.

If it is not possible for students to move around the class freely, follow the following procedure.

- Put students into pairs and give each pair a set of cards **face down** in a pile. Students turn over the cards one by one and write the answers on the cards.
- When a pair has finished, they hand their pile of cards to the teacher for checking.
- The first pair to finish all the cards correctly are the winners.

Learner-training worksheet A
(Using the *mini-dictionary*: introduction)

***You will need:** one copy of the worksheet per student*

The *mini-dictionary* helps students make the transition from bilingual to monolingual dictionaries (see *Teacher's tips: making the most of the* mini-dictionary on pages 9–10 for more details). This worksheet gives students an overview of the type of information contained in the *mini-dictionary*. Before starting the worksheet, check students understand that the *mini-dictionary* only contains words and meanings used in the *Students' Book*.

1. Students do a on their own, then discuss b in pairs. The aim is to show students that they don't always have to understand the definition to grasp the meaning – sometimes the example can be more useful.
2. Students work individually before checking answers with the whole class (see *Resource bank key*).
3. Emphasise that students should do this exercise **without** using the *mini-dictionary*. Ask them to work individually or in pairs before checking answers with the whole class (see *Resource bank key*). In feedback, make sure that students understand the grammar terms and how nouns and verbs are marked in the *mini-dictionary* (noun [C], noun [U], verb [T], verb [I]).
4. Students work individually, then check answers in pairs or with the whole class (see *Resource bank key*).
5. Check that students understand what word stress is, and how it is marked in the *mini-dictionary,* before they do the exercise individually or in pairs. Check answers with the whole class (see *Resource bank key*).
6. Students work individually before checking answers with the whole class.

1B Me too!

***You will need:** one copy of the worksheet per student*

- Words to check: *cousin*, *thriller*, *comedy*, *horror film*. Give each student a copy of the worksheet. Students work individually and make sentences about themselves in the first column on the worksheet.
- Students then work in pairs and, on a separate piece of paper, write down the **questions** that correspond to the sentences on their worksheet. Students must write questions for *you* in the Present simple, and each one must begin with a question word (*Who*, *Which*, *How often*, etc.). For example, for the first sentence on the worksheet, students should write: *What time / When do you usually get up on Sundays?* Do the first two as examples with the whole class before they start.
- Students then move around the room asking the questions. When they find someone who has the same answer as them, they say *Me too!* and write the other student's name in the second column on the worksheet. **Students cannot look at each other's worksheets.** Encourage them to talk to as many different people as possible and to ask follow-up questions where appropriate.
- Students discuss their findings in small groups or with the whole class.

1C Connected lives

***You will need:** one copy of the* Student A worksheet *and one copy of the* Student B worksheet *for each pair of students*

- Divide the class into two groups, A and B. Give a copy of *Student A worksheet* to students in group A, and a copy of *Student B worksheet* to those in group B. Tell students that the other group has the information that is missing from their worksheets.
- Students work individually, or with someone in their group, and decide what questions they need to ask to complete the worksheet. They must use the Present simple in their questions, either with *How often ...?* or with another question word plus an adverb of frequency. Do the first question on each worksheet with the whole class as examples before they start: (1) *How often does Lola sing at the* Flamingo Club? (a) *When / What time does Lola usually finish work?*
- Put students in pairs, so that one Student A and one Student B are working together. Students then ask each other the questions and complete their own worksheets.
- When they have finished, students discuss in pairs how

many connections they can find between the six people before sharing their answers with the whole class.

Learner-training worksheet B
(Using the *mini-dictionary*: irregular verbs – part 1)

***You will need:** one copy of the worksheet per student*

This worksheet helps students to find the infinitive of irregular past tenses in the *mini-dictionary*, and introduces some new irregular verbs that appear later in the *Students' Book*.

1 Students do the exercise individually or in pairs. Check answers with the whole class.
2 Check that students understand how irregular verbs are written in the *mini-dictionary*.
3 Students do the exercise in pairs. Check answers with the whole class. Make sure that students understand the meaning of any new verbs, and know how to pronounce the past tenses.
4 Students work individually. Check answers with the whole class (see *Resource bank key*).

2A Dead famous

***You will need:** one set of cards per three or four students*

- Put students into groups of three or four. Give each group one set of cards **face down**, and ask them to divide them equally among themselves. Allow time for students to read the information on their cards. **They are not allowed to look at each other's cards.**
- Write the following question prompts on the board or on a separate handout. If necessary, check that students can make questions in the Past simple from these prompts by doing an example with the whole class.
  born in America/Europe? nationality?
  live in twentieth/nineteenth century? live in Europe/Asia? married? wife/husband famous too?
  die young? write something? discover something?
  actor / politician / film star / singer? rich/poor?
  play a musical instrument? clever/talented/beautiful?
- Student A chooses one of their cards, and the other students have to find out who the famous person on the card is by asking questions, either based on the prompts on the board or their own ideas. However, they are only allowed to ask questions which require **a *yes/no* answer**. They can ask a maximum of fifteen questions.
- If they haven't guessed after ten questions, Student A reads out the clue at the bottom of the card. If the other students don't discover the person's identity after fifteen questions, Student A can reveal their identity.
- Students take it in turns to be asked questions about a famous person until all the cards are finished.

2B The millionaire's ball

***You will need:** one copy of the worksheet and one role card per student*

- Give each student a copy of the worksheet. Tell them that the line at the beginning of each sentence corresponds to a person's name.
- Students work individually and complete the time phrases by writing *in*, *on*, *at*, *ago*, on the dotted lines. Check answers with the whole class (see *Resource bank key*).
- Words to check: *to leave someone money in a will*; *to play cards/poker*; *caviar*.
- Tell students they are going to a party where everyone is very rich! Revise the following 'getting to know you' questions: *What's your name? Where do you live? What do you do? Are you married? Have you got any children?*
- Give each student a Role card in random order, and allow time for them to read and understand the information. **They must not look at one another's cards.** (If you have more than ten students, the cards can be duplicated without affecting the outcome of the activity.)
- Tell students that they must talk to all the other guests at the party and write their names in the correct place on the worksheet. Students mingle and have short conversations with one another. Encourage them to introduce themselves and use the 'getting to know you' questions to start the conversation, rather than just asking the questions required to complete the worksheet.
- Students check answers in pairs or with the whole class.

2C Invent a story

***You will need:** one copy of the worksheet per student*

- Put students into pairs or small groups. Give each student a copy of the worksheet and tell them that they are going to invent a story. Students must include **at least four** of the items or people at the top of the worksheet in their story. Words to check: *parcel*, *false*.
- The questions on the worksheet provide a framework for the story. Students discuss each question in turn and write their ideas in the appropriate box. Encourage them to write **notes** rather than complete sentences.
- When they have made notes for all the questions, students write their story in their pairs or groups. Encourage them to use the linking words from page 22 of the *Students' Book* (*and*, *because*, *but*, *so* and *then)* when writing their story. Alternatively, the story can be written for homework.
- Students can put their stories up round the classroom and vote on which they like the most.

Learner-training worksheet C
(Noticing and recording collocations)

***You will need:** one copy of the worksheet per student*

The aim of this worksheet is to raise students' awareness of collocation, and to provide them with some useful ways of recording collocations when they come across them in class.

1 Go through the example with the whole class.
2 Students work individually, then check answers with the whole class (see *Resource bank key*).
3 Students work individually or in pairs, checking any answers they are not sure of in the *mini-dictionary*.

Check answers with the whole class (see *Resource bank key*). All the collocations are taken from Modules 1–4 in the *Students' Book*.

4 Go through the examples of how to record collocations with the whole class. Students discuss the questions at the end in pairs or groups.

3A The secret of successful language learning

You will need: *one copy of the worksheet per student; a set of monolingual dictionaries (not the* mini-dictionary*)*

1–5 Give each student a copy of the worksheet. Students work through the exercises individually or in pairs before checking answers with the whole class (see *Resource bank key*).

3B Parents and children

You will need: *one copy of the worksheet per student*

- Words to check: *to dye your hair*; *make-up*; *to do housework*.
- Put students into pairs. If possible, pair one male student with one female student. Give each student a copy of the worksheet and tell them to write their partner's name at the top of the second column.
- Explain that students have to give their opinion on ten statements about parents and children. They also have to guess their partner's opinion. Draw students' attention to the scale at the top of the worksheet.
- Students work individually and circle numbers in both columns. They are not allowed to ask their partner anything at this stage.
- Students compare their answers in pairs and see how many of their predictions are correct. Encourage students to justify their opinions, particularly when they don't agree with each other.
- Students tell the whole class how many of their predictions were correct and discuss any differences of opinion they had.

4A Party guests

You will need: *one role card per student; one copy of* Student A worksheet *or* Student B worksheet *per student*

- Tell students that they are at a party where they don't know anyone. Elicit appropriate questions you could ask a stranger at a party and write them on the board. (Useful ones for the activity are: *Where do you live? Do you live near here? What do you do? What do you do in your spare time? Are you enjoying the party?*)
- Give each student a *Role card*, and allow time for them to read and understand the information. **They are not allowed to look at each other's role cards**. (The activity will work with any number of students, but a minimum of eight is preferable. If there are more than twelve students, distribute duplicate *Role cards*.)
- Give half the class *Student A worksheet* and the other half *Student B worksheet*. Students must find out who the people on their worksheet are by asking questions in the Present simple and Present continuous based on the information provided. **All four pieces of information about each person must match before the student writes down the name.**
- Students move around the room having short conversations and asking one another questions. When they have found someone who **completely** matches the description, they write their name in the appropriate place on their worksheet. The activity continues until students have found out who everyone is.
- Students can compare their answers in pairs/groups or with the whole class.

4B I'm having lunch with Madonna

You will need: *one diary per student*

- Check that students know the following language in **bold** for talking about and making arrangements:
  What are you doing on *Monday (afternoon)?*
  I'm *having lunch with my sister. /* ***Nothing special.***
  Would you like to *go out for a drink? /* ***Let's*** *have lunch. /* ***How about*** *meeting for a coffee?*
  Yes, I'd love to*. /* ***Yes, why not?*** */* ***I'd rather not, thanks***.
- Brainstorm with the class the types of activities that people arrange together, and write them on the board. Include the following: *have lunch/dinner*; *go to the cinema / the theatre / a concert / a football match*; *go shopping*; *go/come to a party*; *come round for a meal*; *go out for a drink*; *meet for a coffee*.
- Give each student one of the diaries and tell them that it contains their arrangements for next week. (If you have more than eight students, use extra copies of the diaries.) Allow time for students to read the information.
- Tell students that they have to make **at least six** new arrangements with their classmates (using the language and ideas previously highlighted) and to write them in their diaries. These arrangements can be made **at any time of the day**. Students move around the room making arrangements. When two students have made an arrangement with each other, they must both write it in the appropriate place in their diaries.
- Remind students to express their arrangements in full sentences using the Present continuous, and not just to read out the notes in their diaries.
- If you have more than eight students, tell them to check they have **different** diaries before they start talking. If they have the same diary, they must find a different student.
- When they have finished, students work in pairs or small groups and tell each other about all the arrangements they have made.

5A Put these in order

You will need: *one copy of the worksheet per student*

- Words to check: *assassination*; *to release somebody from prison*; *recent*.

- Divide the class into teams of three or four. Give each student a copy of the worksheet. Do the example at the top of the page with the whole class.
- Set a time limit of ten or fifteen minutes, and allow students to do the quiz in their teams. They should discuss the answers together and come to a consensus as a team. Encourage students to use comparatives and superlatives while they are deciding on the correct order. For example, *Do you think that Sharon Stone is older than Brad Pitt? / I'm sure Robert De Niro is the oldest.*
- Check answers with the whole class (see *Resource bank key*). Students get one point for each item they have in the correct place. They also get a bonus point if they get all four items correct (a completely correct answer is therefore worth five points). The team with the most points is the winner.
- Students can go through the quiz again in their groups and explain what they got wrong and why, using more comparatives and superlatives: *We thought that the Eiffel Tower was older than the Taj Mahal, but it isn't.*

5B An alien family

***You will need:** one copy of* Picture A *and one copy of* Picture B *for each pair of students*

- Put students into pairs and give one student a copy of *Picture A* and the other a copy of *Picture B*. Tell students that all the aliens in the picture are members of the same family. **Students are not allowed to look at each other's pictures**.
- Students work in pairs. Student A describes one of the aliens in their picture that **hasn't** got a name. They must describe the alien's appearance (using the language on pages 46–47 of the *Students' Book*), **not** where the alien is in the picture.
- When Student A has finished the description, Student B tells them the name of the alien, which Student A then writes in the correct space on the picture. If Student B is unsure which alien is being described, they should ask questions about the alien's appearance to clarify any doubts.
- Students take it in turns until all the aliens are identified. When they have finished, students may look at each other's pictures and check their answers.
- Finally, each pair of students decides how all the aliens are related, giving reasons for their choices. Their ideas can be discussed with the whole class.

Learner-training worksheet D
(Recording new vocabulary)

***You will need**: one copy of the worksheet per student*

When recording new vocabulary, students often make lists of new English words next to translations in their own language. The aim of this worksheet is to encourage students to include more information in their lists, therefore making them more useful.

1 Students work in pairs or small groups and make notes on what extra information is included in List B. Check answers with the whole class. (List B includes the following **extra information**: part of speech (including putting *to* in front of a verb and *a/an* in front of a countable noun); word stress; regular/irregular verbs; dependent prepositions; transitive and intransitive verbs (by writing *someone* or *something* after the verb); countable/uncountable nouns; common collocations and examples; common errors in student's own language; phonemic script.)

2 Students rewrite the list in pairs or small groups. Encourage them to use the *mini-dictionary* to add more information. Check answers with the whole class (see *Resource bank key*).

3 Students work on their own before comparing their ideas in groups. Alternatively, this exercise can be set for homework.

6A Talk about the future

***You will need:** one copy of the board per three or four students; one dice and three/four counters per group*

- Put students into groups of three or four. Give each group a board, counters and dice. If one student has a watch with a second hand, make them the timekeeper.
- Students take it in turns to throw a number. When they land on a future square, they have to talk about the topic or question for twenty seconds without stopping. With a less confident class, you can allow students twenty seconds' thinking time before speaking.
- If a student can't think of anything to say, or stops talking before the twenty seconds are up, then they have to move back to their previous square.
- The student who reaches the *Finish* square first is the winner.

6B Holiday crossword

***You will need:** a copy of each crossword for each pair of students*

- Divide the class into two groups, A and B. Give a copy of Student A crossword to students in group A, and a copy of Student B crossword to those in group B.
- Students work together in their separate groups to check they know the meaning of the words on their half of the crossword. Most vocabulary in this activity is taken from the *Vocabulary and speaking* section on page 54 and the *Listening and speaking* section on page 55 of the *Students' Book*.
- Put students into pairs, so that one Student A and one Student B are working together. **They are not allowed to look at each other's crossword.**
- Students take it in turns to define the words on their half of the crossword. The other student has to guess the words and write them in their own crossword. Encourage students to use collocations and examples from the material in the *Students' Book* where possible.
- Students continue until they both have a completed version of the crossword.

7A Ambition dominoes

You will need: *one set of dominoes for each pair of students*

- All the collocations in this activity are taken from the *Vocabulary and speaking* section on page 62 of the *Students' Book* or from Module 6.
- Students work in pairs. Give one set of dominoes to each pair, and ask them to share them out equally.
- One student places a domino in front of them, and the other student has to make a complete sentence by placing one of their dominoes at either end of the first domino. The students then take it in turns to put down their dominoes at either end of the domino chain. Encourage students to look at the words in **bold** and to consider which words collocate with them.
- If a student thinks their partner's sentence is not grammatically correct or doesn't make sense, they can challenge the other student. If the students cannot agree, the teacher adjudicates. If the sentence is incorrect, the student must take back the domino and miss a turn.
- If a student cannot make a sentence, the turn passes to their partner.
- The game continues until one student has used up all their dominoes, or until neither student can make a correct sentence. The student who finishes first, or has the fewest dominoes remaining, is the winner.
- Students who finish early can test each other on the collocations in **bold** on the cards.

7B Life circles

You will need: *one copy of the worksheet per student*

- Words to check: *primary school*; *recently*; *a personal possession*.
- Give each student a copy of the worksheet. Encourage them to answer as many questions as possible, and make sure they write their answers in **random order**. They should write single words, names or short phrases, **not** complete sentences. Set a time limit of five or ten minutes.
- Students work in pairs. They fold their worksheet in half and swap with their partner. Students then have to ask questions to find out why their partner has written the words in the circles, for example, *Why have you written 'Italy' here? Who's Michael?* The other student must reply using the correct tense: Present perfect or Past simple.
- For each circle, students must ask their partner two or three suitable follow-up questions on the same topic. For instance, for *someone you've known for over ten years* they could ask: *Where did you meet him/her? What does he/she do? How often do you see him/her?*
- At the end, students report back on the most interesting things they found out about their partner.

7C Happy verb families

You will need: *one set of cards for each group of three or four students*

- Put students into groups of three or four. Give each group a set of cards and ask them to deal out **seven** cards to each player. The rest of the cards are then placed **face down** in a pile in the middle of the group.
- **The aim of the activity is for students to get rid of all the cards in their hands**. To do this, students must collect 'verb families' of infinitive, past tense and past participle, which they then place **face up** in front of them.
- Student A begins by asking **one** of the other students (**not** the whole group) if they have a particular card that Student A needs for a verb family. For example, if Student A has cards that say *wear* and *wore,* they can ask: *Jaime, have you got a card that says 'worn'?*
- If the other student does have the card Student A has asked for, they must give it to them. If the other student does not have the card, Student A must pick up an extra card from the pile in the middle. The turn then passes to the next student.
- If a student is asked to hand over their last card to another student, they win the game. So asking a student for their last card is a very silly thing to do!
- When a student gets a verb family, they immediately place it **face up** in front of them. The other students should check that the verb family is correct. Only the verbs in **bold** can be counted as part of a verb family. If necessary, they can check with you or refer to the list of irregular verbs on page 157 of the *Students' Book*.
- If there are no extra cards left, students continue taking it in turns to ask each other for cards until there is a winner. The winner is the first person with no cards left in their hands.
- Groups who finish early can shuffle the cards and play again.

Note: it would be advisable to demonstrate this activity with the whole class before students start playing in groups.

Learner-training worksheet E

(Using the *mini-dictionary*: irregular verbs – part 2)

You will need: *one copy of the worksheet per student*

The aim of this worksheet is to raise students' awareness of how irregular verbs are written in dictionaries, and to increase students' speed at using the *mini-dictionary*.

1 Go through the example dictionary entry.
2 Students work individually and complete the table as fast as possible, using the *mini-dictionary* when necessary. The student who finishes first, with all the answers spelt correctly, is the winner. Alternatively, students can do the activity in pairs. (Note: students are not allowed to look at the list of irregular verbs on page 157 of the *Students' Book*, as the aim of this exercise is to increase dictionary speed.) When they have finished, they can work in pairs to test each other on the verbs. One

student says an infinitive and their partner has to say the correct past tense and past participle.

8A Article snakes and ladders

You will need: *one copy of the board per group of three students; one set of* Question cards *per group; one dice and three counters per group*

- Put students into groups of three and give each group a board, a set of *Question cards*, counters and dice. Tell a student to shuffle the *Question cards* before putting them **face down** in a pile.
- Students take it in turns to throw a number. When they land on a square with a question mark on it, they must take a *Question card* from the top of the pile. The student places the card down next to the board so all the students can see it, then has to answer the question. If the student answers the whole question correctly, they stay on the square and the next student takes their turn. If the student answers the question incorrectly, they must return to their original square.
- If students cannot agree on the correct answer, the teacher adjudicates (see *Resource bank key*).
- If a student lands at the foot of a ladder, they must get the question correct **before** they are allowed to go up it. If a student lands on the head of a snake, they must slide down the snake to its tail.
- The game continues until one student reaches the *Finish* square (or until the group runs out of *Question cards*).
- At the end of the game students can discuss the cards they got wrong, and/or go through the *Question cards* they didn't answer.

8B The Hungry Hippo café

You will need: *one copy of* Worksheet 1 *or* Worksheet 2 *per student*

- Divide the class into two groups. Give copies of *Worksheet 1* to one group, and copies of *Worksheet 2* to the other. Allow time for students to read the information at the top of the worksheet, and check they understand the situation.
- Students work in pairs with someone who has the **same** worksheet. You need **an equal number of pairs** for this activity, so have one or two groups of three if necessary. Students must look at the menu and the pictures, and make three lists: things they have too much/many of; things they don't have enough of; things they don't have any of. Allow about ten minutes for this.
- Group each pair that has *Worksheet 1* with a pair that has *Worksheet 2*. The students tell/ask each other what they've got too much of, not enough of, etc., and swap items where possible. When they swap items, they tick them off their lists.
- Students report back to the whole class on how much they have swapped, and what they still need. (Note: nobody has any ice cream or any cutlery.)

8C Where's the nearest bank?

You will need: *one* Map A *and one* Map B *for each pair of students*

- Check that students know how to ask for directions, for example, *Excuse me, where's the nearest bank?*
- Put students into pairs. Give a copy of *Map A* to one student and a copy of *Map B* to the other. **Students are not allowed to look at each other's maps.**
- Check that students know where they are on the map (at the station). Tell them that the places that are shaded (such as the bus station) are on **both** maps, so they can refer to them when giving directions.
- Students take it in turns to ask for directions to the places listed in the top right-hand corner of their map. (Students can refer to the *Real life* and *Writing* sections on pages 77 and 78 of the *Students' Book* for useful words and expressions.) When a student has been given directions to the place they want to go to, they write the name of the place on their copy of the map.
- When both students have found all six places, they can compare their maps and see if they have marked the places correctly.

Learner-training worksheet F

(Noticing and remembering prepositions and articles in phrases)

You will need: *one copy of the worksheet per student (detach the picture from the worksheet before the lesson)*

The aim of this worksheet is to raise students' awareness of fixed and semi-fixed phrases containing articles and prepositions, and to encourage students to recognise, record and remember these phrases.

1 Students work in pairs. Give each pair a copy of the picture, and allow a few minutes for them to predict what the two teachers are saying. Students discuss their ideas with the rest of the class.

2 Give each student a copy of the second half of the worksheet and allow time for them to check their predictions. Students compare their predictions in pairs or with the whole class.

3 Go through the example phrases with the class, then let students do the exercise individually or in pairs. Check answers with the whole class (see *Resource bank key*). Note that some of the phrases in this activity are 'fixed' (for example, *the other day*), while others can change the tense or the pronoun (for example, *to be not very good at something*). Some of the easier two-word phrases (for example, *on Friday*) have not been included in subsequent exercises or the *Resource bank key*.

4 Students work individually. Suggest they cover the dialogue. Students check answers in pairs, referring back to the dialogue if necessary. Check answers with the whole class (see *Resource bank key*). Students can then practise the conversation in pairs. Two or three pairs can 'perform' their dialogue in front of the class.

9A In the 2020s

You will need: *one copy of* Survey A, B, C *or* D *for each student*

- Words to check: *a survey*; *3D*; *to clone*; *to be extinct*; *IQ*; *to be homeless.*
- Divide the class into four groups A, B, C and D. Give each student in group A a copy of *Survey A*, each student in group B a copy of *Survey B*, and so on. Tell the class they are going to prepare questions on what life will be like in the 2020s.
- Students work in their groups and write down questions based on their *Survey* sheets, for example, for the prompt *people – have more free time?* students should write *Do you think people will have more free time (in the 2020s)?* When they have finished, encourage them to write one or two more questions on the same topic.
- Rearrange the class so that one student from each of the four groups, A, B, C and D, is sitting together. If there are students left over, have some groups of five.
- Write the following answers on the board: *Yes, definitely. / Yes, probably. / Maybe. / No, probably not. / No, definitely not.* Students then ask each other the questions in turn. When responding, students must use one of the answers on the board, and give reasons for their opinion if possible. **All students must make notes on what their classmates think**, based on the five answers on the board.
- Students return to their original groups and collate their answers. The members of the group then add their own answers to the survey, so that their results represent the opinion of the whole class.
- Write the following prompts on the board: *will definitely*; *will probably*; *might/may*; *probably won't*; *definitely won't*. Each group presents their results to the whole class, using the language highlighted on the board. For example, group A might have found out that *Five students think that people will definitely have more free time in the 2020s, but four students think that they probably won't.* Alternatively, you can rearrange the class into small groups again (one student from each of the groups, A, B, C and D) and students can report the results of their survey.
- Students can write up their survey for homework and put the results up round the classroom for others to read.

9B Worried parents

You will need: *one copy of* Student A worksheet *and one copy of* Student B worksheet *for each pair of students*

- Words to check: *to hitchhike*; *to give somebody a lift*; *to get lost*; *to run out of money*; *to go camping*; *a tent*; *a guide*; *a sleeping bag*; *to be fully booked* (of a train).
- Divide the class into two groups, A and B. Give a copy of *Student A worksheet* to students in group A, and a copy of *Student B worksheet* to those in group B. Explain that they are going to do **two** roleplays: one where they are a son/daughter going on a dangerous holiday, and another where they are the son/daughter's worried parent. Allow time for students to read and understand the information on their worksheets.
- Students work individually or in pairs and, using the prompts on the worksheet, prepare questions to ask when they are the **parent** in the roleplay. They should use *you* as the subject of the questions. Do an example with the whole class before they begin: *phone me/as soon as/arrive in Miami? = Will you phone me as soon as you arrive in Miami?* and *what/do/if/get lost? = What will you do if you get lost?*
- Put students into pairs, so that one Student A and one Student B are working together, and tell them to do **roleplay 1**. Allow time for Student B to read the information on their worksheet before they begin.
- When students have finished, they change roles and do **roleplay 2**.

Learner-training worksheet G

(Deducing meaning from context – part 1)

You will need: *one copy of the worksheet per student; a set of* Longman Active Study Dictionaries *(optional)*

The aim of this worksheet is to raise students' awareness of the importance of context when faced with unknown vocabulary, and to give them practice in deducing meaning from context.

1 Students read the text individually, then discuss in pairs what they think really happened. Check ideas with the whole class. (The man had put ketchup on his shirt to pretend he was injured, in order to trick a passer-by into giving him some money.)
2 Students work individually or in pairs. Check answers with the whole class. (Note that, with the exception of *wallet*, these words do not appear in the *mini-dictionary*.)
3 Students work individually. Set a time limit of five minutes.
4 Students compare their answers in pairs or small groups. Check answers with the whole class. Although the success rate will vary, most students should be able to guess the exact meaning for a, b, d, e, f and i, and the general meaning for c, g and j. Students are unlikely to be able to guess the meaning for h. (Note that these words do not appear in the *mini-dictionary*, but students can check the meanings in the *Longman Active Study Dictionary* if necessary.)

10A What can I do for you?

You will need: *one set of role cards for each pair of students*

- Put students into pairs. Give one student a copy of the *Patient A* role card and the other a copy of the *Doctor A* role card. Allow a few minutes for students to prepare their roles. (Most of the vocabulary used in this activity is taken from the *Vocabulary* and *Listening and speaking* sections on pages 88–89 of the *Students' Book*.)

- Students act out the roleplay in their pairs. If there is space in the classroom, rearrange the chairs so that students are facing each other, with room for the doctor and patient to stand up if they wish.
- When each pair finishes, give the *Doctor B* Role card to the student who was the patient in the first roleplay, and the *Patient B* role card to the student who was the doctor. Again, allow a few minutes for them to prepare. Students then act out the second roleplay in their pairs.
- Finally, students report back to the whole class on the advice/treatment their doctor gave them.

10B The Ghost

***You will need:** one set of role cards for each pair of students*

- Words to check: *to burgle*; *a burglar*; *a burglar alarm*; *a criminal*; *to get caught*.
- Divide the class into two groups and give one group *The Ghost role cards* and the other group the *Journalist role cards*. Allow time for them to read the introduction at the top of the cards, and check they all understand the situation. If there is an odd number of students, include an extra journalist.
- Students with the *Journalist role cards* work individually or in pairs to prepare the questions they need to ask. Encourage them to use *used to* where possible in their questions, as well as the Past simple. Students with *The Ghost role cards* work individually to prepare their stories by filling in the gaps in the information on the card. Allow about ten or fifteen minutes for this.
- Rearrange the class so that one student with *The Ghost role card* is sitting next to one student with a *Journalist role card*. The journalists then conduct the interview and make notes of their answers.
- Journalists can write an article for the *Famous Criminals* magazine in class or for homework, and burglars can write their life story.

10C Bob's night out

***You will need:** one set of pictures for each pair of students; one copy of the whole picture story per student (optional)*

- Before the class, cut up and shuffle a set of pictures for each pair of students.
- Put students into pairs and give each pair a set of pictures. Tell students that they have the complete story of *Bob's night out*. Students work together to decide on the correct order of the pictures. Encourage them to discuss their reasons for choosing each picture with their partner while they are working.
- Check the correct order with the whole class (see *Resource bank key*). Other orders may be possible, depending on the students' versions of the stories.
- Students work individually or in pairs and write the story in the past, using the Past simple and Past continuous where appropriate. The stories can be completed for homework (students will need a copy of all the pictures to take away with them in order to finish the story).
- Students can put up their completed stories round the classroom for other students to read.

11A The Lovebug Dating Agency

***You will need:** one set of six* Lovebug Dating Agency *cards (either* Men *or* Women*) for each pair of students*

- Put students into pairs (or groups of three). You must have an **even number** of pairs or groups for this activity.
- Check that students understand the concept of a *dating agency*, and give each pair/group a set of six *Lovebug Dating Agency* cards. Give half the number of pairs/groups the *Men cards*, and the other half the *Women cards*.
- Tell students to look at the pictures on the cards and to fill in the profile with information that they think suits the person's character. Set a time limit of ten or fifteen minutes.
- Group each pair that has *Men cards* with a pair that has *Women cards*. Students tell one another about the people on their cards, then the whole group decides who should go on a date with who, based on the information in the profile. Encourage students to pair up all the men and women if possible, and to give reasons for their decisions.
- Students tell the whole class about their most promising dates. Alternatively, the pairs of cards can be put up round the classroom. Students walk around looking at all the pairs of cards and decide which dates they think will be the most successful.

Learner-training worksheet H

(Using the *mini-dictionary* to find constructions that follow verbs)

***You will need:** one copy of the worksheet per student*

The aim of this worksheet is to show students how to use the *mini-dictionary* to find out what grammatical construction follows a verb, as well as to revise some of the verbs they have already met in the *Students' Book*.

1 Go through the dictionary entries with the whole class. Check they understand what a *gerund* is.
2 Students work in pairs or small groups. All the verbs and verb phrases are taken from Modules 1–11 of the *Students' Book*. Check answers with the whole class (see *Resource bank key*).
3 Students work individually before checking their answers with the whole class (see *Resource bank key*).

12A What's this?

***You will need:** one set of picture cards per three students*

- Put students into groups of three. Give each group a set of picture cards **face down** in a pile. Shuffle the cards beforehand.
- Student A picks up the first card. They must define the object to the student on their right (Student B), without

saying the name of the object. Student B must try to guess what Student A is describing. (Most of the words in this activity are from Modules 9–12, with the exception of *belt*, *corkscrew*, *tin opener*, *ashtray*, *gloves* and *Sellotape*, which should all be familiar items that students are able to define.) Students are not allowed to say the name of the object, or to mime in any way – they should fold their arms when they are defining the words!

- If Student B guesses correctly, Student A gives them the card. If Student B doesn't know the word, the turn passes to Student C. If neither student can guess the word, the card goes back to the bottom of the pile.
- Students continue taking turns defining the objects on the cards to the student on their right. The student who collects the most cards by the end of the game is the winner.

Note: it would be advisable to demonstrate this activity to the whole class before they begin working in groups. Encourage students to use the following phrases for defining the objects: *It's made of …*; *It's used for* + verb *-ing*; *You keep it in your bedroom/bag/pocket*, etc; *You need it to* + verb. Write these phrases on the board to act as prompts.

12B The Handbag Gang

You will need: *one set of pictures for each pair of students; one copy of the* Vocabulary worksheet *per student; one copy of the whole story per student (optional)*

- Before the class, cut up and shuffle a set of pictures for each pair of students.
- Put students into pairs and give each pair a set of pictures. Tell them that they have the complete story of *The Handbag Gang*. Students put the pictures in order, giving reasons for their choices. Check the correct order with the whole class (see *Resource bank key*), and discuss any variations to the suggested order.
- Give each student a copy of the *Vocabulary worksheet*. Students work in pairs again and match the vocabulary with the appropriate picture(s). Tell students that some items of vocabulary can go with more than one picture. Check answers with the whole class. Make sure students understand all the words and expressions, and that they know the past participles of the verbs.
- In their pairs, students tell the story orally, using the new vocabulary. They should tell the main part of the story in the Past simple, and the verbs on the worksheet should be used in the passive form.
- Tell students that they are journalists working for the local newspaper, and they have to write the story for tomorrow's edition. Their report **must** include at least six verbs in the Past simple passive. Encourage students to think of a headline and to lay out the report in newspaper style.
- Students can either write the report in class or for homework. (Note: students will need a copy of all the pictures if they write the story outside class.)
- The finished versions can be displayed round the classroom for other students to read.

13A Century People

You will need: *one set of role cards for each pair of students*

- Divide the class into two groups and give one group *Old person role cards*, and the other group *Interviewer role cards*. Allow time for students to read the introduction on the cards. If there is an odd number of students, include an extra interviewer.
- The old people work individually and fill in the gaps in the information on the role card. Encourage them to be as inventive as possible and to think of interesting details to add to their life story. The interviewers work individually or in pairs and write down the questions they are going to ask in the interview. Make sure students use the Present perfect simple and continuous in their questions where appropriate. Allow the class about ten or fifteen minutes for this.
- Rearrange the class so that one old person is sitting next to one interviewer and allow students to do the roleplay.
- When they have finished, the interviewers can tell the whole class about the old people they have just talked to, and the class can decide which old person has had the most interesting life.

13B Old friends

You will need: one role card per student

- Tell students that they are at a party where there are lots of old friends they haven't seen for ten years. Elicit questions they could ask each other, and write them on the board. Useful questions for this activity are: *What have you been doing since I last saw you? What do you do? Where do you live? Are you married? What does your husband/wife do? What do you do in your spare time?* Also elicit a follow-up question with *How long …?* for each of the preceding questions.
- Give each student a *Role card*, and allow time for them to read the information. **They are not allowed to look at each other's *Role cards*.** (*Role cards 1* to *8* are needed for all students to complete the activity; *Role cards 9* to *12* are optional. If you have more than twelve students, distribute duplicate *Role cards*.)
- Tell students that they have to find at least four old friends they have something in common with. When they find someone they must write down the name of the person, and what they have in common, on their *Role card*. They should write notes (for example, *architect – 7 years*) in the second column, **not** complete sentences.
- Students move around the room introducing themselves and asking one another the questions elicited earlier. Encourage students to ask as many *How long …?* follow-up questions as possible during the conversations.
- Finally, students work in pairs and tell each other what they have found out, using the notes on their *Role card* as prompts. Again, encourage them to use the Present perfect simple or continuous in their answers. For example, *Lisa and I live in New York, and we've both been living there since 1990.*

Learner-training worksheet I
(Deducing meaning from context – part 2)

You will need: *one copy of the worksheet per student; copies of the* Longman Active Study Dictionary *(optional)*

This worksheet follows on from *Learner-training worksheet H* and gives students more practice in deducing meaning from context.

1 Allow students a few minutes to read the story individually, then put them into pairs to reorder the story. Avoid answering questions about the words in italics at this stage. Check answers with the whole class (see *Resource bank key*).

2 Students work in pairs and try to deduce the meaning of the words in italics from the context. Check answers with the whole class. Alternatively, provide the class with copies of the *Longman Active Study Dictionary* and allow them to check their answers themselves. (Note that most of these words do not appear in the *mini-dictionary*.)

3 Students ask and answer the questions in pairs. Encourage both students to answer each question. Students report back to the whole class on their most interesting answers.

14A Get rich quick!

You will need: *one copy of the board and one set of* Money cards *per four students; one dice, four counters per group*

- Put students into groups of four. Give each group a copy of the board, a set of *Money cards* (shuffled), dice and counters. Tell students to put the *Money cards* **face down** in a pile in the middle of the board, and their counters on the *Start* square. Check that students understand what happens when they land on the non-money squares on the board, and that every time they pass *Start* they automatically receive £10,000.
- If you can make some fake money (in £5,000, £10,000 and £20,000 notes!), distribute it amongst the students and make one member of each group the 'banker'. If not, students can write down their running total as they play the game.
- Students take it in turns to throw a number. If Student A lands on a square with some money on it, **another student** takes a *Money card* from the top of the pile and asks Student A the question on the card. If the student gets the answer right, they receive the amount of money on the square and add it to their total. If Student A gets the answer wrong, the other student tells them the correct answer, and Student A receives no money.
- The game continues until all the *Money cards* are finished. When the last *Money card* has been answered, all the students count up how much money they have. The student who has the most money wins the game.
- Groups that finish early can go through the *Money cards* and test each other.

14B Dealing with money

You will need: *one copy of the worksheet per student*

- Give each student a copy of the worksheet. Students work individually to decide what question they will need to ask to complete each statement. Set a five-minute time limit. Circulate and, if necessary, help with questions.
- Students stand up and mingle, asking questions. If another student answers yes to any of their questions, they should write their name on the dotted line. **Students can only write each name once**.
- Students work in pairs and tell their partner what they have found out.

Learner-training worksheet J
(Using the *mini-dictionary* to find dependent prepositions)

You will need: *one copy of the worksheet per student*

The aim of this worksheet is to show students how to use the *mini-dictionary* to find dependent prepositions that follow certain verbs and adjectives.

1 Go through the dictionary entries with the whole class.

2 Students work individually. They are not allowed to use their *mini-dictionary* at this stage. Encourage them to guess if they don't know the answers (see *Resource bank key*).

3 Students work in pairs and check their answers using the *mini-dictionary*.

4 Students work individually and check their answers in the *mini-dictionary* if necessary.

5 Students work in pairs and test each other. Encourage them to repeat the whole phrase (as in the example) as this will help them remember the whole expression.

15A Conditional squares

You will need: *one copy of the worksheet per student*

- Give each student a copy of the worksheet. Students work individually and answer the questions. Make sure they write their answers in **random order**, and encourage them to answer as many questions as possible. They should write single words or short phrases, **not** complete sentences. Set a time limit of five or ten minutes.
- Students work in pairs and swap worksheets with their partner. Students then have to try and guess why their partner has written the words/phrases in the squares. For example, Student A writes *big house*. Student B asks: *Would you buy a big house if you won a lot of money?* Student B writes *seaside*. Student A asks: *Will you go to the seaside if the weather's good this weekend?* Students must ask at least one follow-up question on each topic. For example, *What other things would you buy? / Where do you usually go at the weekend?*

- At the end of the activity, students report back to the class on the most interesting things they found out about their partner.

15B Preposition pelmanism

You will need: *one complete set of cards per three students*

- Put students into groups of three and give each group a set of cards. **Shuffle the cards before the class**. Tell the students to spread the cards out in front of them **face down**, with the bigger cards on one side and the smaller cards on the other.
- Students take it in turns to turn over one big card and one small card. If the preposition is the correct one to fill the gap in the sentence, they keep the cards as a 'trick' and have another turn. If the cards do not match, they must put them back **in exactly the same place**. If students cannot agree, the teacher adjudicates.
- The activity continues until all the cards are matched up. The student with the most tricks is the winner.
- If one group finishes early, they can test each other on the prepositions.

1A Get to know the *Students' Book*

A

Which four pages contain a summary of everything in the *Students' Book?*

Pages .... to ....

B

Where can you find a **pronunciation table**?

....

C

What colour are the **Grammar** boxes in Module 2?

....

D

What topic do you study in the **Real life** section in Module 12?

....

E

On which page is the **Language summary** for Module 10?

Page ....

F

Which activity on page 31 gives you extra pronunciation practice?

....

G

On which page is the **Study ... Practise ... Remember!** section of Module 8?

Page ....

H

Where are the **tapescripts** for Module 7?

Pages .... and ....

I

Which word is studied in the **Wordspot** in Module 4?

....

J

How many **Pronunciation** boxes are there in Module 5?

....

K

What colour is the **Useful language** box in Module 6?

....

L

On which page is there a list of **irregular verbs**?

Page ....

Learner-training worksheet A

Using the *mini-dictionary*: introduction

MEANING

1 **a** Look up the following words in your *mini-dictionary* and read the definitions and examples.

- to gamble
- a witness
- to interrupt

b Do you understand from the *mini-dictionary* what these words mean? What helped you most – the definition, the example, or both?

2 The words underlined in the following sentences have more than one meaning. Look them up in the *mini-dictionary* and write down the number of the dictionary definition that matches each sentence.

a My mother keeps old Christmas cards in a box under the bed. ....
b They run a restaurant in the centre of town. ....
c On Saturday nights, I really enjoy clubbing with my friends. ....

GRAMMAR

3 Match the words in **bold** in this paragraph with the correct grammatical description below. Do **not** look up the words in your *mini-dictionary*.
Mark **woke up** and looked at the alarm clock next to his **bed**. It was eleven o'clock, and he was **late** for **work**. He jumped out of bed, **quickly** got dressed, then **opened** the front door and got into his car. Then he realised it was Sunday!

a an adjective ....
b an adverb ....
c a countable noun ....
d an uncountable noun ....
e a transitive verb ....
f an intransitive verb ....

4 Look in your *mini-dictionary* and find out what part of speech these words are.

a pullover ....
b spacious ....
c protect ....
d hesitate ....
e fame ....
f immediately ....

PRONUNCIATION

Word stress is marked like this in the *mini-dictionary*:

Stress mark

musical /ˈmjuːzɪkl/ *adjective*

5 Look up the following words in the *mini-dictionary* and mark the stress.

- baker
- economics
- independent

6 How do you pronounce these words? (There is a pronunciation table on the inside front cover of the *mini-dictionary* to help you.)

- chaos
- receipt
- pigeon

PHOTOCOPIABLE

1B Me too!

Present simple and question words

YOUR ANSWERS	NAME
1 I usually get up at .... on Sundays.	
2 I go to the cinema once / twice / .... times a week/month.	
3 My favourite food is	
4 My journey home from school takes .... minutes.	
5 At the weekend I usually	
6 I want to learn English because	
7 I've got .... cousins.	
8 I like action films / thrillers / comedies / romantic films / horror films / science-fiction films.	
9 My favourite actor is	
10 I usually go to bed at .... during the week.	
11 I like winter/spring/summer/autumn the most.	
12 I go shopping for new clothes once / twice / .... times a week/month/year.	

1C Connected lives

Present simple questions with *How often ...?* and adverbs of frequency

Student A worksheet

Lola is a nightclub singer, and sings at the *Flamingo Club* (1) ....
She usually finishes work at 3.00 a.m., and always takes a taxi home. She plays tennis with her best friend (2) .... times a week, but loses every time! She goes to the seaside once a year, and stays in a hotel called *The Sea View.*

Tim and Karen own *The Sun Café* in the centre of town. They get up early (5) .... and always open the café at 7.00 a.m. They go on holiday (6) .... times a year, and usually stay in *The Sea View Hotel*.

Bill is a taxi driver, and he usually works (9) .... On Sundays he always gets up at about lunchtime. In the afternoon he usually (10) .... His sister is a dance teacher, and he sees her about once a week.

Molly is a student, and goes to university (3) .... days a week. On Wednesday evenings she always goes to her dance class. She meets her new boyfriend for lunch (4) ...., and plays tennis with her best friend three times a week (Molly always wins!).

Paul works for a computer company, and meets his new girlfriend for lunch in *The Sun Café* (7) .... When he's at work he e-mails her twelve times a day! They go out together (8) ...., and usually go to the *Flamingo Club.*

Student B worksheet

Lola is a nightclub singer, and sings at the *Flamingo Club* three nights a week. She usually finishes work at (a) ...., and always takes a taxi home. She plays tennis with her best friend three times a week, but loses every time! She goes to the seaside (b) .... a year, and stays in a hotel called *The Sea View*.

Molly is a student, and goes to university four days a week. On Wednesday evenings she always (c) .... She meets her new boyfriend for lunch every day, and plays tennis with her best friend (d) .... times a week (Molly always wins!)

Tim and Karen own *The Sun Café* in the centre of town. They get up early every morning (except Sundays) and always open the café at (e) .... a.m. They go on holiday three times a year, and usually stay in (f) ....

Paul works for a computer company, and meets his new girlfriend for lunch in *The Sun Café* every day. When he's at work he e-mails her (g) .... times a day! They go out together every night except Wednesday, and usually go to (h) ....

Bill is a taxi driver, and he usually works at night. On Sundays he always gets up at (i) .... In the afternoon he usually watches football on TV. His sister is a dance teacher, and he sees her (j) ....

Learner-training worksheet B

Using the *mini-dictionary*: irregular verbs – part 1

1 Look at the following sentence and answer the questions below. When you have finished, check your answers in the *mini-dictionary*.

Sally didn't want to go to school yesterday, so she <u>hid</u> under the bed.

a What tense is the verb <u>underlined</u>? ....
b Is this a regular or irregular verb? ....
c What's the infinitive? ....
d Do you know the meaning of this verb? If not, can you guess?

2 Notice how irregular verbs are written in the *mini-dictionary*.

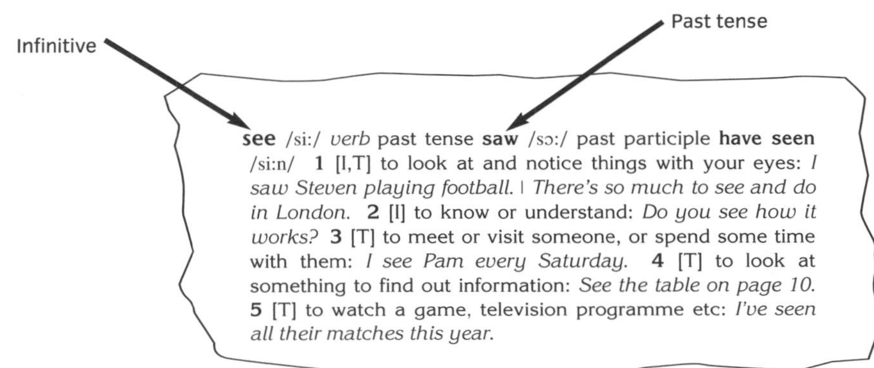

see /siː/ *verb* past tense **saw** /sɔː/ past participle **have seen** /siːn/ **1** [I,T] to look at and notice things with your eyes: *I saw Steven playing football.* | *There's so much to see and do in London.* **2** [I] to know or understand: *Do you see how it works?* **3** [T] to meet or visit someone, or spend some time with them: *I see Pam every Saturday.* **4** [T] to look at something to find out information: *See the table on page 10.* **5** [T] to watch a game, television programme etc: *I've seen all their matches this year.*

3 What's the infinitive of these irregular past tenses? Use your *mini-dictionary* to find the answers or to check your spelling.

INFINITIVE	PAST TENSE	INFINITIVE	PAST TENSE
	brought		taught
	fell		wore
	left		drove
	caught		bought
	rang		broke

4 Fill in the gaps with one of the irregular past tenses from the table above.

a Last summer we .... around Europe in a BMW.
b My grandfather .... English when he was younger.
c Lots of people .... presents to his birthday party.
d Last night Jane .... her favourite dress to the wedding.
e I .... a new computer yesterday.
f I .... my leg when I .... off the roof of my house.
g The phone .... ten times last night.
h We .... the restaurant at 10.30 and .... the last bus home.

2A Dead famous

Past simple *yes/no* questions and short answers

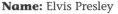

Name: John Lennon
Born: 1940, Liverpool, England.
Died: December 1980, aged 40. He was shot outside his New York home by Mark Chapman.
Famous for: member of the Beatles, and then a solo singer/songwriter. One of his songs (*Imagine*) was voted 'best song of the twentieth century'.
Lived in: Liverpool and New York.
Family life: married twice. His second wife was the musician and artist Yoko Ono.

Clue: his first guitar cost him £17.

Name: Elvis Presley
Born: 1935, Mississippi, USA.
Died: 1977. He was found dead on the toilet in his Gracelands home. He died of a heart attack.
Famous for: 'the king of rock and roll'. He sold millions of records around the world, and also starred in many Hollywood films.
Lived in: Memphis, USA.
Family life: married Priscilla (who starred in the TV series *Dallas*), but they separated in the 1970s.

Clue: he spent two years in the army.

Name: William Shakespeare
Born: 1564, Stratford-upon-Avon, England.
Died: 1616. He was 52.
Famous for: he wrote 37 plays, including *Romeo and Juliet*, *Hamlet* and *Macbeth*. Thought to be the best English writer in history. He became very rich, and lived in a big house in the centre of London.
Lived in: Stratford and London.
Family life: he married Anne Hathaway when he was 18.

Clue: he used to be an actor.

Name: Princess Diana
Born: 1961, Norfolk, England.
Died: 1997, in a car accident in Paris. She was 36. Her boyfriend, Dodi Fayed, also died in the crash.
Famous for: Princess of Wales, wife of Prince Charles. She also did a lot of charity work.
Lived in: London.
Family life: married Prince Charles in 1981. They had two children, William and Harry. They separated in 1992.

Clue: she used to be a kindergarten teacher.

Name: Marie Curie
Born: 1867, Warsaw, Poland.
Died: 1934, aged 67, of leukaemia caused by exposure to radium.
Famous for: discovered radioactivity and radium. Despite her discoveries she was poor all her life.
Lived in: Paris.
Family life: married Pierre Curie, who was also a famous scientist, in 1895.

Clue: she was the first woman to win the Nobel Prize twice.

Name: Albert Einstein
Born: 1879, Ulm, Germany.
Died: 1955, aged 76. He died in his sleep.
Famous for: a brilliant scientist and mathematician. Discovered the theory of relativity, which changed how we see the world.
Lived in: Switzerland, Germany and the USA.
Family life: he was married twice. The second time he married his cousin, Elsa.

Clue: mathematics was the only school subject he was good at.

Name: Mahatma Gandhi
Born: 1869, Porbandar, India.
Died: 1948 in New Delhi. A Hindu who didn't agree with Gandhi's political view assassinated him. He was 79.

Famous for: non-violent leader of Indian independence from British rule.
Lived in: India, England (he did a law degree in London) and South Africa.
Family life: he married when he was 13 and had four children.

Clue: he never wore any shoes.

Name: Christopher Columbus
Born: 1451, Genoa, Italy.
Died: 1506, in Spain. He was 55.
Famous for: he was a sailor and explorer. He went on four long journeys by boat and was the first European to discover South America. He also went to Cuba and the Caribbean.
Lived in: Italy, Portugal and Spain.
Family life: he was married and had one son, named Diego.

Clue: a country is named after him.

Name: Mother Teresa
Born: 1910, Albania.
Died: 1997, of a heart attack. She was 87.

Famous for: in 1950 she started a hostel for the sick and dying in Calcutta, India. She spent her life there and established the Missionaries of Charity, which looks after poor people in over 50 countries.
Lived in: Calcutta, India.
Family life: she became a nun in 1931. She was never married.

Clue: she won the Nobel Peace Prize in 1979.

Name: Marilyn Monroe
Born: 1926, Los Angeles, USA.
Died: 1962, aged 36, from an overdose of drugs. Maybe she killed herself or someone else killed her.

Famous for: movie star. She made 29 films in 16 years.
Lived in: New York and Hollywood, USA.
Family life: she was married four times. Her second (and fourth!) husband was Joe DiMaggio, a famous baseball player.

Clue: her real name was Norma Jean Baker.

Name: Wolfgang Amadeus Mozart
Born: 1756, Salzburg, Austria.
Died: 1791, aged 35, of typhoid fever.
Famous for: composer and musician. He started composing music when he was five, and composed over 600 works during his short life.
Lived in: Vienna.
Family life: he was married, but had no children. Despite his talent, he never made any money and died a poor man.

Clue: there is a film about his life.

Name: Cleopatra
Born: 69 BC, Egypt.
Died: 30 BC, when she was 39. She killed herself by allowing a poisonous snake to bite her.
Famous for: queen of Egypt, and for being extremely beautiful and intelligent.
Lived in: Egypt and Syria.
Family life: she married her ten-year-old brother when she became queen of Egypt. Later she was the lover of Julius Caesar, and then Mark Antony.

Clue: she liked cats.

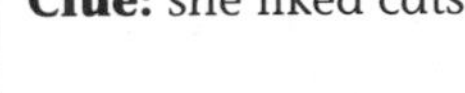

2B The millionaire's ball

Past simple and time phrases

WHO'S WHO AT THE MILLIONAIRE'S BALL?		
1	________________	married someone very rich .... New Year's Day this year.
2	________________	was a very successful film director .... the 1970s.
3	________________	spent $200,000 on a ring .... yesterday afternoon.
4	________________	sold his company for a billion dollars three weeks ....
5	________________	became a millionaire at midnight .... last night.
6	________________	bought an island in the Caribbean three months ....
7	________________	won 50 million pounds .... Saturday night.
8	________________	bought the biggest house in the world .... March last year.
9	________________	invited 10,000 guests to his/her birthday party .... 9th January.
10	________________	sold 10 million copies of his/her first CD .... 1996.

Role card 1

You live in New York with your new husband/wife, who is a *very* famous pop star (you decide who he/she is!). You met him/her in a restaurant last year, where you worked as a waiter/waitress. The wedding took place in Hawaii on New Year's Day this year, and you went to Paris on your honeymoon.

Role card 2

You are now retired and live in a big house in Hollywood. In the 1970s you were a famous film director, and your most successful film, *Bus Driver*, made over $100 million and won seven Oscars. Now you live with your wife (who was an actress in *Bus Driver*) and your three children.

Role card 3

You are a famous actor/actress, and have three houses (you decide where). Last week you started making your new film and fell in love with another actor/actress. Yesterday afternoon you bought a *very* expensive ring (it cost $200,000!) and tomorrow night you're going to ask him/her to marry you.

Role card 4

You are a very successful businessman/woman and live in New York. You aren't married. Ten years ago you started a computer company called *Grey Box*, and now it's one of the biggest companies in the world. Three weeks ago you sold your company to Microsoft for $1 billion.

Role card 5

You live in a small flat and work at *McDonald's*. Your grandfather owned an oil company and was very rich. He died when you were a child, and left you a million pounds in his will – but he also said you couldn't have the money until you were 21. Today is your 21st birthday, so now you're a millionaire!

Role card 6

You are a famous tennis player, and last year you won three big tennis tournaments. You make a lot of money, of course, and three months ago you bought an island in the Caribbean! Now you live on the island with your family, and spend the days swimming and sunbathing on the beach.

Role card 7

You are very rich and live in a big house in the south of France, but you've never worked in your life! You make all your money playing poker. Last Saturday you won 50 million pounds in one game! Tomorrow you're going on holiday with your girl/boyfriend – to Las Vegas!

Role card 8

You own a big car company and have *a lot* of money. In March last year you bought the biggest house in the world, where you now live with your wife/husband and six children. It has 420 bedrooms (each with its own bathroom), 80 living rooms, 65 kitchens and 17 swimming pools!

Role card 9

You are a successful lawyer and live in California with your husband/wife. It was your 30th birthday on 9th January. You invited 10,000 guests to your party, which cost over $1 million. The guests drank 5,000 bottles of champagne and ate 100 kilos of caviar!

Role card 10

You are a famous singer and you live in South America. Your first CD, called *I Want Lots of Money*, sold 10 million copies in 1996. Your second album, *I Love Being Rich*, sold nearly 15 million copies two years later. Now you live by the beach, and have fifteen cars and three boats.

2C Invent a story

Past simple and linkers

Invent a story which includes at least **FOUR** of the following:

A GUN **$10,000 IN CASH** **A WOMAN CALLED KATE**
A LARGE BROWN PARCEL **THE POLICE** **PLANE TICKETS**
A DIAMOND **A FALSE PASSPORT** **A MAN CALLED DYLAN**

Discuss the questions in groups and write your ideas in the box. Then write the complete story in groups, using *and*, *so*, *because*, *but* and *then*.

	WRITE YOUR IDEAS HERE
1 Why was Mark late home from work? How did he feel? Why?	
2 How did his wife Laura feel? Why? What did she do?	
3 What two things did Mark do when he got home?	
4 Mark went into the bedroom and telephoned someone. Who was it? What did they say?	
5 How did Mark feel after the phone call? What did he decide to do? Why?	
6 What did he have in his briefcase? What did he do with it/them?	
7 Laura walked into the bedroom. Why was she angry?	
8 What did Mark say to her? Did she believe him? Why (not)?	
9 Somebody knocked at the front door. Who was it? What did he/she do or say?	
10 Mark left with the person at the door. Where did they go? Why?	
11 How did Laura feel after Mark left? Who did she telephone? Why?	
12 What happened at the end of the story?	

Learner-training worksheet C

Noticing and recording collocations

1 If you want to improve your vocabulary, learning single words is not enough. You often need to learn words that 'go together'. These are called **collocations**. The *mini-dictionary* includes many common collocations for you to learn. They are usually written in **bold**.

> **holiday** /'hɒlədi/ *noun* [C,U] **1** a period of time when you go to another place for enjoyment: *Did you have a nice holiday?* | *Sam is on a camping holiday in Italy.* | *It's only three weeks until I* ***go on holiday.*** | *She needs to* ***have a holiday.*** **2** a day when you do not have to go to work or school: *Next Monday is a holiday.*

2 There are many different types of collocations. Look at the collocations underlined in these sentences and match them with the grammatical descriptions.

1 I always listen to the radio when I'm getting up in the morning.
2 Anne works hard all week, so she usually sleeps a lot at the weekends.
3 Why don't we have a party this weekend?
4 This is a true story about life in the 1960s.

a verb + noun
b verb + preposition
c adjective + noun
d verb + adverb

3 One common type of collocation is verb + noun, for example, *to play football*, *to watch TV*. Which words are missing in these collocations? Use your *mini-dictionary* to help you.

a to surf the _ _ _ _ _ _ _ _
b to _ _ _ _ a mistake
c to rob a _ _ _ _
d to _ _ your homework
e to answer the _ _ _ _ _ _ _ _
f to _ _ _ _ _ your e-mail
g to _ _ _ _ _ for a meal
h to _ _ _ _ a video

4 It is important to write down collocations when you see them. Look at the following examples from students' notebooks, then discuss the questions below with another student.

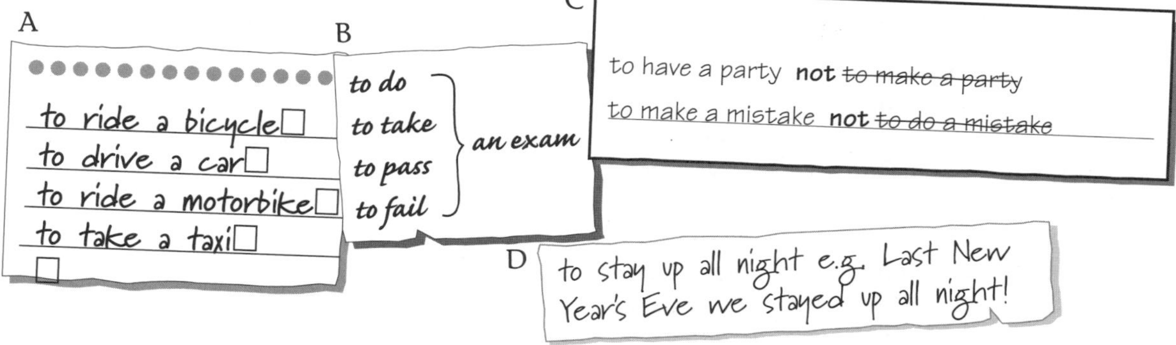

A
to ride a bicycle
to drive a car
to ride a motorbike
to take a taxi
B
to do
to take
to pass
to fail
an exam
C
to have a party not ~~to make a party~~
to make a mistake not ~~to do a mistake~~
D
to stay up all night e.g. Last New Year's Eve we stayed up all night!

- Which do you think is the most useful way to record collocations? Which methods do you use already?
- Find some examples of collocations you have written in your notebook on this course. How did you write them down?

3A The secret of successful language learning

Vocabulary extension (word building)

1 The following words are taken from a magazine article called *What's the secret of successful language learning?* Work with a partner and discuss what you think the relevance of each word has to language learning.

a important
b believe
c imagine
d enjoyable
e successful

2 Are the words above verbs, nouns or adjectives? Write them in the correct column of the table. (Make sure you keep the words **in the same order** as above.)

	VERB	NOUN	ADJECTIVE
a			
b			believable
c			
d			
e			

3 Complete the rest of the table with the verb/noun/adjective forms of the words as appropriate. Use an English–English dictionary to help you. Mark the stress on each word, as in the example.

4 Complete the gaps in the following questions with a word from the table. (Note that the questions do not follow the same order as the words in the table.)

a If you want to s............................ in business, what do you have to do?
b Can you think of something i............................ you have to do tomorrow?
c Do you b............................ that UFOs exist? Why (not)?
d Can you name someone who has a very good i............................?
e What was the most e............................ thing you did last year?
f Can you think of a film or book that is very i............................ .
g Do you think it is important to marry someone with the same religious b............................ ?
h I............................ that you are 100 years old. What do you think the world will be like?
i What kind of things do you e............................ doing in your spare time?
j Can you name a businessman or businesswoman who is very s............................ in your country?

5 Ask another student the questions above, and discuss the answers together.

3B Parents and children

can, can't, have to, don't have to, should, shouldn't

Read these statements about parents and children. Decide whether you agree or disagree with the statement, and circle a number in the **first** column. Then guess your partner's opinion about the same statement, and circle a number in the **second** column.

1 = agree strongly   2 = agree   3 = not sure   4 = don't agree   5 = disagree strongly

	You	Partner's name: ______
1 Children under ten shouldn't watch more than one hour of TV a day.	1 2 3 4 5	1 2 3 4 5
2 Girls over the age of twelve can wear make-up if they want to.	1 2 3 4 5	1 2 3 4 5
3 Children can get up when they want to at the weekends.	1 2 3 4 5	1 2 3 4 5
4 Teenage boys can stay out later than girls of the same age.	1 2 3 4 5	1 2 3 4 5
5 Parents shouldn't tell their children what clothes to wear.	1 2 3 4 5	1 2 3 4 5
6 Teenagers can dye their hair without their parents' permission.	1 2 3 4 5	1 2 3 4 5
7 Girls should do more housework than boys.	1 2 3 4 5	1 2 3 4 5
8 Girls shouldn't go out on their own in the evening before they are eighteen.	1 2 3 4 5	1 2 3 4 5
9 Children over ten years old can decide what time they go to bed.	1 2 3 4 5	1 2 3 4 5
10 Children over sixteen years old don't have to tell their parents where they're going at night.	1 2 3 4 5	1 2 3 4 5

4A Party guests

Present continuous and Present simple

Role card 1

You live in Amsterdam.
You go to Paris every weekend.
You're studying French in the evenings.
You're enjoying the party a lot.

Role card 2

You live in Amsterdam.
You're staying in a hotel around the corner.
You're doing a course in photography.
You like going to the gym.

Role card 3

You work for a television company.
You spend a lot of time surfing the Internet.
You're writing a book in your spare time.
You're enjoying the party a lot.

Role card 4

You work for a television company.
You're learning how to play the guitar.
You're doing a course in photography.
You're waiting for your wife/husband to arrive.

Role card 5

You write for a national newspaper.
You're studying French in the evenings.
You go to Paris every weekend.
You're waiting for a taxi – you want to go home.

Role card 6

You write for a national newspaper.
You're working in London at the moment.
You're writing a book in your spare time.
You like going to the gym.

Role card 7

You have a big house in the country.
You're staying in a hotel around the corner.
You spend a lot of time surfing the Internet.
You're waiting for a taxi – you want to go home.

Role card 8

You have a big house in the country.
You're working in London at the moment.
You're learning how to play the guitar.
You're waiting for your wife/husband to arrive.

Role card 9

You live in Amsterdam.
You're working in London at the moment.
You spend a lot of time surfing the Internet.
You're learning how to play the guitar.

Role card 10

You work for a television company.
You're studying French in the evenings.
You like going to the gym.
You're waiting for a taxi – you want to go home.

Role card 11

You write for a national newspaper.
You're staying in a hotel around the corner.
You're enjoying the party a lot.
You're waiting for your wife/husband to arrive.

Role card 12

You have a big house in the country.
You go to Paris every weekend.
You're doing a course in photography.
You're writing a book in your spare time.

Student A worksheet

You have to find these six people at the party. When you find them, write down their names. Make sure that the person **completely** matches the description.

Person A .... has a big house in the country. ... is staying in a hotel around the corner. ... spends a lot of time surfing the Internet. ... is waiting for a taxi – he/she wants to go home.	**Person B** .... works for a television company. ... spends a lot of time surfing the Internet. ... is writing a book in his/her spare time. ... is enjoying the party a lot.
Person C .... lives in Amsterdam. ... goes to Paris every weekend. ... is studying French in the evenings. ... is enjoying the party a lot.	**Person D** .... writes for a national newspaper. ... is studying French in the evenings. ... goes to Paris every weekend. ... is waiting for a taxi – he/she wants to go home.
Person E .... writes for a national newspaper. ... is staying in a hotel around the corner. ... is enjoying the party a lot. ... is waiting for his wife/her husband to arrive.	**Person F** .... lives in Amsterdam. ... is working in London at the moment. ... spends a lot of time surfing the Internet. ... is learning how to play the guitar.

Student B worksheet

You have to find these six people at the party. When you find them, write down their names. Make sure that the person **completely** matches the description.

Person G .... works for a television company. ... is learning how to play the guitar. ... is doing a course in photography. ... is waiting for his wife/her husband to arrive.	**Person H** .... lives in Amsterdam. ... is staying in a hotel around the corner. ... is doing a course in photography. ... likes going to the gym.
Person I .... writes for a national newspaper. ... is working in London at the moment. ... is writing a book in his/her spare time. ... likes going to the gym.	**Person J** .... has a big house in the country. ... is working in London at the moment. ... is learning how to play the guitar. ... is waiting for his wife/her husband to arrive.
Person K .... has a big house in the country. ... goes to Paris every weekend. ... is doing a course in photography. ... is writing a book in his/her spare time.	**Person L** .... works for a television company. ... is studying French in the evenings. ... likes going to the gym. ... is waiting for a taxi – he/she wants to go home.

4B I'm having lunch with Madonna

Present continuous for future arrangements

DIARY A	
Monday 19th	*Thursday 22nd*
3.00 p.m. coffee – David Bowie (his house)	
Tuesday 20th	*Friday 23rd*
lunch – Madonna – 1.00 p.m. Hilton Hotel	dance class – 2.00–5.00 p.m.
Wednesday 21st	*Saturday 24th*
party – Spice Girls' house! 9.00 p.m. to ???	shopping with Elton John (a.m.)

DIARY B	
Monday 19th	*Thursday 22nd*
party – Leonardo DiCaprio's house 8.00 p.m.	8.00 p.m. cinema – premiere of Leonardo's new film
Tuesday 20th	*Friday 23rd*
	1.00 p.m. – lunch with Steven Spielberg
Wednesday 21st	*Saturday 24th*
9.00 a.m. – breakfast – Sheraton Hotel – Jodie Foster	8.25 p.m. – fly to Hollywood

DIARY C	
Monday 19th	*Thursday 22nd*
8.30 a.m. – arrive back from Bali	**10.00–12.00 – meet accountant**
Tuesday 20th	*Friday 23rd*
9.00 a.m. – collect new Rolls Royce	**7.00 p.m. dinner – US Embassy (with the president)**
Wednesday 21st	*Saturday 24th*
	fly to Monte Carlo (7.40 a.m.)

DIARY D	
Monday 19th	*Thursday 22nd*
	1.00 p.m. – lunch with Frank Einstein (Albert's son)
Tuesday 20th	*Friday 23rd*
Chinese class (evening)	9.00–12.00 – philosophy class
Wednesday 21st	*Saturday 24th*
2.00–5.00 p.m. – take exam (nuclear physics)	1.00–3.00 p.m. – visit National Science Museum

DIARY E

Monday 19th	Thursday 22nd
American Open tennis final (New York) arrive back 10.20 p.m.	9.00–12.00 – play tennis with André Agassi (his house)
Tuesday 20th	**Friday 23rd**
lunch – Maradona (Charlie's Restaurant)	
Wednesday 21st	**Saturday 24th**
8.00 a.m. till ??? - run marathon	3.00 p.m. football – England v Germany

DIARY F

Monday 19th	Thursday 22nd
10.00 a.m. – buy new clothes for Rome trip	**meet Russian president – 1.00 p.m.**
Tuesday 20th	Friday 23rd
fly to Rome – 6.30 a.m. **in Rome all day – interview Pope 3.00–4.00 p.m.** **arrive back 11.00 p.m.**	
Wednesday 21st	Saturday 24th
dinner party – my house – 8.00 p.m.	**a.m. – do TV interview with Tony Blair**

DIARY G

Monday 19th	Thursday 22nd
afternoon - go shopping - Harrods!	*theatre – 7.30 p.m. (with Prince Charles)*
Tuesday 20th	Friday 23rd
breakfast at the Ritz with Tony (Blair)	*opera – 8.00 p.m. (with Charles again)*
Wednesday 21st	Saturday 24th
queen of England coming round for tea	

DIARY H

Monday 19th	Thursday 22nd
engagement party – 9.00 p.m. – parents' house	
Tuesday 20th	Friday 23rd
restaurant – Alex and parents – 7.30 p.m.	*a.m. – buy wedding dress/suit*
Wednesday 21st	Saturday 24th
afternoon – shopping (for honeymoon)	*get married today!!* *party at The Palace Hotel – 8.00 p.m.*

5A Put these in order

Comparatives and superlatives

Example: Put these animals in order, starting with the **biggest**.
☐ a cow ☐1 an elephant ☐ a mouse ☐ a dog

A Put these countries in order, starting with the **smallest**.
☐ Peru ☐ Japan ☐ France ☐ Spain

B Put these oceans in order, starting with the **largest**.
☐ The Atlantic Ocean
☐ The Pacific Ocean
☐ The Indian Ocean
☐ The Arctic Ocean

C Put these countries in order, starting with the one that has **the highest population**.
☐ Poland ☐ Spain
☐ India ☐ Brazil

D Put these famous buildings in order, starting with the **oldest**.
☐ The Colosseum
☐ The Eiffel Tower
☐ The Taj Mahal
☐ The Sydney Opera House

E Put these cities in order, starting with the one **nearest** to the North Pole.
☐ London ☐ New York ☐ Moscow
☐ Tokyo

Put these in order!

F Put these planets in order, starting with the one **furthest** from the sun.
☐ Earth ☐ Mars ☐ Pluto ☐ Mercury

G Put these world events in order, starting with the **most recent**.
☐ the first man on the moon
☐ the assassination of John F. Kennedy
☐ the fall of the Berlin Wall
☐ Nelson Mandela's release from prison

H Put these film stars in order, starting with the **youngest**.
☐ Julia Roberts
☐ Robert De Niro
☐ Brad Pitt
☐ Sharon Stone

I Put these rivers in order, starting with the **longest**.
☐ The Mississippi ☐ The Amazon
☐ The Rhine ☐ The Nile

J Put these films in order, starting with the one that made **the most money**.
☐ *E.T.* ☐ *Titanic* ☐ *Jurassic Park*
☐ *Star Wars*

5B An alien family

Vocabulary: describing people's appearance

Picture A

Picture B

Learner-training worksheet D

Recording new vocabulary

1 Students often write new vocabulary in lists, with a translation into their own language. Look at these two lists of words from Modules 1 and 2 of the *Students' Book*. What **extra** information about the English words is included in List B?

LIST A

rent	=	
yoga	=	
experienced	=	*experto (en)*
explain	=	*explicar*
nervous	=	*nervioso*
check	=	*verificar*
rubbish	=	*basura*
write down	=	*anotar*

LIST B

to rent (a DVD) (reg) *(also a noun – you pay rent for your flat)*	=	
(to do) yoga *(not play yoga)*	=	
experienced (adj) *(e.g. an experienced teacher)*	=	*experto (en)*
to explain something to somebody	=	*explicar*
nervous (adj) /phonemic script/ *to be/feel nervous about something (e.g. an exam)*	=	*nervioso*
to check something *(e.g. the meaning of a word)*	=	*verificar*
rubbish (noun U)	=	*basura*
to write something down *(e.g. in a notebook)* *(write/wrote/written)*	=	*anotar*

2 Look at this list of vocabulary a Polish student has made. Write the list again so that it is more useful. Include as many points as possible from exercise 1. Use your *mini-dictionary* to help you if necessary, and write the translations in your own language.

detective	=	*detektyw*
steal	=	*ukraść*
rob	=	*okradać*
journey	=	*podróż*
wedding	=	*ślub*
embarrassed	=	*zakłopotany*
dress up	=	*przebierać sie*
earn	=	*zarabiać*

3 Look in your vocabulary notebook (or your notes from this course) and see how you wrote down new vocabulary. What extra information can you add to help you use the vocabulary correctly?

6A Talk about the future

going to, would like to, would rather, will/won't

Which of these places would you rather go to? *India Australia the Caribbean* 6	**a country you'd like to visit** 7	GO BACK ONE SPACE 20	somewhere you'd like to go on holiday 21	FINISH
GO FORWARD TWO SPACES 5	how your town/city will change in the next ten years 8	**your plans for this evening** 19	five things that definitely won't happen to you this year 22	**what you'll buy next time you go shopping** 33
something you'd like to buy 4	a place where you'd like to live when you're old 9	GO FORWARD THREE SPACES 18	**someone famous you'd like to meet** 23	MISS A TURN 32
your plans for next month 3	MISS A TURN 10	what the world will be like in a hundred years' time 17	something a friend is going to do soon 24	***how you'll celebrate your next birthday*** 31
THROW AGAIN! 2	**your plans for next week** 11	what you think your children (or grandchildren) will look like 16	THROW AGAIN! 25	**something a member of your family is going to do soon** 30
a job you'd really like to do 1	Which of these jobs would you rather do? ***doctor teacher police officer*** 12	**something you're planning to buy** 15	**a job you *wouldn't* like to do** 26	GO BACK TWO SPACES 29
START	a film or play you'd like to see again 13	GO BACK THREE SPACES 14	your plans for the weekend 27	Which of these places would you rather go to tonight? *restaurant club cinema* 28

6B Holiday crossword

Holiday vocabulary

Student A

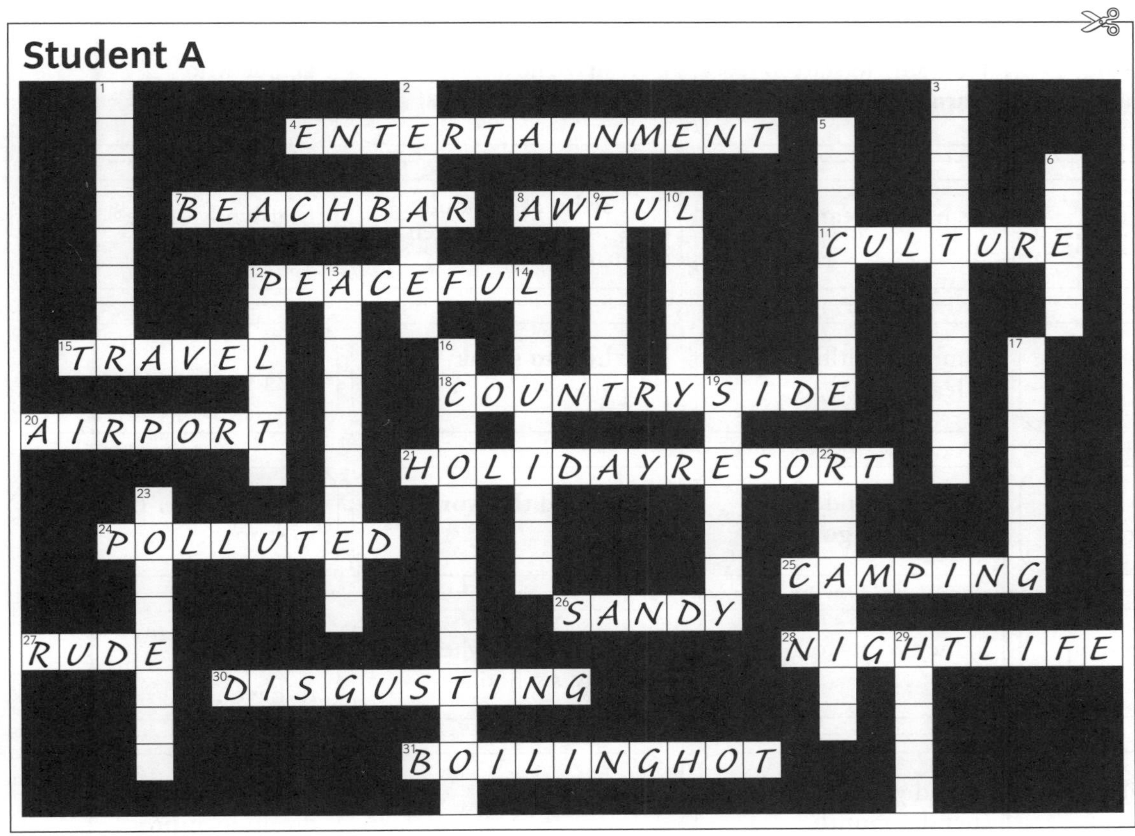

Student B

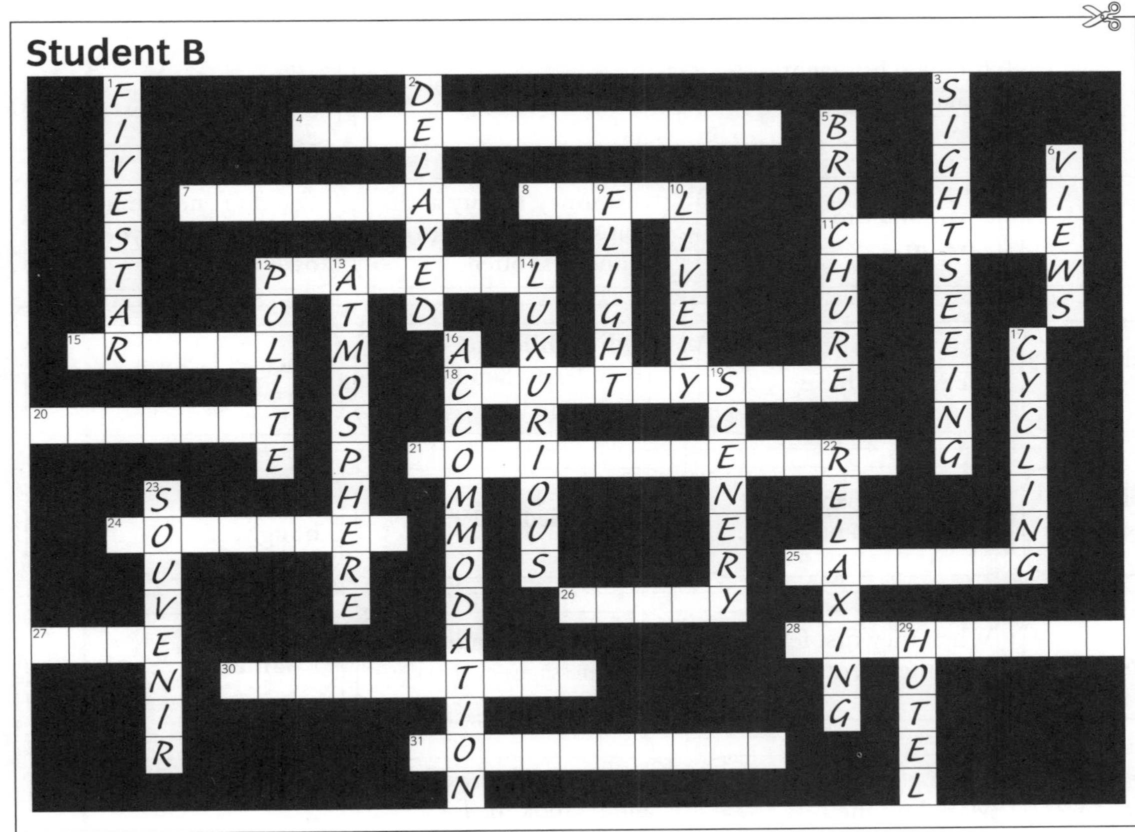

7A Ambition dominoes

Verb/noun collocations

… **be** in a rock band when he was younger.	I'm going to start **learning how to** …	… **drive** next weekend.	People who **become** …
… **famous** have to change the way they live.	It's hard to **learn how to** …	… **swim** as an adult. It's much easier when you're young.	Marilyn Monroe **became** …
… more **famous** after she died.	Tim's new girlfriend **is learning** …	… **how to speak** Japanese.	My uncle **plays** …
… **football** for Manchester United.	My best friend is planning to **go** …	… **round the world** next year.	Have you ever tried to **stop** …
… **smoking?** I gave up last year.	Sidney wants to **go to** …	… **university** when he leaves school.	Nowadays many women don't want to **have** …
… **children** until they're in their thirties.	Would you like to **spend a month** …	… **living** in New York?	It was always Frank's dream to **appear** …
… **on TV** before he died.	It took Chris eight years to **write** …	… his first **novel**.	I'd like to **go** …
… **abroad** next summer.	If you want to **save up** …	… **money to buy** a car, you should go out to dinner less often.	You don't need much money to **start your own** …
… **business** on the Internet.	We want to **have** …	… five **children**. We think larger families have more fun.	Michael Jackson **earned** more than …
… **a million dollars** when he was a teenager.	David Beckham and Victoria Adams **got** …	… **married** in 1999.	Jack and Sally **bought** …
… **a house** last year.	When they first fell in love, they **kept in** …	… **touch** by sending text messages every day.	I **wanted to** …
… **be** a professional tennis player when I was younger.	Mark **bought a** …	… **new car** last week, and he took me for a drive. It's very fast.	My Dad **wanted to** …

7B Life circles

Present perfect and Past simple

Write down **short** answers to the following points in the circles below. Write your answers in any circle you want, but **not** in the same order as the points. You do not have to answer every question, but try to answer at least **ten**.

- the name of someone you've known for over ten years (but not a family member)
- a film you've seen recently (either in the cinema or on TV/video)
- a place you went to on holiday when you were a child
- a personal possession you've had for more than five years
- the name of your best friend when you were at primary school
- a city or country you've been to that you didn't like
- something you got for Christmas last year
- a place you've been to that's very beautiful
- a job you've had in your life that you didn't like
- a film you saw last year that you really enjoyed
- something you've wanted to buy for a long time
- the name of someone you've talked to on the phone this week

FOLD

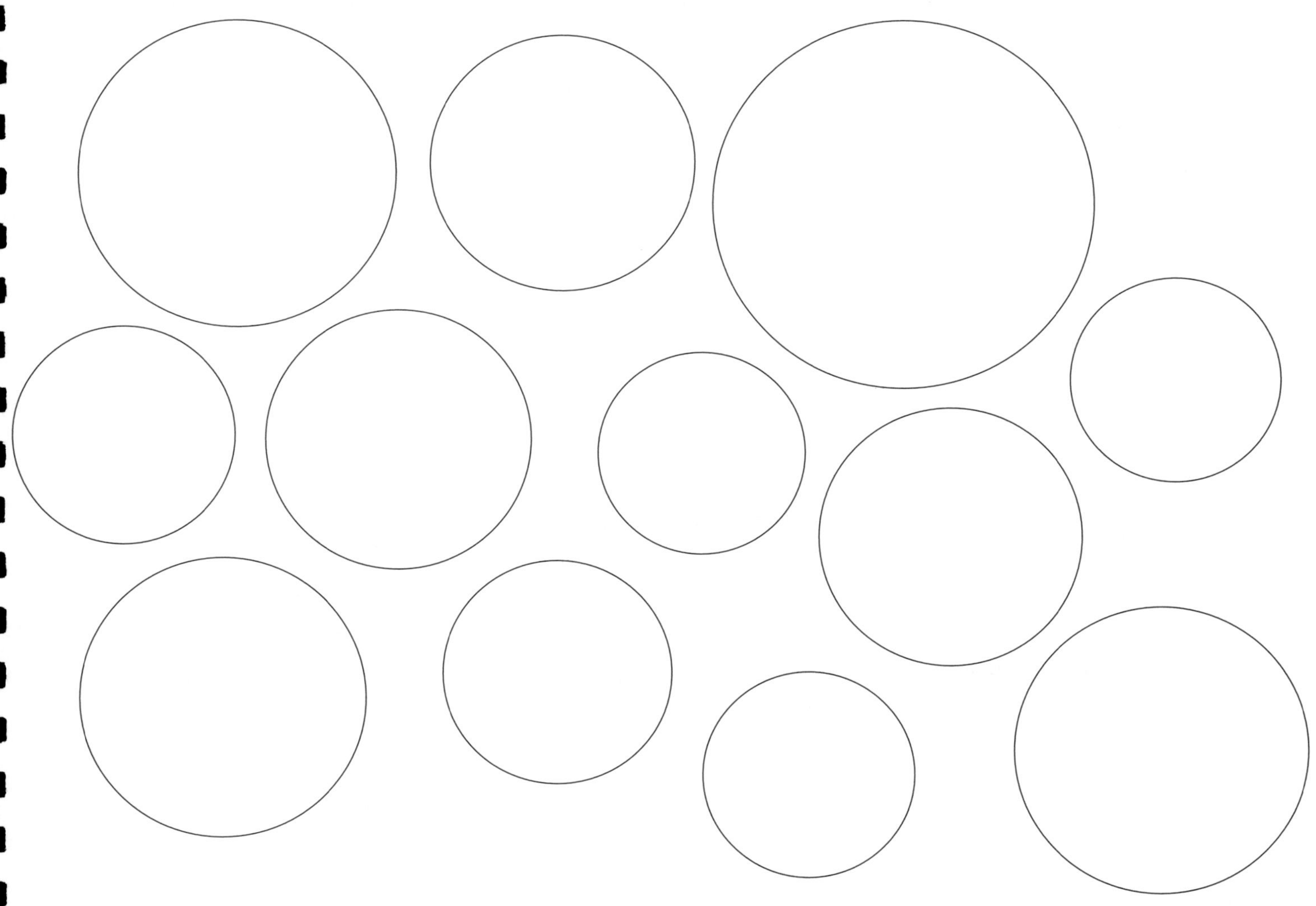

7C Happy verb families

Irregular past tenses and past participles

I'm going to **wear** my favourite dress tonight.	Michael **wore** the same pair of socks all last week!	I've only **worn** these trousers twice, and there's already a hole in them.
I'm planning to **make** a cake for your birthday.	All the students **made** a lot of mistakes in their homework.	My brother has **made** a lot of money this year.
My parents want to **grow** vegetables in their garden.	Rebecca **grew** over five centimetres last year.	These plants haven't **grown** much this summer.
I'd like to **become** a doctor when I'm older.	Kevin **became** ill when he was on holiday.	He's **become** a very good tennis player, hasn't he?
Can you **write** it down for me, please?	Shakespeare **wrote** over forty plays.	I've already **written** to the electricity company.
Will you **take** me home? I'm tired.	George **took** a long time to finish the exercise.	I've **taken** two aspirin and now I'm going to bed.
You have to **tell** him about losing your job.	On Thursday he **told** his girlfriend that he was leaving her.	Have you **told** your father about the car accident yet?
They were planning to **steal** the Mona Lisa!	The boys **stole** sweets from the shop every day.	Help! Someone has **stolen** my handbag!
Will you **send** me a copy of the report?	Aunt Mary **sent** me a letter two weeks ago.	I've just **sent** Mr Robinson an e-mail about the meeting.

Be quiet for a minute. I need to **think**.	They all **thought** that Susan and Tim were married.	Have you ever **thought** of leaving your job?
She's planning to **teach** English in Japan.	I **taught** all my children how to swim.	I've never **taught** children before. I'm scared!
I have to go and **cut** the grass.	Nancy **cut** herself while she was playing in the garden.	I've never **cut** my own hair. Have you?
I'm going to **spend** the weekend with my parents.	Yesterday my girlfriend **spent** over £300 on a dress!	I haven't **spent** much money this month.
Can you **put** that bag on the table?	Polly carefully **put** the injured animal on the table.	Where have you **put** my glasses?
I want to **see** Leonardo DiCaprio's new film.	Everybody **saw** that he was drunk when he arrived at the party.	He hasn't **seen** his brother for years.
My sister is going to **meet** the prime minister next week.	Nick **met** his ex-girlfriend at a party last weekend.	I've never **met** that man before.
I'd like to **lose** some weight this year.	Italy **lost** the 1994 World Cup final on penalties.	Oh no! I've **lost** my keys!
We're planning to **leave** on Sunday.	She **left** home at 10.00, and arrived at the office at 11.00.	Laura has **left** her husband and married his best friend!

Learner-training worksheet E

Using the *mini-dictionary:* irregular verbs – part 2

1 Notice how irregular verbs are shown in the *mini-dictionary*.

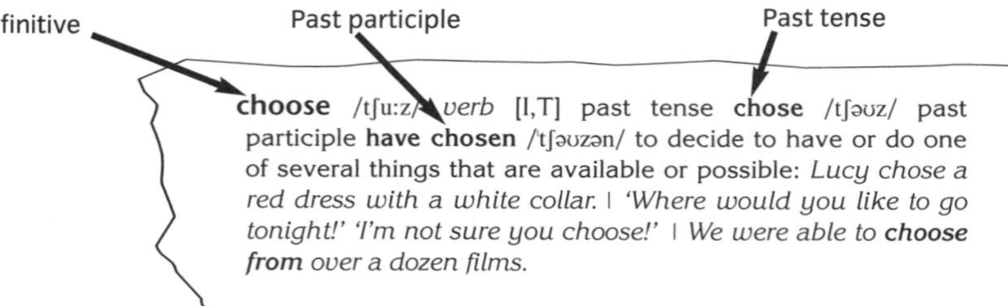

Infinitive
Past participle
Past tense
choose /tʃuːz/ *verb* [I,T] past tense **chose** /tʃəʊz/ past participle **have chosen** /tʃəʊzən/ to decide to have or do one of several things that are available or possible: *Lucy chose a red dress with a white collar.* | *'Where would you like to go tonight!' 'I'm not sure you choose!'* | *We were able to* ***choose from*** *over a dozen films.*

2 Complete the table as quickly as possible to find out who's the fastest *mini-dictionary* user in the class! (Note: You must spell all the words correctly to win!) Then test your partner on the verbs.

INFINITIVE	PAST TENSE	PAST PARTICIPLE
see		
ring		
catch		
fly		
know		
fall		
drive		
become		
throw		
wake up		

8A Article snakes and ladders

Use and non-use of articles

Question cards

1 Which is correct?

Tom is 13, and is still at *a* / *the* / Ø school, but Jim is now at *a* / *the* / Ø university studying English.

2 Find *two* mistakes with articles and correct them.

I live in a flat in city centre, very close to the Oxford Street.

3 Fill in the gaps with *a*, *an*, *the* or Ø.

He went to Italy on .... holiday, and spent a week in .... north of .... country.

4 Is this sentence right or wrong? (If it's wrong, correct it.)

I usually go to work by the train, but yesterday I went by the bus.

5 Which of these should begin with *the*?

Indian Ocean
Mediterranean
Lake Ontario
Amazon

6 *The* or no article?

He's usually at *the* / Ø college in *the* / Ø morning, and at *the* / Ø work in *the* / Ø afternoon.

7 Is this sentence right or wrong? (If it's wrong, correct it.)

In the USA most people go to work by car.

8 Fill in the gaps with *a*, *an*, *the* or Ø.

I met .... queen of .... England when I was in .... UK.

9 Is this sentence right or wrong? (If it's wrong, correct it.)

El Paso is on border of Mexico and United States.

10 Which is correct?

I've got two cars, *a* / *the* Porsche and *a* / *the* BMW.
A / *The* Porsche is much faster, but I usually drive *a* / *the* BMW.

11 Find *two* mistakes with articles and correct them.

Madras is in the south of the India, on east coast.

12 *The* or no article?

The / Ø Lake Titicaca is in *the* / Ø Peru, and it's *the* / Ø highest lake in *the* / Ø world.

Question cards

13 Find *two* mistakes with articles and correct them.

John is standing on left, and Susan is standing in the middle, next to headmaster.

14 *The* or no article?

The / Ø French people love going out at *the* / Ø night, but *the* / Ø English people prefer staying at *the* / Ø home.

15 Which is correct?

Sally lives at *the* / Ø top of *a* / *the* block of flats in *a* / *the* / Ø centre of *the* / Ø Madrid.

16 *A*, *the* or no article?

Mark couldn't find *a* / *the* / Ø job because he was in *a* / *the* / Ø prison for ten years.

17 Fill in the gaps with *a*, *an*, *the* or Ø.

When I was at .... school I lived outside .... London in .... suburbs.

18 Is this sentence right or wrong? (If it's wrong, correct it.)

I think dogs are more intelligent than cats, but horses are the most intelligent animals I know.

19 Which is correct?

They found *a* / *the* / Ø Titanic at *a* / *the* / Ø bottom of *the* / Ø Atlantic Ocean.

20 Find *two* mistakes with articles and correct them.

I bought a picture and a carpet this morning. I've put a picture on the bathroom wall and the carpet on kitchen floor.

21 Fill in the gaps with *a*, *an*, *the* or Ø.

He lives in .... town centre, on .... Park Road, and his house is on .... left.

22 Which of these should begin with *the*?

Andes
Mount Everest
Himalayas
Mount Fuji

23 Is this sentence right or wrong? (If it's wrong, correct it.)

Loch Ness is most famous lake in Scotland, because of Loch Ness Monster.

24 Find *two* mistakes with articles and correct them.

I really hate the mice, but I love spiders.
I have a tarantula at home, and it lives on ceiling!

8B The Hungry Hippo café

Quantifiers (*some*, *any*, *much*, *not enough*, etc.)

Worksheet 1

THE HUNGRY HIPPO CAFÉ

NORTH STREET BRANCH

You are the new managers of this branch of the Hungry Hippo café. You want to open the café **tomorrow**! Look at the menu and the pictures, and decide:

- what you have too much/many of
- what you don't have enough of
- what you don't have any of.

MENU

DRINKS		HOT FOOD	
Tea	80p	Hamburger	£2.40
Coffee	£1.00	Cheeseburger	£2.90
Coke	90p	Pizza	£3.20
Orange juice	£1.00	Chips	£1.20
SANDWICHES		**DESSERTS**	
Egg	£1.30	Chocolate cake	£1.70
Cheese	£1.60	Ice cream	£1.50

Worksheet 2

THE HUNGRY HIPPO CAFÉ

SOUTH STREET BRANCH

You are the new managers of this branch of the Hungry Hippo café. You want to open the café **tomorrow**! Look at the menu and the pictures, and decide:

- what you have too much/many of
- what you don't have enough of
- what you don't have any of.

MENU

DRINKS		HOT FOOD	
Tea	80p	Hamburger	£2.40
Coffee	£1.00	Cheeseburger	£2.90
Coke	90p	Pizza	£3.20
Orange juice	£1.00	Chips	£1.20
SANDWICHES		**DESSERTS**	
Egg	£1.30	Chocolate cake	£1.70
Cheese	£1.60	Ice cream	£1.50

8C Where's the nearest bank?

Language for giving directions

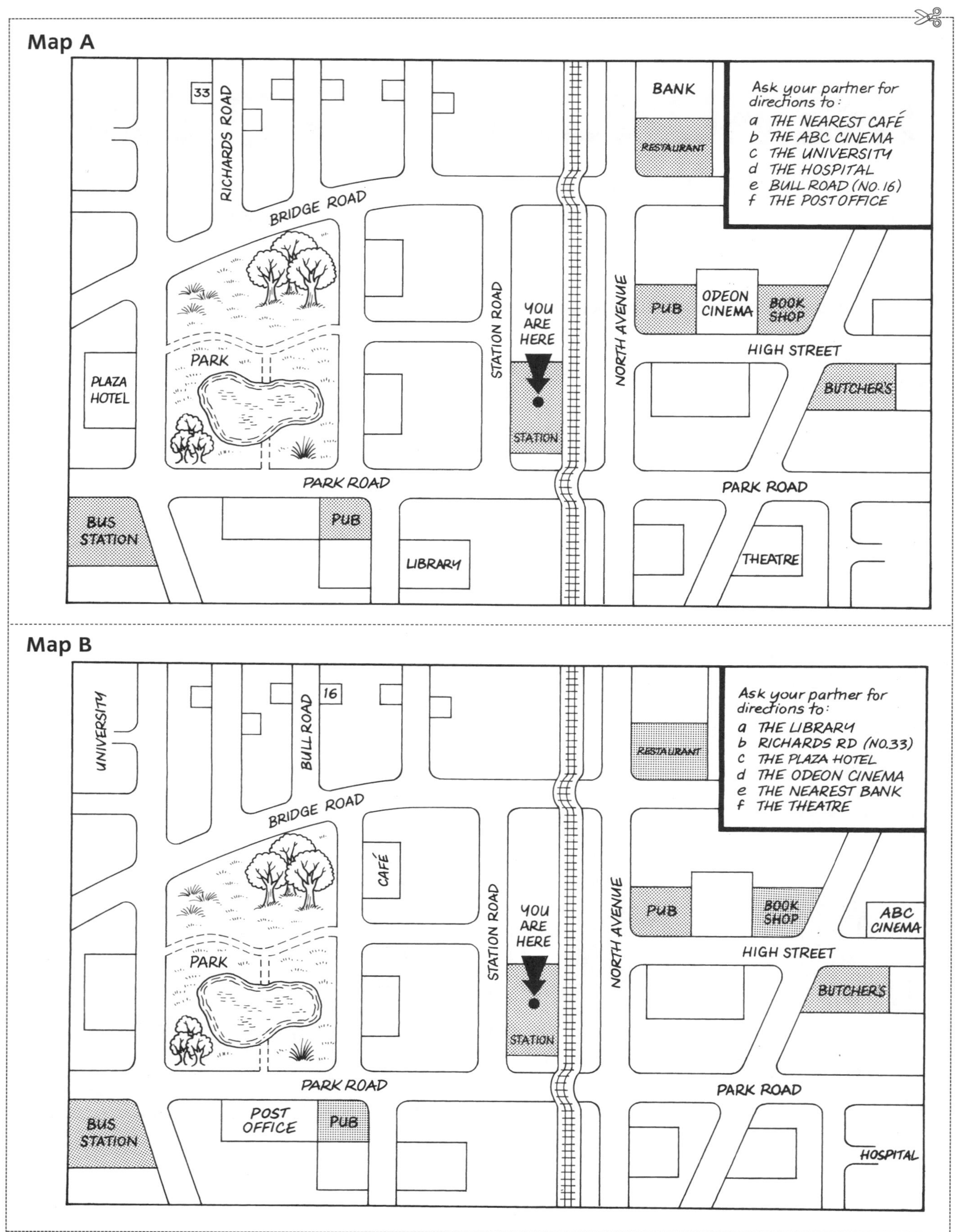

Learner-training worksheet F

Noticing and remembering prepositions and articles in phrases

1 Look at this picture of two English teachers having a break in the teachers' room. What do you think they are talking about?

2 Read the following conversation and see if your predictions were right.

MATTHEW: Hi Jill, have you got a light?
JILL: Yes, here you are. Are you feeling OK?
MATTHEW: Yes, I'm just tired, that's all. I went to a party in the city centre, and didn't get home until three.
JILL: So that's why you didn't arrive on time this morning!
MATTHEW: Er, yes. But you were late for work the other day.
JILL: That was because I went to the doctor, not because I stayed out late!
MATTHEW: Yes, well, I'm not very good at getting up early.
JILL: That's probably why you're always in a bad mood!
MATTHEW: I'm not! Anyway, what are you doing at the weekend?
JILL: I'm going out for a meal with some friends on Saturday. On Sunday I might go for a walk in the countryside. What about you?
MATTHEW: I've got the day off on Friday, so I'm going to visit an old friend who lives on the coast.
JILL: That sounds fun. Look, we're going to be late for our classes. Let's go.
MATTHEW: What, already? Where did I put my books ...?

3 There are lots of phrases in English that are always the same, or only change a little. These phrases often include **articles** (*a*, *an*, *the*) and **prepositions** (for example, *to*, *for*). Look at the conversation above again and underline all the phrases that contain articles and/or prepositions. The first three are done for you.

4 It is useful to write down and learn these phrases as one item of vocabulary. Here are some of the phrases in the conversation. Write in the missing words.

a .... light?
b .... city centre
c to arrive ....
d to be .... work
e .... day
f to go .... doctor
g to stay .... late
h to be (not very) .... doing something
i to get .... early
j to be .... bad mood
k .... weekend
l to go .... meal
m to go .... walk
n .... countryside
o to have the day ....
p .... coast

9A In the 2020s

will, *won't*, *may* and *might* for future possibility

SURVEY A

HOLIDAYS AND FREE TIME

Write questions based on the following prompts.

In the 2020s ...

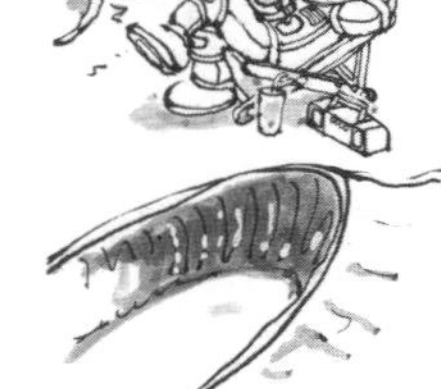

- people – have more free time?
- people – have longer holidays?
- all films – be in 3D?
- people – still read books?
- everyone – spend more time watching TV?
- people – be able to go on holiday to the moon?
- computer games – be more popular than television?

When you have finished, add one or two questions of your own.

SURVEY B

HOMES AND LIFESTYLES

Write questions based on the following prompts.

In the 2020s ...

- robots – do all the housework?
- people – still shop in supermarkets?
- everyone – have videophones in their homes?
- more people – be homeless?
- cars – use water instead of petrol?
- clothes – look completely different?
- students – have robot teachers?

When you have finished, add one or two questions of your own.

SURVEY C

FAMILIES AND CHILDREN

Write questions based on the following prompts.

In the 2020s ...

- people – have smaller families?
- parents – be able to choose the colour of their baby's eyes?
- parents – be able to choose their baby's IQ?
- a lot more people – live to be over 100 years old?
- fewer people – get married?
- men – be able to have babies?
- governments – make laws about how many children you can have?

When you have finished, add one or two questions of your own.

SURVEY D

WORLD NEWS

Write questions based on the following prompts.

In the 2020s ...

- scientists – be able to clone human beings?
- tigers – be extinct?
- there – be a nuclear war?
- a woman – become president of the USA?
- we – make contact with life on other planets?
- China – be the most powerful country in the world?
- we – have enough food to feed the world?

When you have finished, add one or two questions of your own.

9B Worried parents

Present tense after *if*, *when*, *as soon as* and other time words

Student A worksheet

ROLEPLAY 1

Your son/daughter is planning to hitchhike across the USA. He/She is flying to Miami, then going to New Orleans, Las Vegas and San Francisco. You are very worried about him/her, and have lots of questions to ask.

1 phone me / as soon as / arrive in Miami?
2 what / do / if / nobody / give / you a lift?
3 what / do / if / get lost?
4 where / stay / when / get to New Orleans?
5 what / do / when / run out of money?
6 what / do / if / lose all your money in Las Vegas?
7 where / stay / when / arrive in San Francisco?
8 visit me / as soon as / get back home?

ROLEPLAY 2

You're going to the north of India. You're flying to Delhi – you've already booked a hotel there – then getting a train (or a bus) to the Himalayas. You want to go camping in the mountains, and you're planning to find a local guide to come with you. You're going to take a lot of medicine, a tent, some chocolate for emergencies – and a very good sleeping bag!

Your mother/father is very worried about you and is going to ask you lots of questions about the holiday. Use the information above (or your own ideas) to answer the questions, and try to make him/her feel more relaxed!

Student B worksheet

ROLEPLAY 1

You're going to hitchhike across the USA. You're planning to fly to Miami, then hitchhike to New Orleans, Las Vegas and San Francisco. You haven't got enough money for the whole trip, but you've got friends in New Orleans who own a restaurant – you think that you can get a job there. You also have friends in San Francisco. You're planning to take a tent, your credit card and a very big map!

Your mother/father is very worried about you, and is going to ask you lots of questions about the holiday. Use the information above (or your own ideas) to answer the questions, and try to make him/her feel more relaxed!

ROLEPLAY 2

Your son/daughter is planning to go camping in the north of India. He/She is flying to Delhi, then going by train to the Himalayas. You are very worried about him/her, and have lots of questions to ask.

1 where / stay / when / arrive in Delhi?
2 how / get to the Himalayas / if / the trains / be / fully booked?
3 what / do / if / get / very cold in the mountains?
4 what / do / if / get lost?
5 what / eat / if / can't find any food?
6 call me / as soon as / get back to Delhi?
7 what / do / if / get ill?
8 buy me a present / before / leave India?!

Learner-training worksheet G

Deducing meaning from context – part 1

1 Read the following text and decide what really happened!

When Mark was walking home, he noticed a man sitting on the **pavement** with his head in his hands. Mark saw that there was blood all over the man's shirt, so he walked over to him and **tapped** him on the shoulder.

'Are you OK?' asked Mark.

'Three men have just **beaten** me **up** and stolen all my money,' said the man. 'Can you lend me five pounds so that I can get home?'

'Of course,' said Mark, and he took out his **wallet** and gave the man a five-pound note.

'Thanks a lot,' said the man with a **grin**. He stood up and handed Mark a brown paper bag. 'This is for you,' he said, then **sprinted** across the road before Mark could say anything. Mark watched him disappear, then **shrugged** his shoulders and opened the bag. The only thing inside was an empty bottle of tomato ketchup …

2 Look at the words in **bold** in the text above, and answer the following questions.

a Can you guess the meaning of these words from the context?
b Which words can you guess the *exact* meaning of, and which can you only guess the *general* meaning of?
c What other words in the text helped you guess the meaning? Are there any words in **bold** that you can't guess the meaning of?
d When you find a word you don't know in a text, do you always have to know the exact meaning, or is the general meaning sometimes enough?

3 Look at the vocabulary <u>underlined</u> in the following sentences.

Which words
- can you guess the **exact** meaning of?
- can you guess the **general** meaning of?
- **can't** you guess the meaning of?

a He walked down the stairs to the <u>cellar</u> and came back with two bottles of red wine.
b I went to a party last week and <u>bumped into</u> an old friend from school.
c I didn't like him at all. I thought he was very <u>arrogant</u> and unfriendly.
d Sally <u>blushed</u> when her brother started telling his friends about the silly things she did when she was a little girl.
e Frank decided <u>to dig</u> a big hole at the bottom of the garden and put the dead body in it.
f Nobody slept very well because the dogs <u>barked</u> all night.
g Wilf drank nearly a whole bottle of whisky, then <u>staggered</u> out of the pub to look for a taxi.
h Tim walked into the shop and bought a new <u>hammer</u>.
i The bomb <u>went off</u> at exactly 3.47 p.m.
j Tom walked into the room wearing a T-shirt and <u>flares</u>.

4 Discuss your answers with another student. Do you both agree? Which words in the sentence helped you guess the meaning?

10A What can I do for you?

Vocabulary: health problems

Patient A

You have these health problems. Write down what they are in the boxes.

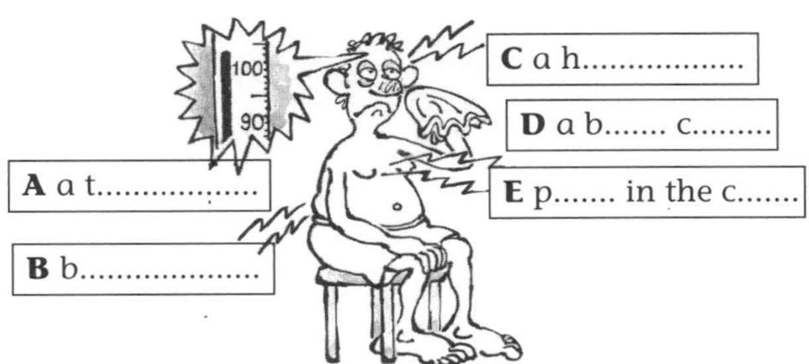

Decide **when** you got problems D and E, and **how long** you've had all your problems. You also cut yourself! (You decide **what** happened.)

You saw your doctor about problems A and B last week. He/She told you to stay in bed and keep warm, but didn't give you anything to take. Now you are going to see him/her again. Tell the doctor about your problems **one at a time**.

Doctor A

This patient came to see you last week with a temperature and a backache. You told him/her to stay in bed and keep warm, but didn't give him/her anything to take. Now the patient is back and doesn't look very well!

Look back at the quiz in the *Students' Book* on page 88 and try to remember all the different treatments and advice you can give.

Useful language

Hello, what can I do for you?
How long have you had (this problem)?
Have you taken anything for it?
You should ...
You must ...

Patient B

You have these health problems. Write down what they are in the boxes.

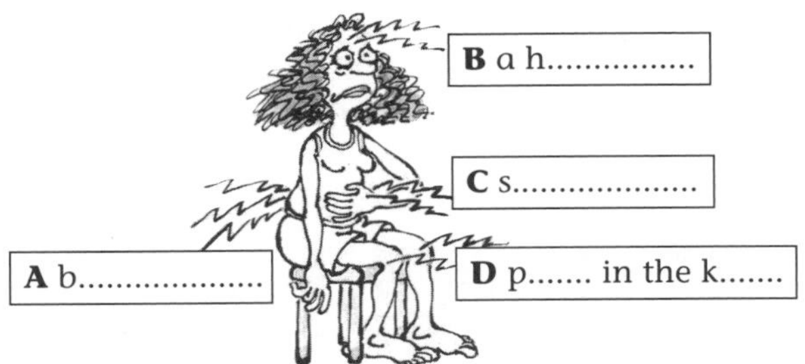

Decide **when** you got problems C and D, and **how long** you've had all your problems. You also burnt yourself this morning! (You decide **how** and **where** you burnt yourself.)

You think you are very ill and want the doctor to send you to hospital (or at least give you a letter saying that you don't have to go to work tomorrow!). Tell the doctor about your problems **one at a time**.

Doctor B

This patient has been to see you quite often. Sometimes he/she has real health problems, but sometimes you think the patient is telling lies so that he/she doesn't have to go to work!

You cannot tell the patient that you think he/she is lying, but you must ask lots of questions about the illnesses to make sure that they are real.

Look back at the quiz in the *Students' Book* on page 88 and try to remember all the different treatments and advice you can give.

Useful language

Hello, what can I do for you?
How long have you had (this problem)?
Have you taken anything for it?
You should ...
You must ...

10B The Ghost

used to and Past simple

The Ghost role card

You are a world-famous burglar called The Ghost. You've spent your life stealing from the houses of rich and famous people all over the world, but last year the police caught you in the middle of a robbery. Now you're in prison! A journalist from the magazine *Famous Criminals* is coming to interview you. Look at the following information and prepare your life story.

The first thing you stole in your life was .... (what?) when you were .... years old.
You started burgling houses in .... (when?). You used to sell burglar alarms to rich and famous people. Then you went back to the house at night, switched off the burglar alarm and stole anything you wanted!
You used to steal .... , ... and .... (what kind of things?) from the houses.
You always used to wear .... and ....
You used to leave .... (what?) in every house to tell them The Ghost was there.
You burgled ....'s house two years ago, and you stole .... from it.
You spent all the money on .... and ....
One night you got caught! You went to burgle ....'s house – but they had a *new* burglar alarm!!

When you've finished, think of some more houses of famous people that you burgled, and what you stole from them!

Journalist role card

You are a journalist from the magazine *Famous Criminals*. You are going to interview The Ghost, a world-famous burglar. The Ghost used to steal from the houses of rich and famous people all over the world, but last year the police caught him/her in the middle of a burglary. Now he/she is in prison.

Look at the following ideas and write down the questions you are going to ask The Ghost in your interview. Use both *used to* and the Past simple in your questions.

- the first thing / steal in your life? Age?
- when / start burgling rich people's houses?
- how / get into / the houses?
- what / steal?
- what / wear?
- what / leave / in the houses you burgled?
- whose house / you burgle two years ago?
- what / steal from him/her?
- what / do with all the money?
- how / get caught?

When you've finished, add some more questions of your own.

10C Bob's night out

Past continuous and Past simple

BOB!
F

...Party...
D

Ten minutes later
J

RING!
B

13th
30th
G

11A The Lovebug Dating Agency

Gerunds; expressions for liking and disliking

Men cards

♥ *Lovebug Dating Agency* ♥

Client A Name: ....

'I really like .... and .... , and I'm very keen on .... I think .... is good fun, and I quite like .... I don't mind .... , but I can't stand .... !'

♥ *Lovebug Dating Agency* ♥

Client B Name ....

'I love .... and .... , and I'm very interested in .... I really enjoy .... , and I quite like .... as well. I don't mind .... , but I absolutely loathe .... !'

♥ *Lovebug Dating Agency* ♥

Client C Name: ....

'I'm crazy about .... I also like .... and .... I find .... very relaxing. I think .... can be fun, but I don't like .... And I really hate .... !'

♥ *Lovebug Dating Agency* ♥

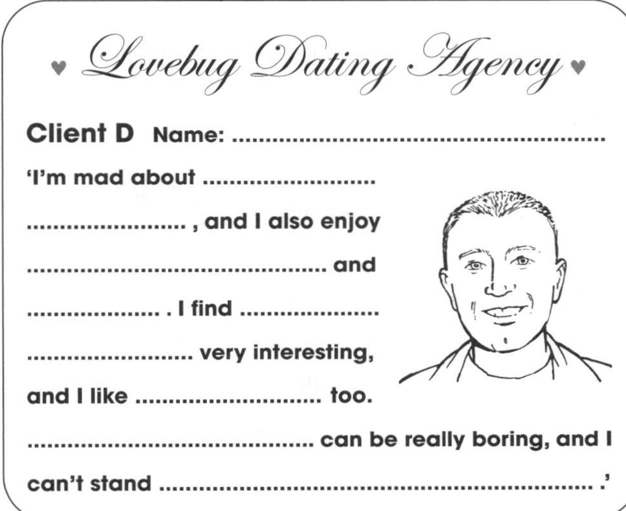

Client D Name: ....

'I'm mad about .... , and I also enjoy .... and .... I find .... very interesting, and I like .... too. .... can be really boring, and I can't stand ....'

♥ *Lovebug Dating Agency* ♥

Client E Name: ....

'I'm very keen on .... and .... I also love .... , and I really enjoy .... I think .... is very relaxing, and I don't mind .... , but I really hate ....'

♥ *Lovebug Dating Agency* ♥

Client F Name: ....

'I'm mad about .... and .... I also really like .... I think .... is very interesting, but I find .... incredibly boring. I don't mind .... , but I absolutely loathe .... !'

Women cards

♥ *Lovebug Dating Agency* ♥

Client 1 Name: ....

'I don't really like .... , but I love .... I'm also very interested in .... and .... I find .... relaxing, but I loathe .... Oh, and I'm crazy about .... !'

♥ *Lovebug Dating Agency* ♥

Client 2 Name: ....

'I'm very keen on .... , and I love .... at the weekends. I also really like .... and .... I think .... can be great fun, and I don't mind .... , but I can't stand ....'

♥ *Lovebug Dating Agency* ♥

Client 3 Name: ....

'I really enjoy .... and .... , and I find .... very interesting. I'm also keen on .... , and I quite like .... too. I think .... is good fun, but I really hate .... !'

♥ *Lovebug Dating Agency* ♥

Client 4 Name: ....

'I like .... and .... , but I can't stand .... I'm mad about .... , and I really enjoy .... I think .... can be very boring, and I absolutely loathe ....'

♥ *Lovebug Dating Agency* ♥

Client 5 Name: ....

'I'm very keen on .... , and I also really like .... I find .... very relaxing, and I quite like .... and .... I don't mind .... , but I really hate ....'

♥ *Lovebug Dating Agency* ♥

Client 6 Name: ....

'I'm mad about .... , and I really like .... as well. I think .... can be fun, and I also enjoy .... and .... I don't really like .... , and I find .... incredibly boring.'

Learner-training worksheet H

Using the *mini-dictionary* to find constructions that follow verbs

1 Notice how the *mini-dictionary* shows which grammatical construction follows a verb.

like /laɪk/ *verb* [T] **1** to think that someone or something is nice or good: *Katie likes John a lot.* | *I really liked that movie.* | *Joe likes playing basketball.* | *What do you like best about school?*

try /traɪ/ *verb* [I,T] past tense **tried** /traɪd/ to make an attempt to do something: *I try to learn a few new English words every day.* | *She tried hard to forget about Rob.* | *Ms. Wood always tries to make the lesson interesting.*

might /maɪt/ *modal verb* used to say that it is possible that something is true or will happen: | *Be careful! You might hurt yourself!* | *Some people might lose their jobs.* | *You might be right.*

2 Look up the following verbs and verb phrases in your *mini-dictionary*, and put them in the correct column in the table below.

~~want~~	have to	enjoy	can	arrange
stop	may	hate	would like	could
learn	intend	don't mind	plan	must

VERB + GERUND	VERB + INFINITIVE WITH *TO*	VERB + INFINITIVE WITHOUT *TO*
	want	

3 Are the following sentences correct? If not, can you correct them?

a I've arranged meeting my brother this evening. ....
b I must to go to the dentist this afternoon. ....
c Stop watching television and do your homework! ....
d Do you enjoy play tennis? ....
e I have to going to work tomorrow. ....
f Jim is learning to drive at the moment. ....
g I'd like to live in France when I'm older. ....
h I hate get up early. ....
i We're planning go to New York for our holidays. ....
j I don't mind looking after the children tonight. ....

12A What's this?

Describing everyday objects

12B The Handbag Gang

Past simple passive

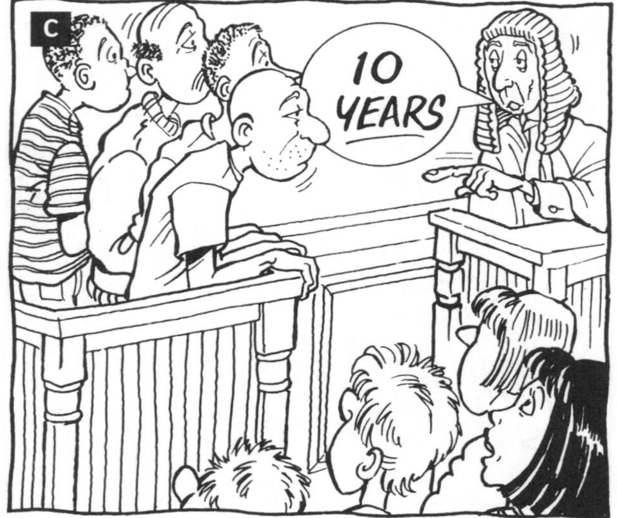

Vocabulary worksheet

Match these words and expressions with the correct pictures. There could be more than one correct answer.

1 to pull out a gun ....
2 to steal money ....
3 to rob a bank ....
4 to arrest someone ....
5 a wig ....
6 a cashier ....
7 to order someone to do something ....
8 to send someone to prison ....
9 to be disguised as women ....
10 a number plate ....
11 a shopping trolley ....

13A Century People

Present perfect simple and continuous for unfinished past

Old person role card

You are over 100 years old! You are going to be interviewed for a TV programme called *Century People*. Before the interview, fill in the gaps in the information below. Use your imagination!

You are .... years old!
You live in .... (where?).
You moved there in .... (which year?).
You got married in .... (when?)
to .... (name?).
He/She is .... years old.
You have .... children, ... grandchildren and ....
great-grandchildren (how many?).
Your oldest friend is .... (who?).
You met him/her in .... (when?).
Your favourite hobby is .... (what?).
You started doing this in .... (when?).
You are studying .... (what?) in the evenings.
You started this .... (when?).
Your oldest possession is .... (what?).
You were given it in .... (when?) by .... (who?).
What is the secret of long life? ....

When you've finished, add more details to the topics above to talk about in the interview.

Interviewer role card

You are an interviewer for the TV programme *Century People*, which every week looks at the life of someone who is over 100 years old. You are going to interview someone for next week's programme. Look at the information below and write questions to ask him/her. Be careful of the tenses you use.

- how old ?
- where / live? how long / live there?
- married? how long / be married?
- children? grandchildren? great-grandchildren?!
- oldest friend? how long / know him/her?
- what do / spare time? how long / do that?
- study anything now? what? how long / study it?
- what / oldest possession? how long / have it?
- what / be / the secret of long life?

When you've finished, think of three or four more questions to ask.

13B Old friends

Present perfect simple and continuous for unfinished past

Role card 1

You've been an architect for seven years.
You live in New York, and you've been living there since 1990.
Your wife/husband has been a primary school teacher for five years.
You study Chinese, but you've only been studying it for two weeks.

Name	What we have in common

Role card 2

You've been an architect for seven years.
You live in Rome, but you've been staying at the Ratz Hotel this week.
Your wife/husband is a waiter/waitress in an Italian restaurant, and he/she has worked there since January.
You go horse riding, and you've had your horse since last April.

Name	What we have in common

Role card 3

You're a lawyer for a computer company. You've been working for them since 1998.
You've been living in London since 1997.
Your wife/husband has been a primary school teacher for five years.
You do yoga, and you've been doing it for nearly three years.

Name	What we have in common

Role card 4

You're a lawyer for a computer company. You've been working for them since 1998.
You live in a flat in the centre of town. You've had the flat for eight years.
Your wife/husband is a waiter/waitress in an Italian restaurant, and he/she has worked there since January.
You love sailing. You've been sailing since you were a child.

Name	What we have in common

Role card 5

You've been studying to be a doctor for three years.
You want to become a GP.
You live in New York, and you've been living there since 1990.
You've been married for exactly one year – it's your wedding anniversary today!
You love sailing. You've been sailing since you were a child.

Name	What we have in common

Role card 6

You've been studying to be a doctor for three years.
You want to become a GP.
You live in Rome, but you've been staying at the Ratz Hotel this week.
You're getting married tomorrow, but you've only known your boyfriend/girlfriend for a few weeks!
You do yoga, and you've been doing it for nearly three years.

Name	What we have in common

Role card 7

You're an actor/actress. You've been appearing in *Romeo and Juliet* since last March.
You've been living in London since 1997.
You've been married for exactly one year – it's your wedding anniversary today!
You go horse riding, and you've had your horse since last April.

Name	What we have in common

Role card 8

You're an actor/actress. You've been appearing in *Romeo and Juliet* since last March.
You live in a flat in the centre of town. You've had the flat for eight years.
You're getting married tomorrow, but you've only known your boyfriend/girlfriend for a few weeks!
You study Chinese, but you've only been studying it for two weeks.

Name	What we have in common

Role card 9

You've been an architect for seven years.
You've been living in London since 1997.
You're getting married tomorrow, but you've only known your boyfriend/girlfriend for a few weeks!
You love sailing. You've been sailing since you were a child.

Name	What we have in common

Role card 10

You're a lawyer for a computer company. You've been working for them since 1998.
You live in Rome, but you've been staying at the Ratz Hotel this week.
You've been married for exactly one year – it's your wedding anniversary today!
You study Chinese, but you've only been studying it for two weeks.

Name	What we have in common

Role card 11

You've been studying to be a doctor for three years.
You want to become a GP.
You live in a flat in the centre of town. You've had the flat for eight years.
Your wife/husband has been a primary school teacher for five years.
You go horse riding, and you've had your horse since last April.

Name	What we have in common

Role card 12

You're an actor/actress. You've been appearing in *Romeo and Juliet* since last March.
You live in New York, and you've been living there since 1990.
Your wife/husband is a waiter/waitress in an Italian restaurant, and he/she has worked there since January.
You do yoga, and you've been doing it for nearly three years.

Name	What we have in common

Learner-training worksheet I

Deducing meaning from context – part 2

1 Put the following story in order, starting with paragraph **D**.

THE BOX

A 'Michael!' said Jennifer when she opened the door. 'What are you doing here?'
Michael took off his hat and *undid* his coat. 'It's Sally,' he said. 'She found the letters. Not surprisingly, she was furious.'

B 'I ... I can explain ...' began Michael.
'Get out, and don't ever come back!' *yelled* Susan. Then she *slammed the door* and ran to the bedroom.

C 'This is going to be a wonderful holiday,' she thought as she started *packing*. Soon she had everything she needed, except for one thing – sun cream. She went to the bathroom to look for some, and when she pulled open the bottom *drawer* she found a small box.

D One afternoon Sally was getting ready to go on holiday. She was going to Jamaica with her husband Michael to celebrate their tenth wedding anniversary, and was looking forward to lying in the sun on a beautiful beach.

E She took the box out of the drawer and opened it. It was full of letters. She lifted the box to her nose and *sniffed* – the letters smelt of expensive perfume! Sally sat on the *edge* of the bath and started reading.

F Michael stood outside the house for a few minutes, then started walking into the centre of town. It was raining hard, and when he arrived at Jennifer's house he was completely *soaked*.

G 'Oh no!,' said Jennifer. 'What are we going to do now?'
Michael put his arms around her and *hugged* her. Then he put his hand into his coat pocket and took out a white envelope. Inside the envelope were two plane tickets.
'Let's go to Jamaica,' he said with a smile.

H Two hours later Michael came home from work. 'Hello, darling!' he said as he opened the front door. Sally was waiting for him.
'I *came across* these when I was packing,' she said, and threw the box of letters at him. 'I know all about you and Jennifer.'

2 With a partner, try to work out the meaning of the words in *italics*, from the context. (Don't use a dictionary.)

3 Ask and answer these questions in pairs or groups.

a What do you always **pack** when you're going on holiday?
b Who was the last person you **hugged**?
c What do you keep in the **drawers** in your house/flat?
d Think of two reasons why people **sniff**.
e Think of three things that have **edges**.
f Have you ever **come across** some old letters or photos in your house?
g Think of two reasons why people **yell**.
h If someone **slams the door**, how do they feel?
i When was the last time you were **soaked**?
j Think of three things you can **undo**.

14A Get rich quick!

Vocabulary: money

GIVE HALF YOUR MONEY TO THE PERSON ON YOUR RIGHT!

£15,000

£10,000

£25,000

£5,000

DOUBLE YOUR MONEY!

£5,000

£20,000

£15,000

THROW AGAIN!

£5,000

£25,000

£5,000

START (EVERY TIME YOU PASS THIS SQUARE YOU GET £10,000 FREE)

£10,000

£15,000

£20,000

£5,000

GIVE HALF YOUR MONEY TO THE PERSON ON YOUR LEFT!

£10,000

£5,000

£15,000

MISS A TURN!

£20,000

£25,000

£10,000

GET RICH QUICK!

MONEY CARDS

Money cards

1 Q: What's the word for someone who bets on horses or goes to casinos? A: *a gambler*	**2** Q: Which preposition? 'I'd like to change a hundred pounds .... dollars.' A: *into*	**3** Q: If you owe somebody money, what should you do as soon as possible? A: *pay him/her back*
4 Q: Which word is missing? 'I'd like to go to Italy on holiday, but I can't .... it.' A: *afford*	**5** Q: Which verb is correct? 'I *win/earn* about £1,000 a month.' A: *earn*	**6** Q: Which of these three verbs is irregular, and what is the past tense and past participle? **save waste bet** A: *bet (bet, bet)*
7 Q: Which verb is correct? 'If you buy that car, you're *spending/wasting* your money. It's over 20 years old!' A: *wasting*	**8** Q: Which preposition? 'He invested all his money .... a new Internet company.' A: *in*	**9** Q: Which word is missing? (at a restaurant) 'Excuse me, is service .... ?' A: *included*
10 Q: Which of these three verbs is irregular, and what is the past tense and past participle? **borrow lose change** A: *lose (lost, lost)*	**11** Q: What do you call money that is round and made of metal? A: *coins*	**12** Q: Which verb is correct? 'Could you *borrow/lend* me some money until tomorrow?' A: *lend*
13 Q: Which preposition? 'Excuse me, could you tell me the price .... that computer?' A: *of*	**14** Q: Which of these three verbs is irregular, and what is the past tense and past participle? **invest win earn** A: *win (won, won)*	**15** Q: Which preposition? 'Frank bets .... football matches every weekend.' A: *on*
16 Q: Which preposition? 'I spend a lot of money .... clothes.' A: *on*	**17** Q: Which preposition? 'John is always very careful .... money.' A: *with*	**18** Q: If you move to a new country and want to put your money in a bank, what do you need to do? A: *open a bank account*
19 Q: Which *two* words are missing? 'Can I pay for this .... card?' A: *by credit*	**20** Q: Which preposition? 'I borrowed £10 .... my brother.' A: *from*	**21** Q: Which of these three verbs is irregular, and what is the past tense and past participle? **lend pay owe** A: *lend (lent, lent)*
22 Q: What do you call the money you leave for a waiter at the end of a meal? A: *a tip*	**23** Q: How do you spell 'businessman'? A: *B-U-S-I-N-E-S-S-M-A-N*	**24** Q: Which of these can't be used with the word 'money'? **earn spend can't afford win** A: *can't afford*

14B Dealing with money

Vocabulary: banking and money

Find someone who:

Name

.... has more than two credit cards.

.... has got a lot of change with them.

.... knows the exchange rate for two different currencies.

.... has changed money recently.

.... knows where you can change money without paying commission.

.... has paid a bill recently.

.... thinks that service shouldn't be included in restaurants.

.... always leaves a tip.

.... knows how much milk costs.

.... has been to a cashpoint machine today.

.... has some foreign currency with them.

Learner-training worksheet J

Using the *mini-dictionary* to find dependent prepositions

1 Notice how the *mini-dictionary* shows which preposition follows some verbs and adjectives.

depend on /dɪˈpend ˈɒn/ *verb* [T] to change because of other things that happen: *'Is the concert indoors or outdoors?' 'It depends on the weather.'*

frightened /ˈfraɪtnd/ *adjective* afraid that something bad might happen: *Liz has always been frightened of spiders.*

2 Circle the correct prepositions in the following sentences.

a Do you ever **worry** *for / about / on* getting old?
b Put this hat on. It'll **protect** you *by / of / from* the sun.
c I'm very **annoyed** *about / with / from* him for being so late.
d He lost control of the car and **crashed** *against / into / onto* a tree.
e Her opinion of the film was very **similar** *for / to / about* mine.
f If you **click** *on / at / onto* this, then you can save your document.
g How much have you **spent** *with / on / for* food this week?
h She's always **arguing** *with / to / for* her boyfriend.
i Jack's aunt **died** *with / of / in* a heart attack last weekend.
j My son is very **good** *for / at / in* playing tennis.

3 Check your answers using the *mini-dictionary*. How many did you get right?

4 Fill in the gaps with a preposition from the box. Check your answers in the *mini-dictionary* if necessary.

a If you eat chocolate every day you'll **put** .... **weight.**
b You should eat more fruit. It's very **good** .... you.
c Don't talk to Tom, he's .... **a bad mood** at the moment.
d Lots of children are **afraid** .... the dark.
e I saw a great film .... **video** last night.
f In England lots of people **complain** .... the weather.
g What's the **difference** .... British English and American English?
h Bruce wrote to me last month, but I haven't **replied** .... him yet.
i Who did you **vote** .... in the last election?
j What are the **disadvantages** .... working at home?

on	for
of	to
about	in
between	on
for	of

5 Test your partner on the prepositions in exercises 2 and 4, like this:

to depend on something

15A Conditional squares

Unreal and real conditionals

Write **short** answers to the following questions in the squares below. You can write your answers in any square you like, but **not** in the same order as the questions. Answer as many questions as you can.

- If you won a lot of money, what would you buy *first*?
- What will you do this weekend if the weather's good?
- If you could go anywhere in the world tomorrow, where would you go?
- If you have enough money for a holiday this year (or next year), where will you go?
- If you could choose one famous person to have dinner with, who would it be?
- If you study English next year, which school will you go to?
- If you could change one part of your body, what would you change?
- If there was a fire in your house, what would be the first thing you'd take outside?
- If you could have any job in the world, what would you like to be?
- If the teacher gives you homework tonight, will you definitely do it?
- If you could only watch one film again in your life, which film would it be?
- What would you do if the doctor told you that you only had two days to live?

15B Preposition pelmanism

Revision of prepositions

He **invested** all his money .... his friend's business.	**IN**	Sometimes it's really nice to be .... **your own**.	**ON**
Hello, doctor. I've got a terrible **pain** .... **my knee**.	**IN**	When we were in London we **went** .... **a tour** of the city.	**ON**
He didn't get married until he was .... **his forties**.	**IN**	Is your new coat **made** .... leather?	**OF**
Can I **change** these yen .... dollars, please?	**INTO**	I'**m really frightened** .... spiders.	**OF**
Mark's **really bad** .... speaking Spanish.	**AT**	We're **going out** .... **a meal** this evening.	**FOR**
Their address is .... **the top** of the letter.	**AT**	I often **go** .... **a walk** after lunch.	**FOR**
Stop **looking** .... **the window** and pay attention!	**OUT OF**	I've **borrowed** £100 .... my brother.	**FROM**
E-mail is a good way of **keeping in touch** .... friends who live abroad.	**WITH**	I'**m looking forward** .... going on holiday.	**TO**
The best thing .... living here is the park opposite.	**ABOUT**	What are you doing **the day** .... **tomorrow**?	**AFTER**
Susannah **knows a lot** .... computers.	**ABOUT**	I went to the theatre **the day** .... **yesterday**.	**BEFORE**

Test one TIME: 45 MINUTES

modules 1–5

A Present simple/continuous and Past simple

Complete the gaps in the following sentences with the correct form (Present simple/continuous or Past simple) of the verb in brackets.

For example:
The average American ..watches.. *(watch)* more than three hours of television a day.

1 I .... *(send)* Stuart a card last Tuesday.
2 Josh normally .... *(practise)* tennis for about four hours a day.
3 I'm sorry, I can't send you an e-mail now because my brother .... *(use)* the computer.
4 All of the students .... *(take)* the exam next week.
5 Anna isn't here. She .... *(go)* out about an hour ago.
6 A good teacher always .... *(correct)* our mistakes.
7 Joan Lloyd .... *(have)* lunch with the Korean president the day after tomorrow.
8 David .... *(live)* with some friends this month, but next month he's going to move into his new flat.

[ ] 8

B Vocabulary

Circle the correct verb in the following sentences.

For example:
(play)/*go* tennis

1 *be / have* a beard
2 *make / have* a shower
3 *go to / go* the gym
4 *take / have* something to eat
5 *fall / feel* asleep
6 *play / do* yoga
7 *go to / want* bed early
8 *have / be* embarrassed

[ ] 8

C Comparing things

Four of the sentences below are correct. Tick (√) the correct ones and correct the others.

For example:
She's ~~more old~~ than me. *older*

1 It's the biggest city of the world.
2 Ruth's more organised than me.
3 My English is badder than Paolo's.
4 Vanessa's friendlyer now than she was a year ago.
5 That man looks as Tom Cruise!
6 German is very different from Italian.
7 Her computer is the same like mine.
8 I'm going to spend more time with my children.
9 Which is better: video or DVD?
10 My surname's similar than yours.

[ ] 10

D Prepositions

Complete the gaps in the following sentences with a preposition from the box.

~~in~~	for	at	off	up	at
for	for	on			

For example:
She started her job .....in..... 1989.

1 It happened .... Thursday afternoon.
2 It was great to see you. Thanks .... coming.
3 Jim had three weeks .... work last month because he broke his leg.
4 I'm going to a wedding on Saturday, so I'll have to dress ....
5 Your driving test will be .... the beginning of June.
6 I'm too tired to cook. Let's go out .... a meal.
7 After work I always go .... a run.
8 I'll be home .... about seven o'clock tonight.

[ ] 8

E Questions

Look at the answer and write the question in the correct tense. Pay attention to the underlined part of the answer and use a question word from the box.

~~Where~~	Which	When	How often	Why
How many	What kind	How long	What … like?	

For example:
Where did you go last night?
We went to the cinema last night.

1 I like rock and jazz music.
2 Karen goes to Spain once a month.
3 Nicolai speaks three languages.
4 I prefer the black boots.
5 Sylvie's going home because it's late.
6 It will take about five minutes to find the information.
7 It was very snowy.
8 I last used my credit card yesterday.

8

F Pronunciation

Put the words below in the correct column of the table according to their word stress.

~~improve~~ enjoy appearance relaxed Internet crowded advert embarrassed frightened relative assistant appear photograph surprised attractive newspaper happened

○●	●○	●○○	○●○
improve			

8

G Vocabulary

Complete the gaps with the missing word.

For example:
Did you buy any *s o u v e n i r s* of your holiday?

1 I haven't got a pen. Can I _ _ _ _ _ _ yours?
2 A: Who's your _ _ _ _ _ _ _ _ _ actor?
B: Tom Hanks. What about you?
3 A: We're celebrating. We got married three years ago today.
B: Happy _ _ _ _ _ _ _ _ _ _ _ _ !
4 A: What's the matter?
B: I feel really _ _ _ _ _ _ _ because I've got a history exam this afternoon.
5 I'm sorry I can't hear you because the baby is _ _ _ _ _ _ .
6 When I wanted to go on holiday, the _ _ _ _ _ _ _ _ _ _ _ was fantastic. She gave really good advice about the best places to go, and got us a cheap flight.
7 Could you _ _ _ _ _ _ the phone, Pat? I'm in the bath.
8 I'm so sorry. I feel really _ _ _ _ _ _ _ _ _ _ _ _ , but I can't remember your name.

8

H Present simple and *how often*

Put the words in the right order, including the word in brackets. Make sure to use the correct form of the verb in each sentence.

For example:
work/at the weekend/He *(never)*
He never works at the weekend.

1 go to work/How/you/do ? *(usually)*
....
2 on holiday/We/go *(twice a year)*
....
3 orange juice/breakfast/have/I/for *(always)*
....
4 my mother/telephone/I *(every week)*
....
5 go to the gym/She/after work *(often)*
....
6 have lunch/They/in the park *(sometimes)*
....

6

I Phrases with articles

Complete the following phrases with *a*, *an*, *the* or Ø. (Note: Ø means 'no article'.)

For example:
She's *an* architect.

1 I can't play .... musical instrument. Can you?
2 Wayne generally goes swimming three times .... week.
3 It's going to rain all .... day. Don't forget your umbrella!
4 Where's Pete? He's surfing .... Internet, looking for a cheap holiday.
5 We saw Jane .... day before yesterday. She sends her love.
6 Let's go out for .... day. The weather's perfect.
7 You're always playing .... video games.
8 I want to rent .... DVD and have a quiet evening at home.

[ ] 8

J *can / have to / should / shouldn't*

Circle the correct form in the following sentences.

For example:
Can I / *Do I have to* / *Should I* smoke in here?

1 I'm sorry, Sir, but you *don't have to* / *can't* / *should* go through that door. It's private.
2 A: I've got a terrible headache and I feel sick.
B: I think you *should* / *can* / *have to* go to bed.
3 You *don't have to* / *can* / *have to* wear jeans or trousers at work if you want to.
4 You *shouldn't* / *can't* / *don't have to* speak English for this job, but it's very useful when you're travelling.
5 You *shouldn't* / *don't have to* / *can* smoke if you want to be healthy.
6 Passengers *can* / *have to* /*should* go through security before they get on the plane.

[ ] 6

K Irregular verbs

Write the Past simple tense of the following irregular verbs.

For example:
write *wrote*

1	meet	6	cost ....
2	wear	7	think ....
3	feel	8	ride ....
4	steal	9	buy ....
5	tell	10	lose ....

[ ] 10

L Opposites

Complete the gaps with the opposite word.

For example:
a fat man   a *slim* man

1	Her skin is pale.	Her skin is ....
2	My job is very safe.	My job is very ....
3	She's got fair hair.	She's got .... hair.
4	I'm excited.	I'm ....
5	to wake up	to ....
6	He's very patient.	He's very ....

[ ] 6

M Pronunciation

Look at the underlined sounds in these words. Match a word in column A to a word with the same sound in column B.

	A		B
1	looked	a	visit
2	weather	b	talked
3	wanted	c	think
4	very	d	when
5	will	e	waited
6	mother	f	yoga
7	thank	g	this

[ ] 6

TOTAL [ ] 100

Test two

TIME: 45 MINUTES

modules 6–10

A Present perfect or Past simple?

Complete the gaps in the following sentences with the correct form of the verb in brackets.

For example:
Patrick ....*sent*..... (*send*) me an e-mail yesterday.

1 Luke Harker .... (*work*) for Unifax from 1993 to 2000.
2 Oh no! I .... (*not buy*) a present for Philip yet.
3 When .... Julie and Pierre .... (*get married*)?
4 The plane to Mexico .... (*leave*) ten minutes ago.
5 .... you .... (*ever go*) to China?
6 This looks delicious! I .... (*never eat*) sushi before.
7 How long .... you .... (*live*) in your present apartment?
8 Where .... (*be*) your children born?

[ ] 8

B Pronunciation: word stress

Put the words below in the correct column of the table according to their word stress.

~~modern~~ temperature stomachache bandage
advice computer luxurious desert climate
scenery mountain canal ambition

●○	○●	●○○	○●○	○●○○
modern				

[ ] 6

C Vocabulary

Read the definitions below and complete the puzzle to find the hidden word.

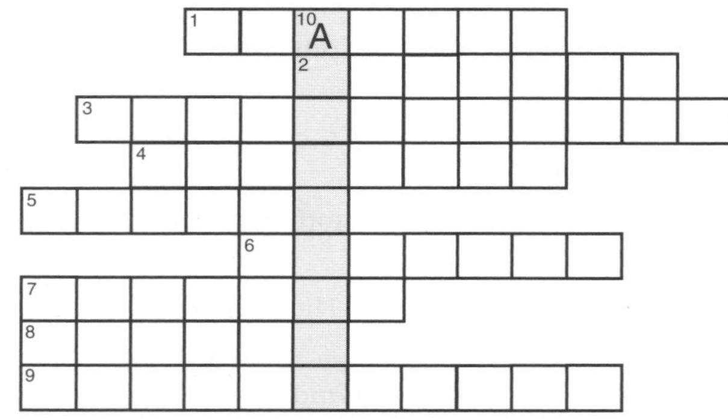

1 If you cut your finger, you can put a .... on it.
2 A place where there are a lot of people is .... The opposite is empty or quiet.
3 This word describes holiday accommodation where you cook your own meals.
4 Something which you want to do one day.
5 If you go to another country, you go ....
6 Our flight was .... so we had to wait at the airport for four hours.
7 A female hero is a ....
8 A very dry place where it never rains.
9 When you travel somewhere as a tourist and you visit the famous places, you go ....
10 The hidden word is ....

[ ] 10

D *will / won't / going to / planning to / would like to / would rather*

Complete the gaps in the following sentences with a phrase from the box.

'd like to ~~'m going to~~ 'll have to 'd rather
won't 'm planning to 'll be able to

For example:
I *'m going to* call my baby Louise.

1 I .... speak to Miss Stacey, please.
2 I'm sure you .... find a hotel easily.
3 I .... travel the world after university.
4 Just a minute. I .... be long!

5 A: Would you like to go out for a drink?
B: Actually, I .... go for a meal.

6 I'm afraid you .... wait. There are ten people before you.

| | 6 |

E Verb forms

Circle the correct verb form in the following sentences.

For example:
I *used to see* / *saw* / *was seeing* Abdul at the station today.

1 Jerry and Meg *used to go* / *have been* / *went* to Goa for their holidays last year.
2 Debra *was playing* / *played* / *used to play* tennis when she slipped and broke her leg.
3 I *was living* / *'ve lived* / *used to live* in Seattle all my life, and I'm not going to move now!
4 *Did you used to like* / *Were you liking* / *Did you use to like* Oasis when you were younger?
5 The hotel gave us dinner as soon as we *have arrived* / *arrived* / *were arriving*.
6 Mikako *has had* / *was having* / *used to have* long hair when she was a child.
7 The football match *wasn't finishing* / *didn't finish* / *hasn't finished* yet.
8 Mark cut his hand while he *has cooked* / *was cooking* / *cooked*.

| | 8 |

F *will/won't/may/might*

Reorder the words to make sentences. The first word is underlined.

For example:
you/night/may/I/tomorrow/see
I may see you tomorrow night.

1 will/race/Schumacher/definitely/win/the
....
2 might/late/I/tonight/be
....
3 probably/down/Computer/go/will/prices
....
4 rain/It/definitely/tomorrow/won't
....
5 to/may/Jayne's/not/come/We/party
....
6 ten/won't/father/o'clock/My/probably/before/arrive
....

| | 6 |

G Articles

Complete the gaps with *the*, *a*, *an* or Ø. (Note: Ø means 'no article'.)

For example:
I can't put pictures on ...*the*..... wall in my room.

1 Budapest is on .... River Danube.
2 You should never look directly at .... Sun.
3 London is in .... south of England.
4 In London you should stand on .... right on escalators.
5 It's easy to book holidays on .... Internet.
6 What's .... best film you have ever seen?
7 .... Atlantic Ocean is between .... Europe and America.

| | 8 |

H Quantifiers

Four of the sentences below are correct. Tick (√) the correct ones and correct the others.

For example:
Are there any special celebrations at New Year? √

1 Henman didn't win no matches in the last championship.
2 There aren't many beaches in the south.
3 A lot people play computer games just to relax.
4 We had to cancel the concert because not enough people bought tickets.
5 People shouldn't spend too many time on their computers without a break.
6 A few students knew the answer, but not many.
7 I'm having days off next week.
8 There's some beautiful scenery in Tuscany.

| | 8 |

I Vocabulary

Circle the odd one out in the following groups.

For example:
headache cold toothache relationship

1 river beach ocean canal
2 hotel villa office apartment
3 friend neighbour customer fit
4 headache dizzy temperature happy

| | 4 |

J Prepositions

Complete the gaps in the following sentences with a preposition from the box.

~~on~~ of on in for into for at on

For example:
We've got a summer house ..*on*.. the coast.

1 Eating chocolate is bad .... you.
2 Get off the bus .... the first stop.
3 What do you want .... Christmas?
4 You should put a plaster .... that cut.
5 The bank is .... the corner of North Street and Victoria Avenue.
6 My brother fell .... the river when he was younger.
7 A lot of people are frightened .... snakes.
8 Well, here I am .... France! The weather's fantastic and …

8

K Past participles

Write the past participles of the following words.

For example:
bring .*brought*.

1	make	9	pay ....
2	win	10	do ....
3	break	11	take ....
4	drink	12	think ....
5	read	13	say ....
6	catch	14	buy ....
7	write	15	eat ....
8	know	16	fly ....

8

L *if / when / before / as soon as*

Three of the sentences below are correct. Tick (√) the correct ones and correct the others.

For example:
If it snows tomorrow, we'll probably stay in. √

1 We can leave as soon as Kevin will find his car keys.
2 If you want to, we could go to the beach tomorrow.
3 Before you leave, don't forget to give me your telephone number.
4 When the film is ending, why don't we go for a meal?
5 Yasmin wants to go back to India before she will die.
6 Could you e-mail me the report when you finish it?

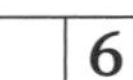
6

M Vocabulary: collocations

Complete the following sentences with a word from the box.

~~change~~ keep become go have start take

For example:
I want to ....*change*.... my e-mail address.

1 When did you .... your business?
2 When I .... famous, I'm going to buy a much bigger house.
3 You look tired. I think you should .... a rest this weekend.
4 What are you going to study when you .... to university?
5 You should go to bed and try to .... warm.
6 Go home and .... these tablets three times a day.

6

N Missing words

There is one word missing from each of the sentences below. Put one word from the box in the correct place in each sentence.

~~in~~ for just already yet last ago when never

For example:
The first men went to the moon ....*in*.... 1969.

1 José started learning English four months.
2 Oh no, I've lost all my work on the computer!
3 I've used a DVD player before. Can you help me?
4 We spoke on the phone week.
5 Lee and Oliver have known each other ten years.
6 A: Julie, this is John.
B: Actually, we've met. Hello, again!
7 Chris left school he was sixteen.
8 Mel hasn't heard the results of her exam.

8

TOTAL 100

Test three TIME: 45 MINUTES

modules 11–15

A Vocabulary

Complete the gaps with the missing word.

For example:
If the weather is a.*wful*., it's very bad.

1 You can keep money in a w........................ .
2 A hobby or interest which becomes the most important thing in your life, it becomes an o................. .
3 You can use a t........................ to dry yourself.
4 A show at the theatre in which there is a lot of singing and dancing is called a m................. .
5 If a man doesn't want to grow a beard, he needs a r................. to shave.
6 A person who offers to do something without being paid is a v................. .
7 The money you give to a waiter because you are happy with the service is a t................. .
8 If you break the law, sometimes the punishment is that you have to pay a f................. .

	8

B Verb forms: Past simple / Present perfect / Present perfect continuous

Circle the correct verb form in the following sentences.

For example:
Shakespeare (wrote) / *has written* over thirty plays.

1 Yesterday it *rained* / *has rained* all day!
2 Tom and I are good friends. We *have known* / *have been knowing* each other for six years.
3 Hi! I *tried* / *'ve been trying* to phone since three o'clock. How are you?
4 How long *have you had* / *have you been having* your car?
5 Between 1998 and 2000, the Juice Bar *opened* / *has been opening* over 200 new shops around the world.
6 I *shopped* / *'ve been shopping* all morning! Let's have lunch.

	6

C *like*

Rewrite the following sentences by adding the word *like* in the correct form.

For example:
I enjoy playing tennis.
I like playing tennis.

1 You look very similar to your sister.
....
2 I want to become famous.
....
3 How was the weather on your holiday?
....
4 If you hire a car, you can go where you want.
....
5 He sounds the same as a cat when he tries to sing.
....
6 Do you want tea or coffee?
....

	6

D Active or passive?

Put the verb in brackets in the correct active or passive form.

For example:
The film *Gladiator* .... *(direct)* by Ridley Scott.

1 The new art gallery .... *(finish)* before the end of next year.
2 We .... *(tell)* Redman the bad news.
3 In Japan, kimonos .... *(wear)* for special occasions, for example, when a woman gets married.
4 Two people.......................... *(hurt)* when their car went over a bridge last night.
5 My parents remember where they were when John F. Kennedy .... *(kill)*.
6 The government .... *(build)* three new hospitals next year.
7 I'm sorry I'm late. My train .... *(delay)*.
8 Thanksgiving Day .... *(celebrate)* in the USA in November every year.

	8

E *like doing / would like to do*

Circle the correct form in the following questions.

For example:

(*Do you*) / *Would you* like dancing?

1 Where *do you / would you* like to go on holiday?
2 What *do you / would you* like doing at weekends?
3 What *do you / would you* like to do this weekend?
4 *Do you / Would you* like *going / to go* to the cinema? this evening?
5 *Do you / Would you* like eating Chinese food?
6 *Do you / Would you* like *studying / to study* English?

F Pronunciation

Put the words below in the correct column of the table according to their word stress.

~~afford~~ hobby collect collection sunglasses compass organised committed envelope commission expert honest divorced currency wallet salary model

● ○	○ ●	● ○ ○	○ ● ○
afford			

8

G *for* and *since*

Write F (*for*) or S (*since*) beside each of the time expressions below.

For example:

Monday
...*S*...

1 1988 ....
2 three days ago ....
3 the day before yesterday ....
4 three days ....
5 ten o'clock this morning ....
6 twenty minutes ....

6

H Past perfect or Past simple?

Look at the Past simple verbs in bold in the text. Some of them should be in the Past perfect. Tick (√) the ones that are correct, and change the others into the Past perfect.

Last year we [1] **went** on holiday to Buenos Aires. We [2] **were** very tired and quite dirty when we [3] **arrived** because the plane [4] **left** six hours late. When we [5] **got** to the city centre we [6] **looked** at the map which the travel agent [7] **gave** us in London. We [8] **walked** along the street and [9] **found** our four-star hotel.

'McDonald,' I said to the receptionist.

'No,' she said. 'Go out of the hotel and take the second street on the left. McDonald's restaurant is on the right.'

When she realised she [10] **made** a mistake, she [11] **was** very embarrassed!

1 ....✔.......... 2 .... 3 ....
4 .... 5 .... 6 ....
7 .... 8 .... 9 ....
10 .... 11 ....

10

I Vocabulary: word formation

Complete each sentence with the correct form of the word in capitals.

For example:

People in America were very .... HELP

1 Sam Taylor hasn't got very much .... IMAGINE
2 Has anybody seen my .... licence? DRIVE
3 My father's got lots of different hobbies and .... so he's always busy, even though he doesn't go to work any more. INTEREST
4 The manager of this office needs to be very well .... ORGANISE
5 Sue's a really good person to talk to if you have a problem. She's very .... SYMPATHY
6 Lianne is an .... teacher. EXPERIENCE
7 To be a doctor you need to be a good .... LISTEN
8 Becoming an Olympic athlete requires a huge .... COMMIT

8

J Pronunciation

Are the underlined sounds the same (S) or different (D)?

For example:
furniture waste *D*

1	patient	tissues	4	heaven	jeweller
2	violent	licence	5	building	profit
3	enough	storey	6	purse	earn

6

K Prepositions

Circle the correct preposition in the following sentences.

For example:
How about going out (for)/to a meal?

1 My brother's crazy *over/about* skiing.
2 I'm really interested *in/about* ghost stories.
3 I lent my copy of the book *to/from* John.
4 It took our grandparents twenty years to save up *with/for* an apartment.
5 I'm not very keen *about/on* Chinese food, to be honest.
6 Mary often borrows things *from/to* me but she never gives them back!
7 Chris is applying *for/on* a new job.
8 The supermarket is *in/on* the right, next to the bank.

8

L Conditionals

Complete the gaps with a suitable form of the verb in brackets. Think about whether the situation is real or imaginary.

For example:
If I ..*had*.. *(have)* more money ..*I'd move*.. *(move)*

1 If you .... *(give)* me your e-mail address, I .... *(send)* you the information.
2 If I .... *(have)* my mobile phone with me, I .... *(ring)* them now.
3 What .... you .... *(do)* if you .... *(win)* the lottery?
4 If I .... *(knew)* the answer, I .... *(tell)* you!
5 If you .... *(leave)* your telephone number, I .... *(ask)* Steve to call you later.
6 If I .... *(not be)* so tired, I .... *(go out)* tonight.
7 If I .... *(be)* seventeen again, I .... *(do)* a lot of things differently.
8 If we .... *(wake up)* early tomorrow, we .... *(go)* swimming.

8

M Past perfect or Past simple

Choose the best form of the verb in brackets to complete the story, using the Past perfect or Past simple.

Jackie [1] .... *(come)* home from work exhausted. She [2] .... *(had)* a terrible day. When she [3] .... *(arrive)* at work, she [4] .... *(realise)* that she [5] .... *(forget)* to prepare for an important meeting. However, she [6] .... *(ask)* her colleague to help her, and they [7] .... *(be)* ready just in time. Later, she [8] .... *(drop)* coffee all over her desk, and then her computer [9] .... *(crash)*. The worst thing of all was that she [10] .... *(left)* her car windows open. When she [11] .... *(get)* in the car to go home, she [12] .... *(get)* wet!

6

N Pronunciation

Look at the underlined sounds in these words. Match a sound in column A to a word with the same sound in column B.

	A		B
1	/h/	a	liked
2	/s/	b	hope
3	/sh/	c	imagination
4	/z/	d	played
5	/t/	e	wants
6	/d/	f	nothing
7	/ng/	g	flies

6

TOTAL 100

Resource bank key

1A Get to know the *Students' Book*

A pages 2 to 5 B in the front of the *mini-dictionary* C purple D making suggestions E page 154 F **Pronunciation spot** G page 79 H pages 167 and 168 I *day* J two K green L page 157

Learner-training worksheet A

2 a meaning 1 b meaning 2 c meaning 1

3 a late b quickly c bed d work e open f woke up

4 a countable noun b adjective c transitive verb d intransitive verb e uncountable noun f adverb

5 baker economics independent

1B Me too!

1 **What time / When** do you usually get up on Sundays?
2 **How often** do you go to the cinema?
3 **What**'s your favourite food?
4 **How long** does your journey home from school take?
5 **What** do you usually do at the weekend?
6 **Why** do you want to learn English?
7 **How many** cousins have you got?
8 **What kind of** films/movies do you like?
9 **Who**'s your favourite actor?
10 **What time / When** do you usually go to bed during the week?
11 **Which** season do you like the most?
12 **How often** do you go shopping for new clothes?

Learner-training worksheet B

4 a drove b taught c brought d wore e bought f broke; fell g rang h left; caught

2B The millionaire's ball

1 on 2 in 3 Ø 4 ago 5 Ø 6 ago 7 on 8 in 9 on 10 in

Learner-training worksheet C

2 1 b 2 d 3 a 4 c

3 a Internet b make c bank d do e question f check g go out h rent

3A The secret of successful language learning

1 There are no right or wrong answers in this discussion. Accept any logical answers.

2 and 3

	VERB	NOUN	ADJECTIVE
a		importance	important
b	believe	belief	believable
c	imagine	imagination	imaginative
d	enjoy	enjoyment	enjoyable
e	succeed	success	successful

4 a succeed b important c believe d imagination e enjoyable f imaginative/important g beliefs h imagine i enjoy j successful

5A Put these in order

A 1 Japan (377,000 sq km)
2 Spain (505,000 sq km)
3 France (551,000 sq km)
4 Peru (1,285,000 sq km)

B 1 The Pacific Ocean
2 The Atlantic Ocean
3 The Indian Ocean
4 The Arctic Ocean

C 1 India (1 billion)
2 Brazil (160 million)
3 Spain (40 million)
4 Poland (36.6 million)

D 1 The Colosseum
2 The Taj Mahal
3 The Eiffel Tower
4 The Sydney Opera House

E 1 Moscow (latitude 56°)
2 London (latitude 51.5°)
3 New York (latitude 41°)
4 Tokyo (latitude 36°)

F 1 Pluto (5,900 million km from the sun)
2 Mars (228 million km from the sun)
3 Earth (150 million km from the sun)
4 Mercury (56 million km from the sun)

G 1 Nelson Mandela's release from prison (February 1990)
2 the fall of the Berlin Wall (November 1989)
3 the first man on the moon (July 1969)
4 the assassination of John F Kennedy (November 1963)

H 1 Julia Roberts (born 28th October 1967)
2 Brad Pitt (born 18th December 1963)
3 Sharon Stone (born 10th March 1958)
4 Robert de Niro (born 17th August 1943)

I 1 The Nile (6,741 km)
2 The Amazon (6,440 km)
3 The Mississippi (3,780 km)
4 The Rhine (1,390 km)

J 1 *Titanic* ($515 million)
2 *Star Wars* ($460 million)
3 *E.T.* ($399 million)
4 *Jurassic Park* ($356 million)

Learner-training worksheet D

2 *Example answer*

a detective = (also 'a detective story')
to steal something (steal/stole/stolen) =
(you steal things and money)
to rob someone/somewhere (reg) =
(you rob people and banks)
a journey /dʒɜːni/ = (to go **on** a journey)
a wedding = (to go **to** a wedding)
embarrassed (adj) =
to be/feel embarrassed **about** something
to dress up (reg) (e.g. for a party, to go out for a meal) =
to earn /ɜːn/ (money by doing a job) (reg) =

8A Article snakes and ladders

1 Ø, Ø
2 I live in a flat in **the** city centre, very close to ~~the~~ Oxford Street.
3 Ø, the, the
4 I usually go to work by ~~the~~ train, but yesterday I went by ~~the~~ bus.
5 the Indian Ocean, the Mediterranean, the Amazon
6 Ø, the, Ø, the
7 The sentence is correct.
8 the, Ø, the
9 El Paso is on **the** border of Mexico and **the** United States.
10 a, a, The, the
11 Madras is in the south of ~~the~~ India, on **the** east coast.
12 Ø, Ø, the; the
13 John is standing on **the** left, and Susan is standing in the middle, next to **the** headmaster.
14 Ø, Ø, Ø, Ø
15 the, a, the, Ø
16 a, Ø
17 Ø, Ø, the
18 The sentence is correct.
19 the, the, the
20 I bought a picture and a carpet this morning. I've put **the** picture on the bathroom wall and the carpet on **the** kitchen floor.
21 the, Ø, the
22 the Andes; the Himalayas
23 Loch Ness is **the** most famous lake in Scotland, because of **the** Loch Ness Monster.
24 I really hate ~~the~~ mice, but I love spiders. I have a tarantula at home, and it lives on **the** ceiling!

Learner-training worksheet F

3

MATTHEW: Hi Jill, have you got a light?
JILL: Yes, here you are. Are you feeling OK?
MATTHEW: Yes, I'm just tired, that's all. I went to a party in the city centre, and didn't get home until three.
JILL: So that's why you didn't arrive on time this morning!
MATTHEW: Er, yes. But you were late for work the other day.
JILL: That was because I went to the doctor, not because I stayed out late!
MATTHEW: Yes, well, I'm not very good at getting up early.
JILL: That's probably why you're always in a bad mood!
MATTHEW: I'm not! Anyway, what are you doing at the weekend?
JILL: I'm going out for a meal with some friends on Saturday. On Sunday I might go for a walk in the countryside. What about you?
MATTHEW: I've got the day off on Friday, so I'm going to visit an old friend who lives on the coast.

JILL: That sounds fun. Look, we're going to be late for our classes. Let's go.
MATTHEW: What, already? Where did I put my books ...?

4

a **Have you got a** light?
b **in the** city centre
c to arrive **on time**
d to be **late for** work
e **the other** day
f to go **to the** doctor
g to stay **out** late
h to be (not very) **good at** doing something
i to get **up** early
j to be **in a** bad mood
k **at the** weekend
l to go **out for a** meal
m to go **for a** walk
n **in the** countryside
o to have the day **off**
p **on the** coast

10C Bob's night out

The correct order is E, C, I, A, H, F, D, J, B, G.

Learner-training worksheet H

2

VERB + GERUND	VERB + INFINITIVE WITH *TO*	VERB + INFINITIVE WITHOUT *TO*
enjoy stop hate don't mind	arrange would like learn intend plan	have to can may could must

3

a I've arranged **to meet** my brother this evening.
b I must **go** to the dentist this afternoon.
c correct
d Do you enjoy **playing** tennis?
e I have to **go** to work tomorrow.
f correct
g correct
h I hate **getting** up early.
i We're planning **to go** to New York for our holidays.
j correct

12B The Handbag Gang

The correct order is E, H, B, F, J, A, D, I, G, C.

Learner-training worksheet I

1 The correct order is D, C, E, H, B, F, A, G.

Learner-training worksheet J

2

a about
b from
c with
d into
e to
f on
g on
h with
i of
j at

4

a on
b for
c in
d of
e on
f about
g between
h to
i for
j of

Test one (modules 1–5)

A

1 sent 2 practises 3 is using 4 are taking
5 went 6 corrects 7 is having 8 is living

B

1 have 2 have 3 go to 4 have 5 fall
6 do 7 go to 8 be

C

1 It's the biggest city **in** the world.
2 correct
3 My English is **worse** than Paolo's.
4 Vanessa's **friendlier** now than she was a year ago.
5 That man looks **like** Tom Cruise.
6 correct
7 Her computer is the same **as** mine.
8 correct
9 correct
10 My surname's similar **to** yours.

D

1 on 2 for 3 off 4 up 5 at
6 for 7 for 8 at

E

1 What kind of music do you like?
2 How often does Karen go to Spain?
3 How many languages does Nicolai speak?
4 Which boots do you prefer?
5 Why is Sylvie going home?
6 How long will it take to find the information?
7 What was the weather like?
8 When did you last use your credit card?

F *(half a mark each)*

○● enjoy, relaxed, appear, surprised
●○ crowded, advert, frightened, foreign, happened
●○○ Internet, relative, photograph, newspaper
○●○ appearance, embarrassed, assistant, attractive

G

1 borrow 2 favourite 3 anniversary
4 nervous 5 crying 6 travel agent 7 answer
8 embarrassed

H

1 How do you usually go to work?
2 We go on holiday twice a year.
3 I always have orange juice for breakfast.
4 I telephone my mother every week.
5 She often goes to the gym after work.
6 They sometimes have lunch in the park.

I

1 a 2 a 3 Ø 4 the 5 the 6 the
7 Ø 8 a

J

1 can't 2 should 3 can 4 don't have to
5 shouldn't 6 have to

K

1 met 2 wore 3 felt 4 stole 5 told 6 cost
7 thought 8 rode 9 bought 10 lost

L

1 tanned 2 dangerous 3 dark 4 bored
5 fall asleep 6 impatient

M

2 g 3 e 4 a 5 d 6 f 7 c

Test two (modules 6–10)

A

1 worked 2 haven't bought 3 did; get married
4 left 5 Have; ever been 6 've never eaten
7 have, lived 8 were

B *(half a mark each)*

●○ bandage, desert, climate, mountain
○● advice, canal
●○○ temperature, stomachache, scenery
○●○ computer, ambition
○●○○ luxurious

C

1 plaster 2 crowded 3 self-catering 4 ambition
5 abroad 6 delayed 7 heroine 8 desert
9 sightseeing 10 accidents

D

1 'd like to 2 'll be able to 3 'm planning to
4 won't 5 'd rather 6 'll have to

E

1 went 2 was playing 3 've lived
4 Did you use to like 5 arrived 6 used to have
7 hasn't finished 8 was cooking

F

1 Schumacher will definitely win the race.
2 I might be late tonight.
3 Computer prices will probably go down.
4 It definitely won't rain tomorrow.
5 We may not come to Jayne's party.
6 My father probably won't arrive before ten o'clock.

G

1 the 2 the 3 the 4 the 5 the 6 the
7 The, Ø *(2 marks)*

H

1 Henman didn't win **any** matches ...
2 correct
3 A lot **of** people play ...
4 correct
5 People shouldn't spend too **much** time ...
6 correct
7 I'm having **a few** days off ...
8 correct

I

1 beach 2 office 3 fit 4 happy

J

1 for 2 at 3 for 4 on 5 on 6 into
7 of 8 in

K

1 made 2 won 3 broken 4 drunk 5 read
6 caught 7 written 8 known 9 paid
10 done 11 taken 12 thought 13 said
14 bought 15 eaten 16 flown

L

1 We can leave as soon as Kevin **finds** his car keys.
2 correct
3 correct
4 When the film **ends**, why don't we go for a meal?
5 Yasmin wants to go back to India before she **dies**.
6 correct

M

1 start 2 become 3 have 4 go 5 keep
6 take

N

1 José started learning English four months **ago**.
2 Oh no, I've **just** lost all my work on the computer!
3 I've **never** used a DVD player before. Can you help me?
4 We spoke on the phone **last** week.
5 Lee and Oliver have known each other **for** ten years.
6 A: Julie, this is John.
B: Actually, we've **already** met. Hello again!
7 Chris left school **when** he was sixteen.
8 Mel hasn't heard the results of her exam **yet**.

Test three (modules 11–15)

A

1 wallet 2 obsession 3 towel 4 musical
5 razor 6 volunteer 7 tip 8 fine

B

1 rained 2 have known 3 've been trying
4 have you had 5 opened 6 've been shopping

C

1 You look very **like** your sister.
2 **I'd like** to become famous.
3 **What** was the weather **like** on your holiday?
4 If you hire a car on holiday, you can go where you **like**.
5 He sounds **like** a cat when he tries to sing.
6 **Would** you **like** tea or coffee?

D

1 will be finished 2 told 3 are worn
4 were hurt 5 was killed 6 will build
7 was delayed 8 is celebrated

E

1 would you 2 do you 3 would you
4 Would you; to go 5 Do you 6 Do you; studying

F (*half a mark each*)

●○ hobby, compass, expert, honest, wallet, model
○● collect, divorced
●○○ sunglasses, organised, envelope, currency, salary
○●○ collection, committed, commission

G

1 S 2 S 3 S 4 F 5 S 6 F

H

2 ✓ 3 ✓ 4 had left 5 ✓ 6 ✓ 7 had given
8 ✓ 9 ✓ 10 had made 11 ✓

I

1 imagination 2 driving 3 interests 4 organised
5 sympathetic 6 experienced 7 listener
8 commitment

J

1 S 2 S 3 D 4 D 5 S 6 S

K

1 about 2 in 3 to 4 for 5 on 6 from
7 for 8 on

L

1 give; 'll send 2 had; 'd ring 3 would, do, won
4 knew; 'd tell 5 leave; 'll ask 6 wasn't; 'd go out
7 were/was; 'd do 8 wake up; 'll go
(*half a mark each*)

M

1 came 2 'd had 3 arrived 4 realised
5 had forgotten 6 asked 7 were 8 dropped
9 crashed 10 had left 11 got 12 got

N

2 e 3 c 4 g 5 a 6 d 7 f